The Stress

Myth

By

Serge Doublet, Ph.D.

Science & Humanities Press
PO Box 7151
Chesterfield MO 63006-7151
636-394-4950
sciencehumanitiespress.com

I

Graphics Credits:

Original Cover design by Dr. Bud Banis

Published simultaneously in Australia by
IPSILON Publishing
PO Box 3160
Freemans Reach NSW 2756
(ISBN 0646393707)

ISBN 1-888725-36-2
    Library of Congress Cataloging-in-Publication Data

Doublet, Serge, 1946-
  The stress myth / by Serge Doublet.
     p. cm.
Includes bibliographical references and index.
  ISBN 1-888725-36-2
  1. Stress (Psychology) 2. Stress management. I. Title.
  BF575.S75 D68 2000
  155.9'042--dc21
                                        00-009698

Science & Humanities Press

PO Box 7151

Chesterfield, MO 63006-7151

(636) 394-4950

on the web at

 sciencehumanitiespress.com

CONTENTS

IV

PREFACE

Hardly a day goes by without someone around us uttering the word 'stress'. Many speak of being 'stressed out', 'stressing', and having all this 'stress' in their life. Yet ask many of these people, as I have, what they actually mean by 'stress' and you soon realize that they are not so sure. Nevertheless, some readily accept that stress is bad for us but at the same time think that in small doses it can be beneficial, if not necessary. They may even believe that it is responsible for many diseases or even death. Alternatively, other people just use the word to describe any unpleasant situation or feeling.

Stress is part of a growing number of conditions that have been claimed to be either discovered or better understood in recent years. The 'discoveries' have included ADHD, formerly ADD, Chronic Fatigue Syndrome and lately Road Rage. In the meantime, depression is now blamed on a chemical imbalance. Alcoholism, criminal behavior, homosexuality and anything else you can think of are traced back to genes. The overall message seems to be that we cannot really be responsible for our behavior. Everything apparently has some sort of physical origin for which we cannot be blamed.

This appears to have extended to other aspects of our life. Thirty years ago, if you tripped and injured your ankle because of a pothole on the footpath, you would curse for not watching where you were going. Today, people sue the authority that maintains the footpath. Likewise, if a child does badly at school, teachers or learning difficulties are blamed rather than the child.

Stress is probably the most significant of the many conditions which blame external events for some of our problems. Just about any adverse situation can be labeled 'stress' or a cause of it. Stress can then be used to explain any sort of crisis be they minor or great. Things are getting a bit too much, it must be stress. Can't cope with problems at work, can't cope with relationships, can't sleep or eat, difficult to diagnose conditions, or unknown causes of disease, are all at some time blamed on stress. Stress is a wonderful blanket that can be thrown over any problem. There is only one small hiccup though. Whatever the difficulty is, blaming it on stress for it does not solve the problem.

What is this ravaging and devastating 'thing' which seems to be present in every little corner of our lives? Well, none of us can really describe it in a way that makes sense. So how could we be ever certain that we are right in blaming stress for many of our ills if we don't really know what it is? Perhaps, we should not really do so without knowing the full story.

Few, if any, know the whole story about stress. This is not limited to lay people. Claims that stress affects many aspects of our lives have resulted in studies being conducted in many specialized areas of knowledge such as psychology, biology, immunology as well as various branches of medicine. The growth in knowledge in these disciplines has meant that many scientists are more likely to specialize in specific, sometimes narrow, fields of knowledge. When this is the case, specialists with particular expertise may have to accept, on face value, some of the evidence from specialists in other fields.

In fact, it appears that many people, scientists and lay people alike, have taken the concept of 'stress' for granted. Presented with this easy 'one-fit-all' concept that can at once be an excuse and an explanation for everything, many people have grabbed it. No more need for long searching explanations or solutions. Stress can do it all and quickly. It seems, however, too easy, too convenient. This is why I decided to look a bit deeper.

My suspicions about stress grew when I realized that even stress 'experts' could not really explain adequately what stress was. A bit more probing into what had been written about the topic made me realize that there was a fair amount of confusion about most of the things to do with stress. This is when I decided to conduct a thorough study of stress to determine whether or not it was a legitimate condition.

The psychological aspect of stress did not present any problem. My training in that field taught me both the background knowledge and the jargon necessary to understand the content of articles written about stress. (last year there were over 15,000 journal articles written about stress in psychology alone). The other fields concerned with the study of stress were more of a challenge. I was, however, fortunate to be married to a very knowledgeable lady who had studied medical science, microbiology, immunology and genetics. After a crash course in many of these areas and equipped with a good understanding of the rules of science, I was able to start my investigation.

I soon realized that it was worse than I thought. Not only could I not find any evidence for the existence of this 'thing' called stress, it became evident that most 'experts' in the field were actually talking about different 'things' altogether. No, not different types of stress, just different phenomena. As for the connection with disease, there was little evidence to support the numerous claims which had been made. Nor was there any proof that stress was going to kill us.

This book, therefore is about a myth. It is the untold story about stress. Untold, simply because no one to my knowledge has ever taken the trouble to investigate the whole story. You may wonder why I feel there is a need to debunk stress. If you think of it, the emergence of the concept has not helped one person out there. Most of the stress management techniques that have been proposed have been attempts to deal with the symptoms rather than the causes. This is mostly because their proponents have accepted not only that stress exists but also that it is an inevitable part of life. Starting from this understanding, coping is all that seems left. If we accept this as true, then we are contemplating a life of eternal remedial coping, no doubt with the assistance of ever-willing stress managers.

I intend to demonstrate that this is not necessary. You are not, nor will you ever be a victim of stress, for stress is not a genuine scientific condition. Stress is merely an abstraction. No one has ever seen touched or felt stress. By never felt I mean never felt physically. You may have felt it psychologically but this is a different matter. The only way you can feel stress is through your imagination. I am not suggesting that when you say you feel 'stressed' you are not feeling anything. What I am suggesting is the something you feel is not stress. There is no physical object, thing, animal, bacterium or virus that can be identified as 'stress'.

The debunking of stress will begin with a description of various popular views about stress. This will be done by showing what sort of explanations and claims are made about stress and what solutions are offered to deal with it. I felt it was important to start with popular views because these views have helped shape people's beliefs about stress. Before the theories about stress became popularized by the media, the label was never used at the popular level. Another reason for highlighting these popular views is that they can later be compared with the scientific claims and findings about the topic. The popularization of science often results in outlandish and misleading claims. Stress has certainly been no exception to the rule.

The popular views also raise a few questions about stress which will subsequently be answered in the following chapters. One of these questions is whether stress has always been part of life or whether it's a recent development in modern times.

The chapter on historical perspective will show that stress is the last in the long list of labels that have been introduced throughout history. These labels have emerged as a result of attempts to understand the effects of life on health. At the peak of their popularity, they have had the same sort of respectability and credibility that the label of 'stress' enjoys today, only to be eventually discarded, sometimes after a very long reign. This historical journey will also reveal that the notion of a 'fast pace of life' started with the introduction of improved transport and communication. It also situates stress in relation to its predecessors.

The next chapter, I believe, is the most pivotal chapter of the book. It discusses important linguistic considerations with regard to stress. Stress, as its inventor Hans Selye sometimes acknowledged, is an abstraction. As such stress cannot be or do anything. Abstractions, in a way, are conceptual inventions. They are meant to provide us with explanations about our world. This is especially true for our social world, itself an abstraction.

The chapter will show that because stress is an abstraction, there can never be a universal agreement as to what it is or what it can do. It should not really defy the imagination to suggest that if we don't know what something is, we hardly have a chance to know what it does or doesn't do. Most of our knowledge about things involves some sort of observation or measurement. Stress, as an abstraction, could never be observed or measured. This in my view constitutes fatal and sufficient evidence that stress can ever be a scientific fact. Furthermore, if stress cannot be observed then no claim or theory about stress, no matter how sophisticated, is ever going to provide evidence for either its existence or its effects. No matter what is claimed, it can only be based on assumptions rather than facts.

The section on the theories of stress will show that Hans Selye's original conceptualization of stress was messy from the beginning. Contradictions, changes of mind and poorly argued points made his theory difficult to follow. Several later attempts to improve on its original incoherence have only resulted in stress being whatever anyone wanted it to be. Subsequent theories by other researchers have only succeeded in increasing rather than decreasing the confusion. Despite the enormous volume of writing about stress in the last five decades, several key issues have remained unresolved.

The chapter titled *Other theoretical problems* deals with three important problems. The first is the impossibility of ever proving the purpose implied in explanations about stress and homeostasis. The second relates to the important differences between psychological and physical 'stressors' and that found between various 'stressors' of the same type.

Because of this, findings about a particular 'stressor' cannot be generalized to other 'stressors'. The last problem is about the issues involved in animal studies that are designed to study human psychological stress.

Finally the last two chapters on stress investigate the methodological problems encountered in the study of the effects of stress on people. The role of stress in causing various diseases is also discussed. On the basis of the evidence which is offered, no conclusive link between stress and diseases can be found.

In the last chapter, I introduce an alternative explanation to stress. This explanation will tackle the problem rather than the symptoms. It is based on a practical approach which has helped people who have sought my help. The approach I have developed is aimed to simplify rather than complicate what is a confused rather than a complex issue. Once relieved from the burden of believing in stress, it is easier to accept that we are the makers of happiness and misery. The chapter gives a basic yet useful understanding of what we feel but also of why we feel the way we do. I have already begun to write another book which will go into more detail about the why.

In concluding, there are a few things I would like to clarify. To begin with, I want to say that I did not start my study of stress with a bias or any great desire to prove that stress did not exist. In fact, when I started, I believed as most people do in some sort of homeostasis or balance state for the body. I also believed that too much adversity, or rather the resulting negative emotions such an adversity created, could eventually cause some sort of physical damage or even disease. After reading a huge amount of literature on the subject, however, I am no longer convinced that these beliefs were justified.

It was surprising and interesting to also note that when our reactions to life events were studied in relation to emotions rather than in terms of stress, there were seldom any suggestions that emotions or feelings could be detrimental to our health. Alternatively when these reactions or feelings were labeled 'stress', there were always suggestions that our health was affected.

The other point I want to make is about the coverage of the book. Some of you may feel that I have omitted some important pieces of research or that I don't seem to be aware of the latest theory or findings about stress. The latter is likely to be true. I have no doubt that some studies or explanations have escaped my scrutiny. At the same time, I can assure you that I have not omitted anything on purpose. I have no reason to do so.

There is nothing that can be said or found about stress that would ever prove conclusively that it either exists or that any of the claims that have been made can be justified. All apparent evidence will always be reliant on assumptions rather than facts. For this reason alone stress can never be shown to be a valid scientific concept.

In parting, I want to state that while the main purpose of this book is to make you the reader aware of the full story about stress, it is also about more than just stress. In a world in which sheer volume of information impedes understanding, we can sometimes have the impression that we know more and more about some aspects of the world when we, in effect, only know more of them.

INTRODUCTION

From a modest beginning 63 years ago, stress has now become a widely studied area. In scientific journals, in books and in the media, we are constantly reminded of its detrimental effects on our life and health. The Internet has many sites giving advice on dealing with it. Experts and ordinary people alike seem to agree that the demands faced by individuals in living in our modern world are responsible not only for our unhappiness but also for many of our health problems. Insurance companies are reportedly paying out enormous sums of money for stress related claims. Employees are said to be taking stress leave. Pressure from more and more demanding jobs coupled with the specter of unemployment is said to add to the level and occurrence of stress (Humphries, *The Sydney Morning Herald*, 1998). Many health specialists tell us that it is all because of our busy life style. In the United States, the American Academy of Family Physicians estimates that two thirds of visits to doctors are attributable to stress related symptoms (Wallis, *Times*, 1983). Recently, in Australia, the Australian Council of Trade Union (ACTU) declared a national stress day.

A whole new industry to combat the 'epidemic' has emerged. The stress management industry has been estimated to be worth billions of dollars in America alone (Goldstein, 1995). The public is told about stress from a wide variety of people. A mixture of 'experts', stress management practitioners, doctors and scientists offer many different points of view of what stress is and how it should be treated or handled. These points of view are often contradictory and result in a great deal of confusion.

It seems that the time has come to conduct an evaluation of the vast amount of writing that has been devoted to the concept of 'stress'. This will require an investigation of the many claims that have been made about stress. This can only be done adequately by examining critically all aspects of the stress discourse. Over the last six decades, the discourse on stress has diverged in many directions. This is in part due to the many issues that the concept has raised since its introduction. Specialists in many areas of social science, biology and medicine have conducted their own research often focusing on relatively narrow aspects. The extent and the complexity of some of their findings may have given the impression that the knowledge necessary to investigate all aspects could be beyond the understanding of a single individual. Certainly, to understand some aspects of the stress discourse requires a more than casual acquaintance with some biological, medical and psychological concepts but what is more important is an understanding of the philosophical, linguistic and methodological elements of this discourse.

Many writers in the field of stress research have expressed serious doubts about the usefulness of the concept. Others have been critical of certain aspects of the research but no one has seemingly ever undertaken a complete evaluation of the field. A possible explanation for this may be found in the fact that most of the writing on stress has assumed the existence of stress in the first place. A large majority of researchers in the field seem to be prepared to take much of the evidence from disciplines other than theirs for granted. This study, in contrast, starts from the position that stress does not exist. This is why throughout the book terms like 'stressors' and 'stressful' or 'stressed', which essentially depend on the existence of stress for their own validity, will be used with single quotes. Once the existence of stress is questioned, obvious flaws start to appear and contradictions become more obvious. Once common sense rather than faith is used it becomes evident that the more the literature has grown the greater the confusion has become. A revealing aspect of my study was that most of the evidence, which ultimately show that 'stress' is not a valid scientific concept, comes from writers who have never questioned such a validity. Another was that my initial preparedness to accept the notions of 'psychosomatic illness' and 'homeostasis' is now greatly diminished. Both these concepts, homeostasis in particular, are important

2

foundations of modern medicine, yet they remain largely unproven.

Once many of the assumptions underpinning the concept of 'stress' have been investigated and shown to be flawed, there is still a need to understand the various issues the concept of 'stress' was trying to address. In the last part of this book I discuss these issues and offer various strategies to deal with them.

POPULAR VIEWS

An analysis of the concept of 'stress' might well start at the popular level for this is where the word 'stress' is commonly used and the feeling of being 'stressed' is seemingly experienced by lay people and scientists alike. In fact, when scientists from various disciplines try to test some of the hypotheses that have emerged from various theories, they do so with the belief that stress is a legitimate source of inquiry. After all, there seems to be much agreement that the concept of 'stress' is not only a legitimate source of inquiry, it also appears to be describing a very real state that most people can relate to. It would be easy to dismiss the use of 'stress' as a useful linguistic abbreviation (Goldstein, 1995) if it were not for the many claims that have been made about the effect of stress. Thompson, Murphy, and Stradling (1994), for instance, have suggested that:

> One of the main reasons why stress is such an important area of study is its heavy cost in terms of the damage it does to individuals, to relationships and to organizations.

A difficulty for the study of stress is that the term 'stress' has a different meaning for researchers in various disciplines. In the biological literature it is used in relation to single organisms, populations of organisms, and ecosystems. Biologists refer to things such as heat, cold, and inadequate food supply as being sources of stress. Human biologists add to this microbial infection and taking of toxic substances. Social scientists, for their part, are more concerned about people's interaction with their environment and the resulting emotional disturbance that can sometimes accompany it (Hinkle, 1987).

There would have been less of a problem had scientists restricted their studies to their area of expertise. However, this has not been the case in relation to psychological stress which is the main area of interest in my examination. Many claims have been made about the physiological consequences of stress. The implication of

5

neurotransmitters, hormones and their effects on many body systems has meant that specialists in areas such as physiology, endocrinology, cardiology, neurology and other branches of medicine have been involved in the debate on psychological stress. Sometimes their studies have involved human subjects but ethical concerns have meant that often their experiments have been carried out on animals. A consequence of this has been that the proper distinction that exists between psychological and physical stress has not always been made. Furthermore, this has helped reinforce the view that stress is an all-encompassing condition. Therefore, findings have often been generalized from physical stress to psychological stress and from animals to humans.

A logical consequence of the studies of physiological responses to stress has been attempts to establish a link between stress and disease. Immunologists have played an important part in this quest but like many of the other human biologists, their definition of stress has not always been clear. Booth (1998) when asked to define stress, described it as a perception or a feeling. Bonneau(1998) also replying to an E-mail answered: "We immunologists/ virologists treat stress as a rather simple concept in our experimental model systems. However, it clearly is not!" A further question relating to the difference between stress and emotions gave a clearer indication of his views on stress when he replied "I guess I have a difficult time understanding the definitions of 'emotions' and 'stress'. Is not stress itself an emotion in response to an environmental stimulus?" and in the same e-mail "Basically, we *(immunologists/virologists)* [italic added] consider stress any stimulus that induces activation of the HPA axis and sympathetic nervous system. Perhaps this is too simplistic for psychology folks" (personal correspondence, 1998).

These comments illustrate that the many facets of the stress discourse make it difficult for a researcher to have an adequate understanding or awareness in all these facets. This is also true for social scientists. Many of them have not always understood the consequences of their

6

pronouncements concerning the physiological aspects of stress.

Under the circumstances, gaining a thorough understanding of all the issues relating to stress would seem even more problematic for lay people. Seldom versed in the rules of science or philosophy, members of the public can only but trust the many 'experts' and their findings. Unable to evaluate the validity of their claims, they are more likely to accept these claims, basing their judgments on the reputation of their author. For the lay person, scientific information is acquired or received in many forms. Popular books, magazine and newspaper articles, radio and television and increasingly the Internet, are where most of this information is available. The media address the public with regard to stress usually by adopting a basic and often simplistic approach. Metaphorical expressions are often used to this effect. In these instances stress is portrayed alternatively as 'the spice of life' or a 'silent killer'. Away from academic scrutiny, uncertain or cautious findings become certainties, estimates become facts and fanciful claims are more likely to be made. A recent article in a popular scientific magazine provides an example:

STRESS...IT'S WORSE THAN YOU THINK. The effects of stress are even more profound than imagined. It penetrates to the core of our being. Stress is not something that just grips us and, with time or effort, then lets go. It changes us in the process. It alters our bodies—and our brains (Psychology Today, 1996).

When these sorts of statement are uttered by people that are presumed to know about these things, they can often take on an absolute truth-value for many people.

In the remainder of this chapter an attempt will be made to show how stress is understood at the popular level, that is, at a non-scientific level. The reason why this evaluation is needed is that a popular view is often the only one available to most people. As for scientists, this is often the level at which many of them have gained their first understanding of stress. This may partially explain why most studies try to prove the existence of stress and its side effects rather than disprove them.

However, an attempt to depict various individuals' understanding of stress would not necessarily provide the best picture of what stress means for many people. While most people 'know' about stress, many find it difficult to describe what it is. For this reason, it would seem that looking at the various messages available to the public might give a better understanding of how stress is conceived at that level. Furthermore, the variety of explanations that are on offer may help to explain the confusion in many people's minds as to what constitutes stress.

To achieve this, extracts from newspapers and magazine articles and various Internet sites about stress are used. These have been written by members of various professions such as journalists, counselors, psychologists, psychiatrists, doctors, traditional and alternative health workers and stress management consultants. Discussions about the evidence for the existence of stress, its nature, its causes, its symptoms and effects are presented as is advice for stress management. This, hopefully, will help provide an understanding of the diverse perspectives that are offered to the public about stress.

The existence of stress

Many commentators on stress usually offer statistics to support the notion that stress exists. The three most common aspects that will be discussed refer to the belief by people that they are 'stressed', the relationship between stress and disease in the form of visits to the doctors and the cost of stress to the economies of countries where stress is said to be a problem.

People's belief that they are 'stressed'

Bernik, a Brazilian psychiatrist, claims that "The incidence of stress in the general population has been increasing at a rate of 1 % per year and in some professions, like for executives, it can affect up to 60 % of all individuals. This, alone, would make stress the 'disease of the century', or perhaps the 'disease of the third millennium'" (1997). To support his claim, he tells of a nationwide poll in the USA in which 89% of Americans reported that they often experience high levels of stress and 59% claimed that they feel great stress at least once a week.

In the USA, in a health bulletin about stress issued by the *Rose Medical Center* (1993), it is claimed that "a five-year study of the American workforce conducted by the Families and Work Institute showed that 30% of employees often or very often feel burned out or stressed by their jobs, 27% feel emotionally drained from their work and 42% feel used up at the end of the work day." The author of the bulletin concludes "Balancing work pressures and family responsibilities leaves many workers feeling burned out."

An article in *Newsweek* (1988) contains the findings of a survey by D'Arcy, Masius, Benton and Bowles, in which three quarters of Americans said that their jobs caused stress.

Davidson (1998), in an article in *Public Management*, quotes a Gallop Poll survey of a cross section of Americans which found that in the answer to the question: how often do you experience stress in your daily life? 40% answered 'always', 39% 'sometimes', 17% 'rarely' and 4% 'never'. A further finding, that three quarters of the respondents agreed that their stress was under control, led him to conclude that "After all, with all the psychology we've been exposed to in the last several decades, most people understand that they bear the most responsibility for the quality of their lives".

In England, *The Mental Health Foundation* (1997), a charity for people with mental health problems or learning disabilities, in a reply on its web site to a question concerning the number of people affected by stress and anxiety, states that "Research has shown that in the course of a year 12 million adults attending GP surgeries have mental health problems; of these the great majority (80%) suffer from anxiety and depressive states."

A press release by a trade union, the Manufacturing, Science & Finance Union [MSF] (1997), announces that:

Government minister Angela Eagle MP will tomorrow join MSF, the union for more than 400,000 skilled and professional people, to release a survey which shows stress in the London workplace has doubled in the last five years, making London the most stressful place to work.

It also features claims that eight in ten people say stress is a major problem in their workplace and that it is worse now than it was 5 years ago. The fact that so many people are prepared to say they are 'stressed' seems at odds with a claim by Rees (1997) in the *Sunday Times* that:

> ...while stress - and the effects inflicted on individuals by prolonged or excessive amounts of pressure - is nothing new, it is emerging slowly from the shadows of ignorance and prejudice. Okay, the stigma still exists and an admission of stress is still perceived by some as a sign of weakness. The unspoken fear encapsulated in the phrase, 'I'll never get promoted if I admit to being stressed, remains. It is revealing to note that, when a stress-management seminar was staged in the City of London last year, attendance was poor. People didn't turn up because they didn't want to display weakness.

Nevertheless, another survey conducted by the Office for National Statistics (1997) on behalf of the *Health Education Authority*, titled *Health In England: What People Know, What People Think, What People Do,* reveals that 69 per cent of women and 62 per cent of men reported they had experienced a 'moderate' or 'large' amount of stress in the 12 months before the interview. Over two fifths of all men and more than half of all women felt stress had had a harmful effect on their health.

An earlier survey of workplace union safety representatives, carried out by the Trade Union Congress [TUC] (1996), allegedly showed that occupational stress was the major health and safety issue in British workplaces, affecting workers in all sectors, regardless of company size. It found that 68% of safety representatives identified stress as one of the top five health and safety concerns of their work colleagues and that "An alarming 89% of safety reps in the voluntary sector cited stress as a major health and safety issue, the highest rate of all sectors". In education, the percentage was 80%.

When 699 personnel and human resources professionals were surveyed by the Industrial Society, only 7% said stress was regarded as an excuse for taking time off work. That compared with 83% who confirmed stress was a problem in their organizations (Rees, 1997).

In Belgium, an article in the newspaper *Le Soir* (1997) contains an estimate of professional stress that puts the figure at about 30% of the work population. The author of the article, however, admits that "In Belgium, the extent of the phenomenon is more difficult to capture (than in the USA) notably because it is not recognized as a professional disease."

In France, the newspaper *Les Dernières Nouvelles D'Alsace* (1996) reports a study by 101 workplace doctors of 1070 truck drivers in Normandy in 1994. Describing the problem alternatively as 'nervous tension' and 'stress', the study found that 16% of respondents reported always feeling very tired, with 30% feeling 'nervous' and 'tense' and 20.7% being often angry. Despite this, 78% of the truck drivers were fairly or very satisfied with their job.

In 1997, a Canadian Mental Health Survey, sponsored by *The Canadian Mental Health Association*, found that when compared to a similar survey in 1992, there was a five percentage point increase in the number of respondents who said their stress levels were higher than two years before. This, however, did not happen to people in Quebec, their number dropping from 54% to 40%. Yet in British Columbia and the Atlantic regions only 30% of respondents reported increased stress (the Canadian Mental Health, 1997). Commenting on the survey, National President of the Canadian Mental Health Association, Sharron Gould, declared in the same news release, that "This new survey confirms that Canadians are experiencing disturbing levels of stress in their lives."

Doctor's visits

Stress is often described as an epidemic affecting the Western World *(The American Institute of stress*, 1998; Humphries & Delvecchio, 1998; Rose Medical Center, 1993; Rees, 1997; Stress Free Net, 1998). It is estimated that over two-thirds of office visits to physicians are for stress related illness (Stress Free Net, 1998).

On their internet site promoting seminars in stress reduction, Karen and David Gamow (1998) use a quote from *The American Institute of Stress* stating that "75-90% of employee visits to hospitals are for ailments linked to stress." but they do so despite some reservation about its veracity (personal communication, 1998).

Gould, (1997) describing himself as a leading psychiatrist and expert in adult development and self-care software, suggests that stress accounts for 40-60% of all doctor's visits and that 23 million people are affected by anxiety disorders. He also claims that "At any given time 3% of the population seek help while another 23% suffer from the same amount of stress but avoid getting help for fear of what others might think." While he does not offer evidence to support his claim, he offers a self-help computer program called *Mastering Stress* to remedy the problem.

The Cost of Stress

Estimates of the cost of stress vary wildly in most countries. In the USA, stress-related illness is thought to cost businesses over $150 billion a year (Kiechel III, 1986; Gould, 1997). Bernik (1997) feels that the figure is more likely to be between 50 to 75 billion dollars lost each year, directly or indirectly, due to stress and that this would represent around 750 dollars per year per worker. Karen and David Gamow (1998) use an estimate by George Pfeiffer, WorkCare Group, costing the loss to industry for stress-related ailments at $200 billion per annum. Seppa (1997) quotes a 1989 Gallup poll survey which found that roughly 16 workdays are lost per year for each reported case of stress on the job.

In England the estimates also tend to fluctuate. According to *The Mental Health Foundation*, about 45 million working days are lost each year through anxiety and stress conditions with a cost to industry of over £3000 million. The MSF survey (1997) found that cost to be around £7000 million. This was calculated on the basis that 130 million days were lost every year through stress, equivalent to one week for every working person in the country. That same year, a report by the *Industrial Society* showed that absenteeism (due to stress) costs Britain at least £13 billion a year, with the highest absence rates in the public and voluntary sectors (Spiney, *Electronic Telegraph*, 1997). Tyler (1998), thought that the number of lost working days "through the ravage of misunderstood stress" was over 100 million. Rees' claim, that every day in the UK some 270,000 people take time off work for stress-related illness is more modest as it amounts to around 65 million days per annum (1997).

In Australia, a claim in *The Sydney Morning Herald* by Humphries and Delvecchio (1998,) that 'stressed' workers cost companies $60 million annually is difficult to compare to that of the ACTU, a labor organization, which suggests that between 1990 and 1994, compensation claims for stress in the New South Wales public sector had more than quadrupled, at a cost of $35.7 million (Trinca, *The Sydney Morning Herald*, 1997). A later estimate put the cost of compensation in Australia at over $200 million and the overall cost of stress at $1.2 billion. (Jacobsen, *The Sydney Morning Herald*, 1999)

In South Africa, *Business Day Online* (1996) in its Internet edition reports that 'thinking skills' mogul Richard Broome said that transcendental meditation can halt the stress-induced absenteeism costing local business 1.5 billion Rand annually.

Other claims implying the existence of stress

There have been suggestions that advances in science and technology have made it possible to observe and measure either stress itself or its effects. In an article in *Free Press*, Boyd (1997) announces that:

> Recent advances in biology are allowing scientists to determine why recent declines in stock prices—or a myriad of other stuff— makes people feel so stressed. They are now able to see how stress actually changes the physical structure and chemistry of the brain, sometimes leading to lifelong disability.

For others, these advances can be located in both psychology and technology. In an article published by

Stress Free Net (1998) it is claimed these advances have made "…it possible to accurately assess and measure levels of stress in the individual and in the workplace". Meyer (1998) states that "developments in computer technology have made it possible to watch your body's stress reactions and muscle tension on a graphically displayed video monitor. This is called Biofeedback".

Definitions of stress

There is much confusion in popular discourse about what stress actually is. Rees (1997) after alleging that "Stress is affecting more and more lives - and one of the easiest places to catch it is in the workplace" adds that "Of course, there is no such thing as a stress-free life. As one expert puts it, stress is a life circumstance not a pathological condition." Bernik (1997) has a different perspective and offers that stress "… designates the aggression itself, leading to discomfort or the consequences of it. It is our organism's response to a challenge, be it right or wrong." Yet, for natural therapist Bowman (1998), it is the body's automatic response to any physical or mental demand placed upon it. When pressures are threatening, he claims that the body rushes to supply protection by turning on 'the juices' and preparing to defend itself. "It's the 'flight or fight' response in action". This is similar to the understanding expressed in a publication on the Internet by *Rose Medical Center* (1993) in which stress is also reduced to the 'flight or fight' response. The difference is that it is also described as an adaptive response and the body's reaction to an event that is seen as emotionally disturbing, disquieting or threatening.

In an article in *Forbes Magazine* (1995), stress is explained as being "...nature's way of putting your body on red alert—something that can come in handy if, for instance, a lion has just taken a large chunk out of your backside." That same notion of 'attack' is reflected in nutritionist Mindell's (1997) definition of stress as "… a wonderful word to describe what happens when we humans are assaulted by a difficult, frightening, unpleasant or anxiety provoking situation." Morgan, a natural therapist, does not

14

directly refer to 'flight or fight' but suggests that "If the body is surprised or alarmed from an outside stimulus, the body's startle system is triggered" (1998). Stress, according to Morgan, is "the body's main code for healing and restoring the body to its perfect state", when such a state is inhibited by the muscular tension which itself is caused by mentally holding on to 'stressors'.

A writer for *The Mental Health Foundation* (1997) views stress as the body's reaction to difficult situations, while a psychiatrist, Gould (1998) describes stress as a natural physical and emotional response to events or thoughts that impact on our well-being. He explains "Stress is our signal that we must make some adjustment in our lives. Prolonged stress occurs when we are stuck, when we can't take appropriate action because we are in conflict about what to do or are afraid to take the necessary steps." Another psychiatrist, Posen (1994) quotes Hans Selye, 'the father of stress theory', as having defined stress as "the nonspecific response of the body to any demand made upon it". Then he adds that the 'demand' can be a threat, a challenge or any kind of change which requires the body to adapt, the response to that demand being automatic and immediate.

Counseling centers at universities have varying explanations of stress. Members of the staff at the University of Illinois at Urbana-Champaign (1996) describe stress as the 'wear and tear' our bodies experience as we adjust to our continually changing world. At the University of Texas Counseling Services (1998), it is felt that "stress is unique and personal to each of us. What is relaxing to one person may be stressful to another. One person may find 'taking it easy' at the beach relaxing while another may find it boring". Finally, a page on the Internet from Bilkent University Counseling Center (1998), in Turkey, proposes that we experience destructive stress as "overload on our physical and psychological strength" when our usual coping strategies are insufficient to handle the 'stressful' situation.

Other organizations and individuals offer yet more explanations as to what stress may be. For Arbetter, a journalist with *Current Health*, stress, it seems, is a personal thing but at the same time she defines it "as any extra demand made on the system"(1992). This is similar to the view expressed on behalf of Stress Free Net (1998). It argues that "Stress is a state of tension that is created when a person responds to the demands and pressures that come from work, family and other external sources, as well as those that are internally generated from self imposed demands, obligations and self-criticism." James (1994) writing for the *Medical Consultants Network, Inc* [MCN] states that "Pictures of stress may include freeway traffic, a dog's bark in the tedium of insomnia, a mother-in-law visiting over the holidays or a boss drumming his fingers on a conference table. No matter how diverse the images, the physical imprint of stress on the body is remarkably uniform. There is a medically recognizable process that all these images evoke." However, she concedes that "Defining stress is difficult, but one of the well-accepted concepts is that occupational stress comes from jobs that make high demands and allow little control."

Kelly Gray, a school student writing for her school newspaper, appears to agree with these previous definitions by also declaring that stress is the tension you feel when faced with new, unpleasant or threatening situations. However she adds, "Although stress may seem bad, it can really be very good for teenagers. It helps them face many of life's challenges" (1998).

For *The American Institute of Stress* (1998) "Stress comes in all shapes and sizes and has become so pervasive, that it seems to permeate everything and everybody…. Stress is an unavoidable consequence of life. Without stress, there would be no life". Yet, Kiechel III (1986), writing in *Fortune Magazine*, concedes that "…a few conceptual difficulties remain: even the experts can't agree on what stress is, how it works or what can be done about it". Davidson (1998), on the other hand, has no doubt as evidenced by his statement that "Stress is an ever-present reality. You don't need a ton of data-supporting evidence to know that you're experiencing it on a daily basis. It hits you in the face or the gut or wherever you happen to feel it, often enough. It's real for you and that's all that counts."

The stress reaction

Stress is mostly defined by its reaction or its effects. This section attempts to show how various commentators in the public domain have explained the stress reaction. Bowman (1998) largely follows Hans Selye's description of the three stages of his General Adaptation Syndrome and suggests that under stress, change is experienced as a threat which triggers the release of hormones from the brain. The body goes through the stage of alarm when the body recognizes a 'stressor' and prepares for it. This includes release of hormones and neurotransmitters, rise of blood pressure, perspiration, etc. This is followed by the stage of resistance during which, Bowman claims, the body repairs the damage done during the alarm stage. Ultimately, the final stage is that of exhaustion. This stage only occurs when either the 'stressor' does not go away, multiple 'stressors' occur or the capacity for adaptation is exhausted. If any of these happen then "...the sign of the alarm reaction reappears and the individual becomes impaired." The description given by Bernik (1997) is much simpler and stipulates that "The perception of an imminent danger or traumatic event is made by a part of the brain named cortex."

Other explanations of the stress response are linked with the 'flight or fight' response. Talk of alarm and emergency abounds. For instance, people are told:

> When you're feeling overwhelmed, or encounter a major stressor of some kind in your environment, your adrenaline kicks in and your sympathetic nervous system takes over. Your body is suddenly prepared for action. But when there's no dinosaur to slay or damsel in distress to rescue, your body reacts with heart palpitations, sweating, increased stomach acidity, stomach spasm, skeletal muscle spasms and increased blood pressure (*Rose Medical Center*, 1993).

Morgan (1998) on the other hand believes that:

> If the body is surprised or alarmed from an outside stimulus, the body's startle system is triggered, and adrenaline is injected into

the system. Among the things adrenaline does is constrict the cardiovascular system and inject clotting factors into the blood to restrict bleeding in battle...This Fight, Flee or Freeze mechanism is triggered by our mental process. After time, this situation leaves deposits of oxygenated fats in our arteries and veins, restricting the flow of blood and raising blood pressure to dangerous levels, setting us up for a heart attack or stroke[1]

The author of the article written on behalf of the *Health Response Ability Systems, Inc.* (1995) also proposes that it is the body which reacts to stress with a 'flight or fight' response. The body's response is in preparation to do something, either fight and eliminate the 'stressor' or flee from the 'stressor' but "Usually, it's not practical to fight or to leave a stressor. As a result, individuals internalize stress...and then they get sick."

Prosen (1998) and staff at Bilkent University Counseling Center (1998) offer remarkably similar depictions of the stress response. Also reducing such response to the 'flight or fight' response, they both talk of "outpouring of adrenaline, a stimulant hormone, into the blood stream" and of protective changes in the body which "...provide the strength and energy to either fight or run away from danger." However, the counselors at Bilkent conclude from this that:

> Our physiological response to stress hasn't evolved beyond the days when we lived in caves. Our cave-dwelling ancestors, by running or fighting, got the source of the stress out of their lives. Modern man is frequently unable to avoid or overcome the stress causes in his environment, and therefore spends a major portion of his life in a state for which he isn't really designed—like a car kept constantly at full throttle, even when it is sitting at a stop light.

This ancestral origin of the stress response is also promoted by Sandberg (1998) who explains that it "... is one of a number of instincts our ancestors developed thousands of years ago that is passed down to us through our genes....

---

[1] It is worth noting that the body is first described as the trigger to the body's startle system, when this system is renamed the 'fight and freeze' system it is triggered by mental processes.

This instinct is built into our DNA. And, whether we like it or not, it's with us for good." He further elaborates on the development of the stress response by claiming that whilst our brain can do a certain number of things at the same time, like a computer chip it can only hold on to a certain number of unfinished things at one time. So over time, the brain has developed an 'overflow control' which is in effect the stress response. This response 'kicks in' when we try to keep too many things going at once and "gives us the sensation of stress". "If we try to ignore it, the stress response just kicks in harder and hands out more stress", then as stress rises the body triggers another primitive response the 'flight or fight' response. It is clear that for Sandberg the stress response is not the 'flight or fight' response itself, but rather causes that response.

Finally as far as Riddering (1998) is concerned, stress is all about homeostasis. In fact, he contends that "Homeostasis is a mechanism geared towards counteracting the stresses of living, creating a new balance every time." and that when the body "meets the stress challenge" it does so by creating a new homeostasis.

The nature of stress

Three common basic points are continually found in popular and sometimes academic, explanations regarding the nature of stress. The first is that stress is not all that bad after all and that, in fact, it can be beneficial in the right but usually unspecified amount. The second is that too much stress will do much harm and the last is that stress is an inevitable and necessary part of life and that life without stress would not be worth living.

Bowman (1998) promotes the view that not all stress is bad and that the stress reaction is necessary and can be beneficial. He tells how stress can assist us in threatening situations by allowing us to run faster or fight harder and does so by giving us 'strength body fuels' in emergency situations. Others believe that:

> In metered doses, it can be helpful...it can even make you better at what you do, and help give you the competitive edge. If we

can harness stress, it may help to make us more alert, energize us, or give us 'a motivational kick in the pants'. It's the major-league, non-stop, never-let-up stress you have to watch out for. Because, man, it can kill you (*Rose Medical Center*, 1993).

Morgan's (1998) contribution is that stress itself is neither good nor bad and that light stress such as exercise can help strengthen the system.

A company press release promoting the 'Power of flowers' to beat the stress blues (Bach Flower Remedies, 1996) declares that everyone suffers from stress at some points "...it is normal, natural and indeed necessary for us to work better." The author of *The American Institute of Stress*' home page (1998)[2] goes a bit further by stating that "stress is an unavoidable consequence of life. Without stress, there would be no life." He continues by saying that although distress causes disease, this is offset by the good stresses which themselves 'promote' wellness. He further suggests that up to a point increased stress results in increased productivity and that point depends on the individual. Comparing the stress on people to that exercised on a violin string, he tells us that:

"Not enough produces a dull, raspy sound. Too much makes a shrill, annoying noise, or causes the string to snap. However, just the right degree can create magnificent tones. Similarly, we all need to find the proper level of stress that promotes optimal performance, and enables us to make melodious music."

Causes of stress

Many things, it seems, are said to cause stress. The following is a list of alleged 'stressors' by many of the previously mentioned writers:

Environmental (noise, air pollution), social (over-crowding), interpersonal (behavior or others), personal (feelings or thoughts), and physical (illness, injury) (Bowman, 1998).

Illness, job changes, moving, separations and divorces, deaths in the family, and financial difficulties. But even joyous events, like marriage, the arrival of a baby, or entertaining guests, can be

---

[2] Hans Selye was the founder of *The American Institute of Stress*.

stressful... overwhelming responsibilities at home or work, loneliness, the fear of losing our jobs (*Rose Medical Center*, 1993).

Management style and working conditions are the biggest causes of stress (MSF, 1997).

External stressors include: physical environment: noise, bright lights, heat, confined spaces. Social (interaction with people): rudeness, bossiness, or aggressiveness on the part of someone else. Organizational: rules, regulations, "red tape," deadlines. Major life events: death of a relative, lost job, promotion, new baby. Daily hassles: commuting, misplacing keys, mechanical breakdowns. Internal stressors include Lifestyle choices: caffeine, not enough sleep, and overloaded schedule. Negative self-talk: pessimistic thinking, self-criticism, over-analyzing. Mind traps: unrealistic expectations, taking things personally, all-or-nothing thinking, exaggerating, rigid thinking. Stressful personality traits: type A, perfectionist, workaholic, pleaser (Posen, 1994).

External stressors can include relatives getting sick or dying, jobs being lost or people criticizing or becoming angry. Social (interaction with people): rudeness, bossiness or aggressiveness on the part of someone else (Health Response Ability Systems, Inc., 1995).

There are 4 major causes of disease: radiation stress, chemical stress, emotional stress, and nutritional stress (Boschen, 1997).

There are two basic causes of stress - excessive workload and traumatic memories. The hereditary vulnerability, plus the concern about the future in a time of economical or political uncertainties, of decreasing quality of life, of looming unemployment, of fear of old age, and of becoming destitute; has led to a general increase of persons who report stress. Other contributing factors are the lack of regular leisure or physical activity, bad or scarce food, an inadequate family structure and support, etc. In general, acute or chronic stress can be attributed to the biggest problems we have during our life courses. Certain events in our lives are so severe in terms of stress, that they are characterized as a trauma (lesion or damage) of a psychic origin (Bernik, 1997).

It's official - women are the biggest cause of stress in a man's life! The nineties man, beset by changing work patterns and job uncertainties, tied down with mortgages and higher purchase loans ... still blame a nagging girlfriend or an annoying mother-in-law for a rise in blood pressure or the onset of a tension

21

headache. When asked what the major cause of stress in their life was, the answer was bad news for girlfriends. Over 20 per cent of the men questioned said that the thought of their future mother-in-law gave them a huge headache - more than career worries, financial fears or football blunders. And an irritable or demanding girlfriend presented a problem for many. This was just one of the surprise findings revealed by a survey of FHM readers, commissioned by leading painkiller Nurofen to find out how men cope with pain (Nurofen, 1997).

Stress is a part of every student's daily life. Your personal stress requirements and the amount which you can tolerate before you become distressed varies with your life situation and your age. As a college student, the greatest sources of events you experience as stressful are likely to be relationships, academic and social situations, environment and lifestyle. Leaving home or commuting daily, managing finances, living with roommates and juggling a job, classes, and relationships all contribute to the normal stress of being at the University. It is also not uncommon for students to feel overwhelmed and anxious about wasting time, meeting high standards or being lonely. In addition, stress can also come from exciting or positive events. Falling in love, preparing to study abroad or buying a new car can be just as stressful as less happy events (University of Texas Counseling Services, 1998).

Scientists say stress can be caused by anything from a bad day at the office or a nasty letter from the IRS to something deeply traumatic like combat in war, sexual abuse or a baby's lack of motherly love (Boyd, Free Press Washington Staff, 1997).

Rapid changes in science and technology have led to increased stress levels for individuals (Davidson, 1998).

A Press release from Ohio State University (1998) reports a study by one of its researchers, which found that:

Both married men and women identify economics, finances, and budgeting as the top stressors... Also high on both lists is not spending enough time together and disciplining the children. But beyond that, husbands and wives disagree about what causes stress in their lives. That disagreement alone may be a big cause of stress—and it's one many families overlook...husbands more often mentioned difficulty in communicating with children, over-scheduled family calendars, unhappiness with their work situation and television. Wives more often mentioned lack of shared responsibilities in the family, housekeeping standards, guilt about not accomplishing more and self-image or self-esteem.

Finally, unions blame longer working hours and growing pressure on staff to sell financial products for the extra stress (Banking Insurance and Finance Union [BIFU], 1996).

In Australia, a survey by the ACTU found that workers thought that the main causes of stress were of lack of communication and consultation (53 per cent), increased workload (42 percent), job insecurity and lack of career paths (36 percent), organizational change and restructuring (29 percent). Many of the respondents said they were treated like slaves, robots, machines or children (Trinca, *The Sydney Morning Herald*, 1997).

The effects of stress, including diseases

Not only are many things held responsible for causing stress, stress itself is blamed for causing many conditions or at least playing a part in them. The following physical symptoms are suggested "...fatigue, headache, insomnia, muscle aches/stiffness (especially neck, shoulders and lower back), heart palpitations, chest pains, abdominal cramps, nausea, trembling, cold extremities, flushing or sweating and frequent colds" (Posen, 1994).

A stress management company on the Internet also names cool skin, rapid breathing, dry mouth, a desire to urinate, diarrhea, change in appetite and illness such as asthma, digestive problems, skin eruptions, sexual disorders, aches and pains (Mind Tools, 1996) The consequences of stress, Boyd (1997) proposes, "range from trivial—like the abnormal eating pattern like 'midnight munchies' to such crippling disabilities as ulcers, colitis, anxiety, irrational fear and major depression."

More alarmist, however, is Tyler (1998) who warns us 'STRESS CAN KILL!' and declares that:

Heart attacks, strokes, nervous breakdowns, drink abuse, drug abuse, divorce, suicides. So-called modern day stresses are responsible wholly or in part. At its extreme it is accepted as a killer...Stress is a major contributing factor either directly or indirectly, to coronary artery disease, cancer, respiratory disorders, accidental injuries, cirrhosis of the liver and suicide; the six leading causes of death in the United States....

The suggestion that stress merely aggravates other conditions such as multiple sclerosis, diabetes, herpes, mental illness, alcoholism, drug abuse, and family discord and violence seems somehow more reassuring (Stress Free Net, 1998).

Some writers imply some scientific respectability for their claims by alleging that "Stress is medically known to cause gastritis, ulcerative colitis, irritable bowl syndrome, peptic ulcers, hypertension, asthma, depression, etc. to name just a few." (Riddering, 1998) or by proposing that there is a "...growing confirmation of the role of stress in Heart Disease, Hypertension, Sudden Death, Depression, Anxiety, Smoking, Obesity, Alcoholism, Substance Abuse, Cancer, Arthritis, Gastrointestinal, Skin and a host of infections and immune system disorders." (*The American Institute of Stress*, 1998).

Others seem less certain, as evidenced by the statement by staff at the *Rose Medical Center* (1993) indicating that "Researchers tell us that stress may play a role in the development of high blood pressure, though more studies are necessary to tighten up the connection. Stress also appears associated with heart disease, even if a direct causal relationship has yet to be proven."

Many newspapers and magazines have published stories relating to the role of stress in specific diseases or conditions.

Heart disease

Bairey-Merz (1997), writing for *Newsweek*, tells us that: "Studies show that 75% of coronary patients experience ischemic heart dysfunction, an early sign of a heart attack, as a result of various kinds of mental stress. Stress also causes high blood pressure and other conditions that contribute to heart attacks.

Despite such a positive start, he admits later in the article that:

Although studies of this nature are intriguing, they can only teach us about associations between stress and heart disease. They do not prove that the two entities are directly related, and do not help us understand the mechanisms of how they might be related. Studies that demonstrate causality and mechanisms are necessary for definitive identification of linkage between mental stress and heart disease, and for treatment development.

Blindness

She's got the blinding blues: link found between stress and blindness. With this dramatic headline in the magazine *Health*, Pine (1988) tells of a 32 year old seemingly happily married woman. When her husband suddenly left her we are told that she spent hours 'submerged in memories' but that "she really hit rock bottom the day she woke up partially blind, a victim of 'central serious chorioretinophathy', a stress-induced weakening of the retina resulting in blindness in one eye". Pine then quotes a study of 33 patients with vision loss which found that stress was a factor in 30 of those examined. This was deduced from the fact that these patients had apparently suffered a 'stressful' event weeks or even hours before their loss of vision. "...What's more" she comments:

97 percent of the patients qualified as hard-driving type A perfectionists. The researchers speculate that the effects of stress, soaring blood pressure and a release of 'flight or fight' hormones, injure the blood vessels near the retina. When these vessels and capillaries around the retina leak, the structure that attaches the retina to the eye weakens, gradually resulting in blindness. In severe cases, the retina eventually totally detaches.

Fortunately, we are told that the condition is reversible if the person can get over his or her source of stress and can also be corrected by such methods as laser surgery.

Irritable bowel syndrome

Adessa (1989), in *Psychology Today* argues that there is growing evidence that emotional stress and ineffective ways of dealing with it may play a major role in Irritable Bowel Syndrome.

Esophageal pain

McKeown (1989), in an article in *Nation's Business* titled *'Esophageal pain: another price of success'*, reports a statement by Dr. Joel Richter, an associate professor at *The Bowman-Gray School of Medicine Business*. Richter claims that 90,000 to 150, 000 new cases of esophageal pain are diagnosed every year in the USA and that business people are particularly vulnerable to esophageal pain because they constantly face 'stressful' situations that can activate the condition.

Multiple sclerosis

A *Reuters News Service* dispatch, published in the electronic newspaper *Nando Times* (1998), tells of a study that shows that multiple sclerosis worsens with stress. It quotes David Mohr, a clinical professor of neurology at the University of San Francisco, who claims that his study of 48 patients indicated a clear correlation between stress and the development of the brain lesions characteristic of MS. He found that major 'stressful' events as well as small daily hassles were related to the development of new lesions in the brain two months later. The article concludes that this provides clear evidence of increased disease activity in the brain.

Less threatening conditions

Loss of hair

A press release in 1997 by *Organics*, a hair care product manufacturer in England, announces that:

> Recent newspaper headlines have highlighted a growing concern among working women and one which represents a nightmare vision - working so hard, under so much stress that their hair falls out. Leading celebrity hair stylist, Denise McAdam has been observing the phenomenon of thinning hair and even hair fall-out among some of her high-powered female clients in the last few years. Denise joined forces with psychologist, Dr. David Lewis in June this year to examine the causes of hair loss and both agreed that stress was a strong contributing factor (1997).

The psychologist suggested that the "scalp tightening effect of stress restricts blood flow to the scalp, slowing or hampering the hair's growth and making it appear dull and lifeless." The hairdresser's contribution was that "The hair is the body's natural barometer, it gives clues to how someone's lifestyle is taking its toll on their health." and that a visit to a "... salon is one of the greatest stress-relievers."

Infertility

Goodman (1994), in the magazine *Health*, informs us that:

It has been known that infertility, with its ongoing disappointments, causes stress, but some are beginning to believe that stress itself may bring about infertility. Relaxation and stress management classes and techniques may be an effective approach to the infertility problem.

Disorders of the mind

Stress, according to Bernik (1997), may also be accompanied by a wide range of disorders of the mind, either temporary or permanent. Exacerbation of previously existent neurotic, psychopathic or sociopathic disorders can also be experienced. Further symptoms that can also be due to stress include irritability, weakness, nervousness, fears, obsessive thoughts, failed acts, compulsive rituals, etc. He adds:

Anguish is very common, and there is an increase in emotional sensitivity to small, unimportant events, which usually provoke unjustifiable violent discussions or aggressive behavior. On the other hand, there are also depressive symptoms associated to [sic] stress, such as the decrease of appetite, sleep disturbances, apathetic behavior, affective bluntness (emotionless people) and loss of libido and sexual interest.

Newman (1998), a BBC Science journalist, reports on a study by Dr. Amy Arnsten from Yale University School of Medicine in the United States in which the different regions of the brain that become active at different times were observed. He also describes how the team, led by Dr. Arnsten, claims to have discovered that stress suppresses the part of the brain that makes us rational. Their leader explains that:

When we're stressed, we produce a family of nerve chemicals that act on our body, preparing our heart and muscles to respond to danger. But they also act on our brain, where they stimulate a region long known to be the seat of emotion… Meanwhile, the same chemicals turn-off the part of our brain that allows us to cut out distractions.

This, she, feels is important because "We need to organize and concentrate and remember things better than ever now, in order to deal with the great complexities of modern life."

A short anonymous article in Forbes Magazine titled 'Stress can cause - um, I forgot. (Research shows that long-term stress may shrink part of the brain that keeps people intelligent)' suggests that there is "another good reason to chill out: stress might make you stupid" (1996). The author of the article relies on a study undertaken a few years earlier by Sapolsky, which claimed that in rats, months of stress shrink the hippocampus permanently.

Weight problems

An *Associated Press* news wire published in *Nando Times* (1998) with the headline *'Stress hormone linked to high-fat snacking in women'*, informs us that "Gobbling down that handful of potato chips when you're under stress may have more to do with hormones than hunger, according to a preliminary study by Yale University researchers." Researchers, we are told, examined the eating habits of 60 women and measured levels of cortisol in their saliva. The women were given a variety of 'stressful' tasks to perform such as counting backwards, trying to solve an unsolvable puzzle and giving a speech within unrealistic time constraints. It was found that the women who secreted the most cortisol ate the greatest amount of high fat food after the 'stressful' tasks. Those who didn't eat any high-fat food had secreted the least amount of cortisol. Later in the article, two researchers are quoted; one of them cautioning that other hormones have a bearing on eating and another calling the research 'over simplistic'.

Effect of stress on medication

'Watch the washout: can stress affect your medications?' warns and asks Munson (1995) in the publication *Prevention*. He reports a study which indicated that stress could inhibit the effectiveness of blood-thinning

medications in the form of a fish-oil regimen. The study claims that the benefits of the medication regimen were destroyed after just eight minutes of stress. The stress was measured by distracting subjects while they were focusing on a task or trying to make a good social impression.

Dealing with stress

Some of the contributors to the popular discussion on stress hold the view that stress is inevitable and a majority implicitly accept that 'stressors' are a feature of our environment. From these points of view, stress cannot be eliminated and all that can be done is to deal with its consequences. To this effect, many strategies are offered. For instance, Gould (1997) thinks it is just a matter of understanding what is causing stress and developing a plan of action.

Bernik (1997) proposes that we should rethink our life, "...mostly by identifying the sources of stress" and that a psychiatrist may be helpful as he can assist with prescription drugs:

> ...but sometimes simple changes, such as doing more exercise, getting more free time for leisure, or changes in life habits are enough to do good... The true and old wisdom, however, says that our main attitude towards avoiding stress should be to learn how to deal sensibly with our own emotions, and how to live well and without tension, at home as well as at work.

Bowman (1998) believes: that

> Many of us use negative methods to cope with stress. Such behaviors as drinking alcohol and caffeine, smoking, using drugs, or overeating only add more stress to the body. More positive coping methods are beneficial to the body and mind in the long run. Positive coping methods are: exercise, meditation, yoga, self-hypnosis, healthy diet, positive attitude, being assertive, expressing feelings, talking problems out with a friend or counselor, time management, modifying the environment and taking breaks and vacations.

Counselors usually offer highly detailed programs to deal with stress. At the University of Illinois (1996), a six-point plan is proposed which requires constant practice to be effective:

1. Become aware of your stressors and your emotional and physical reactions.

Notice your distress. Don't ignore it. Don't gloss over your problems. Determine what events distress you. What are you telling yourself about meaning of these events? Determine how your body responds to the stress. Do you become nervous or physically upset? If so, in what specific ways?

2. Recognize what you can change.

Can you change your stressors by avoiding or eliminating them completely? Can you reduce their intensity (manage them over a period of time instead of on a daily or weekly basis)? Can you shorten your exposure to stress (take a break, leave the physical premises)? Can you devote the time and energy necessary to making a change (goal setting, time management techniques, and delayed gratification strategies may be helpful here)?

3. Reduce the intensity of your emotional reactions to stress.

The stress reaction is triggered by your perception of danger...physical danger and/or emotional danger. Are you viewing your stressors in exaggerated terms and/or taking a difficult situation and making it a disaster? Are you expecting to please everyone? Are you overreacting and viewing things as absolutely critical and urgent? Do you feel you must always prevail in every situation? Work at adopting more moderate views; try to see the stress as something you can cope with rather than something that overpowers you. Try to temper your excess emotions. Put the situation in perspective. Do not labor on the negative aspects and the 'ifs.'

4. Learn to moderate your physical reactions to stress.

Slow, deep breathing will bring your heart rate and respiration back to normal. Relaxation techniques can reduce muscle tension. Electronic biofeedback can help you gain voluntary control over such things as muscle tension, heart rate, and blood pressure. Medications, when prescribed by a physician, can help in the short term in moderating your physical reactions. However, they alone are not the answer. Learning to moderate these reactions on your own is a preferable long-term solution.

5. Build your physical reserves.

Exercise for cardiovascular fitness three to four times a week (moderate, prolonged rhythmic exercise is best, such as walking, swimming, cycling, or jogging). Eat well-balanced, nutritious meals. Maintain your ideal weight. Avoid nicotine, excessive caffeine, and other stimulants. Mix leisure with work. Take breaks and get away when you can. Get enough sleep. Be as consistent with your sleep schedule as possible.

6. Maintain your emotional reserves.

Develop some mutually supportive friendships/relationships. Pursue realistic goals which are meaningful to you, rather than goals others have for you that you do not share. Expect some frustrations, failures, and sorrows. Always be kind and gentle with yourself—be a friend to yourself.

Not to be outdone, the University of Texas Counseling Services (1998), has a 14-point plan. The following is a short version of it:

1. Take a Deep Breath!

2. Manage Time by giving priority to the most important and unpleasant things first and not overworking.

3. Connect with others and seek activities involving others.

4. Talk It Out. When you feel something, try to express it (appropriately, of course!). 'Bottled up' emotions increase frustration and stress. Share your feelings. Perhaps a friend, family member, teacher, clergy person, or counselor can help you see your problem in a different light.

5. Take a 'Minute' Vacation. Create a quiet scene. You can't always run away, but you can dream. Imagining a quiet country scene can take you out of the turmoil of a stressful situation. ...Or change your mental 'channel' by reading a good book or playing relaxing music to create a sense of peace and tranquillity.

6. Monitor Your Physical Comfort. Be as physically comfortable as the situation will allow. Wear comfortable clothing. If it's too hot, go somewhere where it's not. If your chair is uncomfortable, change it. If your computer screen causes eye-strain or backaches, change that, too.

7. Get Physical. Try to find something you enjoy and make regular time for it. Running, walking or swimming are good options for some people, while others prefer dance or martial arts. Working in the garden, washing your car, or playing with your dog can relieve that 'uptight' feeling, relax you, and often will actually energize you! Remember, your body and mind work together.

8. Take Care of Your Body. You are special! Take care of yourself. Healthy eating and adequate sleep fuels your mind as well as your body. Avoid consuming too much caffeine and sugar.

9. Laugh. Maintain your sense of humor, including the ability to laugh at yourself. Rent or take yourself to a funny movie: the sillier the plot the better. Laughter is good for you!

10. Know Your Limits. A major source of stress is people's efforts to control events or other people over whom they have little or no power. When confronted with a stressful situation, ask yourself: is this my problem? There are many circumstances in life beyond your control, starting with the weather and including in particular the behavior of others. Consider the fact that we live in an imperfect world.

11. Must You Always Be Right? Consider cooperation or compromise rather than confrontation. A little give and take on both sides may reduce the strain and help you both feel more comfortable.

12. Have a Good Cry. Big boys and girls do cry. A good cry during periods of stress can be a healthy way to bring relief to your anxiety... However, if you are crying daily, seek a consultation with a counselor or a physician. This can be a sign of depression.

13. Avoid Self Medication. Alcohol and other drugs do not remove the conditions that cause stress... Prescription medications should be taken only on the advice of your doctor.

14. Look for the 'Pieces of Gold' around you. Pieces of gold are positive or enjoyable moments or interactions. These may seem like small events but as these 'pieces of gold' accumulate they can often provide a big lift to energy and spirits and help you begin to see things in a new, more balanced way.

At the University of Bilkent Counseling Center (1998), the staff members' advice sounds rather more scientific:

You cannot control certain stressful events such as death of a significant other. In this case, experiencing negative feelings for a certain time is unavoidable. However, to control the long-term effects of an event, accepting its occurrence will help you. In other words, you can control your reactions—indirectly, your feelings—to a certain event but not the event itself.

Strategies are separated into two categories, behavioral and cognitive. The behavioral strategies include many of those mentioned previously. In addition, the use of informative resources, written by experts on the subject, is mentioned as well as enriching one's life with rewarding activities that will help people to cope. For it all to work the drawing of a contract with oneself is suggested. On the cognitive side, positive talks, challenge of negative beliefs by analyzing them "as would a scientist", and mental visualization of coping with the problem situation are offered as additional ways of coping with stress.

The counselors at *The Mental Health Foundation* (1997) offer much of the same, stating that you first must recognize the signs of stress or anxiety. The next step is to review your lifestyle either on your own or with counseling help. Time must also be made for relaxation. Furthermore, they feel that "Striking a balance between responsibility to others and responsibility to yourself is vital to reducing levels of stress in your life." Minimal amounts of tobacco and coffee are also recommended. Seeking help is again emphasized "...so that you can begin to get better." They conclude with a few quick tips for managing stress such as: avoid hassles, control change, take a break and find help/access resources.

At the *Rose Medical Center* (1993), the standard offering is complemented by some further advice. For instance, it is suggested that "learning to relax in the face of your stressors may be your most valuable weapon." This supposedly will replace the stress response with the relaxation response. Relaxation is possible through a 'menu of choices' which includes meditation, breathing exercises, yoga, creative visualization, progressive muscle relaxation, stretching and biofeedback. "Good old regular exercise works well, too and may be used separately or in conjunction with the preceding options." Getting a pet, a massage, listening to the tunes ("music can indeed soothe the savage beast and help minimize the stress response"), writing about your problems and laughing are also promoted. Finally, under the rubric "Other Techniques For Banishing Stress From Your Life", more advice is offered.

It advances the benefits of many factors such as the maintenance of good social relationships, being realistic, improving one's communication with assertiveness training, making time for self-renewal/rejuvenation with music, dance, meditation, sports, prayer, painting, Tai Chi, hiking in the mountains, visiting the ocean or "...anything else you enjoy that makes your spirit soar". The importance of "defining yourself to others" is also emphasized. Ultimately, we are told that we are responsible for the stress that we suffer because "Much stress is the product of faulty expectations". These expectations evidently also need to be corrected.

Posen (1994) feels that the management of stress requires changing lifestyle habits such as decreasing intake of junk food, eating slowly, getting adequate sleep (figure out what you need, then get it is his simple advice). Changing 'stressful' situations using time and money management and problem solving or by possibly leaving a job or relationship is also suggested. Finally changing one's thinking is recommended by seeing problems as opportunities, refuting negative thoughts and keeping a sense of humor.

Jane Kirby (1997), a nutritionist, urges the readers of *American Health for Women* to consume an adequate amount of magnesium and protein-rich foods, such as chicken and turkey. This, she explains, will prevent a deficiency in the amount of serotonin hormone which, she alleges, causes stress [3]. Reducing stress, she adds, will also be achieved by drinking eight glasses of water daily and including fruits and vegetables in daily meals.

Sandberg (1998) informs us that:

> The secret of successful stress reduction is to...learn to relax at will - to quickly and easily achieve a deep state of inner peace and calm, wherever and whenever you want. To achieve this we recommend the use of biofeedback trainers, sound therapy tapes and devices to balance your body's own surrounding electromagnetic fields. Use all three of these together, for thirty

---

[3] Serotonin is in fact a neurotransmitter.

minutes a day, and we can pretty much guarantee that after one month you'll be feeling completely transformed!

Not surprisingly Sandberg sells these devices and after promising that "Permanent stress reduction is within your grasp now", he urges readers to "Visit our product page and get started".

Contradictory views of stress

The majority of the commentaries on stress support the view that stress exists. There are, however, some rare dissenting views.

Charles Gordon (1990) a columnist with the *Ottawa Citizen*, in an article in *Maclean's*, commented on the urgency in most people's life in the 80's and the 90's. He felt that the urgency was not caused by events but that it was carried within and that:

> We have given that urgency a name. It is called Stress... And why is that? Because we, as a society, have legitimized stress. First we gave it a name. Then we gave it a deluge of publicity. Four years ago, about the time stress hit big, there were 643 articles containing the word 'stress' in *The Ottawa Citizen*. Last year, there were 813.... Last year, there were 67 uses of the word 'stress' in headlines in *The Toronto Star*. That means about every five days a *Toronto Star* reader would be reminded of the stressfulness of his existence....Stress, we read every day, comes from the pressures of everyday life, particularly work life. It is a jungle in there, we are told. The race is to the swift. ...In fact, many people probably like the idea of stress. They like to think of themselves as stressed people. It means, according to what our mass communications have been telling them, that they are trying hard, that they are fighting the odds. Conversely, if they are not stressed, it means that they are doing something wrong in their lives. It has been clear for quite some time now that stress is not good for us. But because we have legitimized it, not everyone is going to pay attention to that fact. It is even possible that we have gone beyond legitimizing stress and have romanticized it. Stress is like alcohol and tobacco—recognized as harmful, yet seen as necessary by some. Just as generations of creative writers grew up thinking that alcoholism equaled creativity, so generations of business and professional people, students and athletes have come to think that stress equals effectiveness.

A Belgian journalist, writing for the *Le Soir* daily, also shows some reservations and remarks that:

Anyway, one must look at the word [stress] with much circumspection and when one says that one person out of two encounters an episode of stress at least once a week, it must be understood...that this means nothing. And that we have to be suspicious of these figures that serve to feed the businesses of these merchants of the temple of modern times who would be very much at pains to demonstrate the efficiency of the anti-stress methods they market (1997).[Translated from French].

Morrish (1996) writing in the *Sunday Telegraph*, on semantics, discusses the various usage of stress in history and explains that:

The word has had this ambiguity all along. 'Stress' began life as a variant on 'distress' in the 14th century. It meant the experience of physical hardship, starvation, torture, and pain.

and concludes that:

These days, however, the term is bandied around so imprecisely that we are almost back with the medieval definition, in which 'stress' simply meant 'hardship'. It will be interesting to see how language adapts to recent scientific developments, which insist that 'stress' is actually good for us.

Horin (1997), an Australian journalist diagnosed with breast cancer writing for *The Sydney Morning Herald* discusses how:

Among the secular-minded, the belief that stress is to blame for many serious ailments has reached epidemic proportions. Too sophisticated to believe in the wrath of God, many bright people seek equally esoteric explanations for the bad things that afflict their bodies from ulcers to cancers. And stress is the easy candidate. Often it is not a helpful - or sound - explanation... Blaming stress is another way of blaming the victim...Some loving friends, and the raft of self-help books I consulted, strongly suggested that a 'stressful' lifestyle doubtless contributed to my condition. As well as that, I should look to my diet. Whatever, it was something I did or ate (or didn't do or didn't eat) that had suddenly propelled me into the clutches of surgeons, oncologists and radiologists. Cut down, slow down, drop out... men who worked 60 or 70 hours a week saw no irony in blaming my cancer on my 'stressful' four-day a week job. Stay at home more and I would be cured... A couple of decades ago, before stress reared its head, people with cancer were burdened with a different character defect: emotional repression. The cure was to get in touch with their rage. Now raging working mothers are told to calm down. Personally, I find the notion of having to 'live each day as if it could be your last a pain in the neck. And practicing 'positive thinking' is a drag. I prefer to get on with the life I loved, stress and all. But I understand the urge of others to 'battle' with their cancer, to try every potion and every therapist, to analyze, visualize, psychologize, to change things. If you believe you were responsible, you can also believe you have control, even if in reality, you don't.

Conclusion and consequences

This presentation of some of the views expressed by various participants in the popular discourse on stress has revealed some important issues. Several of these will be investigated in the rest of this work. To begin with, an examination of the historical context of stress will test the notion of 'stress' as a 'disease of our times'. This should assist in revealing whether stress has always been with us or whether it is a phenomenon or construction of 'modern times'. At the same time the views and beliefs relating to the mind/body connection at various times in history will also be considered. These are important as they underpin the concept of 'stress'.

Linguistically, it has been shown that a single definition of stress has hardly been agreed upon. The chapter to follow on the linguistic aspect of stress will not only look at the different definitions offered by various theorists, it will also show that this definitional problem is not unique to stress. Many abstract concepts, other than 'stress' share this problem. An analysis of the problems of abstraction in language, in the broader context of how language is socially used, will reveal and explain the variability of most definitions. Others linguistic elements and their contribution to the belief in the existence of stress will also be discussed.

At a theoretical level, the validity of claims made by many of the popular writers introduced above will be

37

investigated. This will be accomplished by analyzing the major theories that underpin some of these claims. This will reveal the lack of cohesion and the contradiction among the various theories. While this is not unusual in Science, it is more critical in this instance because stress as a scientific or medical condition was actually constructed by a specific individual, Hans Selye. Thus, attempts to redefine the condition by later researchers underscore its original inadequacy.

At the scientific level, it is clear that some of the claims identified in this chapter have been based on assumptions that stand in need of rigorous scientific scrutiny. For instance, the idea that some stress can either be necessary or lethal warrants more detailed analysis. Similarly, the notion that stress can cause many diseases and even kill us will also require investigation by reviewing the evidence that is supposed to link stress and various deleterious conditions..

At the philosophical level, the teleology of the theories of homeostasis, adaptation and stress will be discussed, as will reification and personification in language. An analysis of the teleological aspect will show the difficulty in 'proving' the purpose implied in most theories of stress while the discussion on reification and personification will show how these linguistic fallacies have assisted in making an improbable concept like stress acceptable to many people.

Ultimately, this analysis of the construction of stress will show that nothing underpinning the 'stress' concept can be redeemed. Despite this, the concept has continued to enjoy a growing popularity and this may be mainly due to the fact that in everyday life it serves as an easy 'one-fit-all' term to describe everything adverse or unpleasant. Most people do not fully understand the scientific debate and possibly do not feel as badly 'stressed' as researchers and stress management promoters would like to believe. When Rees (*Sunday Times*, 1997) discussed the poor turnout in a stress management seminar in London, she may have overlooked the point that to many people stress may be just a word, not a condition that requires strategies or treatment.

Incidentally, the situation she describes is not unique: workshops available for teachers at Technical Colleges of Advanced Education in Western Sydney were rarely run due to insufficient demand, despite the fact that teaching is frequently ranked highly as a 'stressful' profession.

HISTORICAL PERSPECTIVE

The concept of 'stress' over the past six decades has been the source of immense interest. The widespread belief that stress plays a part in many diseases has been largely responsible for its current acceptance as a legitimate concept. Many writers in the area of stress have included, in their preamble, the commonly accepted claim that three quarters of diseases are caused by stress. However, the origin of such a claim is to be found in a study in which doctors, members of the American Academy of Family Physicians, estimated that two thirds of visits to doctors are attributable to stress related symptoms (Wallis, *Times,* 1983). Despite an apparent lack of direct evidence, many scientists and lay people continue to believe that stress is, at least, a significant contributor to disease. This belief is not totally new to modern times. Historical records show that over at least the last twenty-four centuries, various non-physical phenomena have been advanced as either possible causes of diseases or factors contributing to diseases. At times, the prevailing view has been so overwhelming that it seems to have been difficult for the scientists of the time to even contemplate other points of view. This has sometimes resulted in alternative views taking many years, sometimes even centuries, to finally become accepted. In what follows, various beliefs and explanations of disease that were advanced at different times in history will be discussed. Other significant events that contributed to these beliefs and explanations will also be mentioned.

Early history: magic, the supernatural and astrology

In ancient Egypt, as early as 2450 BC, medicine known as "the necessary art" was partly magical. Magic, alongside anatomy and surgery, played a big part in "pharonic" medicine. The belief that various diseases were caused by the acts of specific gods, may help explain why spells and verbal rituals were used for healing. Magic was also used in

41

conjunction with other treatments for wounds and diseases that were not otherwise treatable or that were of unknown origins (Dawson, 1929).

In Mesopotamia, a region between the Tigris and Euphrates rivers, 40 tablets were found in the 1920's, which contained a medical treatise known as the "Treatise of Medical Diagnosis and Prognoses". The oldest surviving copy, which dates back to 1600 BC, represents the amalgamation of several preceding centuries of Mesopotamian medical knowledge. It revealed, amongst other things, that diseases were often blamed on gods, spirits or ghosts, each one being responsible for a specific disease in any one part of the body (University of Indiana, undated).

In the Western Asian region of Babylonia, evidence from 2000 BC was uncovered which also suggests that medicine was heavily intertwined with a belief that supernatural forces were involved in the causes of diseases. This belief was influenced by a strong emphasis in Astrology (Bores, 1996). This astrological component was still evident many centuries later. In the 15th century an Englishman, William Forrest, would lose a court case against three surgeons who had maimed his right hand. The judge ruled that "any defect to the aforesaid right hand is due to the aforesaid constellation" (Van Urk, Duin & Sutcliffe, 1992).

In Ancient Greece, the benefit of spiritual healing was also recognized and coexisted with a theory that stipulated that the four humors of blood, phlegm and yellow and black bile needed to be balanced. This type of healing was used as a last resort. Patients would stay overnight in one of the many temples where the god Asklepios would supposedly provide them with "dream" drugs or surgery (Van Urk, Duin & Sutcliffe, 1992). The Greek influence was still in evidence in Rome where Asklepios was credited to have eradicated the plague in 293 BC.

Magical cures and spiritual healing were employed for a long period of time in history. They are still in use in many parts of the world today, when traditional Western medicine is perceived as not being adequate to provide the cures and remedies that are needed to restore health.

The Greeks And The Romans

Plato (427-347 BC) embraced a dualistic theory in which mind and matter were separate phenomena (Stone, 1997,). His pupil, Aristotle (343-322 BC), claimed that the brain condensed vapors emanated from the heart (Stone, 1997). Hippocrates of Cos (c.460-380 BC) is generally regarded as the "Father of Medicine" but little is known about him. Most historians estimate him to be a contemporary of Socrates and there is some evidence that he was a practicing physician. Many of the treatises that have been attributed to Hippocrates were in fact, written between c.510 and c.300 BC, so that it is unlikely that he would have been responsible for all of them. This is why the treatises are often referred to as the Hippocratic Corpus. Despite some contradictions, they share many common views in the way they explain illness and are unanimous in their rejection of sorcery and magic as useful means of treating disease (University of Indiana, undated).

According to the Hippocratics, each person had an individual humoral balance, with a particular humor, blood, phlegm or yellow and black bile dominating (Bynum, 1993). The most common labels for disturbed behaviors were mania, melancholia, hysteria and paranoia. Mania, associated with excitement and melancholia and depressed states were both thought to be caused by an excess of 'black bile' whereas terrors and fear attacks were thought to be due to a change in the brain (Brown, 1993).

Hysteria was thought to affect only women since it was theorized that it resulted from the womb (hyster, in Greek) traveling periodically to the brain. Marriage, preferably early marriage, was the prescribed cure. This view, slightly modified through suggesting that vapors from the uterus rather than the uterus itself were the cause of hysteria, would persist well into the 18th century (Stone, 1997).

The notion of the brain being involved in emotions had not been universal. Unlike the ancient Egyptians, Mesopotamians, Hebrews and some of the Greeks who believed that the heart was the essential organ, the Hippocratics identified the brain as being not only the seat

43

of the mind, but also where most emotions originated (Stone, 1997). Even today, despite our modern understanding of the role of the brain in emotion, the notion of emotions originating from the heart is still persistent in ordinary language.

A few hundred years later, a less known Greek physician, Soranus of Ephesus (98-138 AD), who had introduced the concepts of 'anger', 'grief' and 'anxiety', was the first to mention that study, commerce and other ambitious pursuits could result in intense straining of the senses and the mind (Brown, 1993).

Galen

In the second century, Galen would expand on the Hippocratic Corpus's theory of the four Humors. Not only did he divide the world into Earth, Air, Fire and Water, he also added Dry and Moist, Spirits and Solids to the Humors (Mayeaux, 1989). He further distinguished between three types of spirit: The *spiritus vitalis* (life spirit) coming from the heart and flowing through the arteries, the *spiritus animalis* (animal spirit), found in the brain and nerves and the *spiritus naturalis* (natural spirit) originating in the liver. Galen was mostly in agreement with Hippocrates about the existence of the four basic human temperaments, each of which was caused by a predominance of one of the four humors. The *sanguinicus* was endowed with a sturdy, confident, cheerful and lively temperament that was produced by the dominance of the blood. The temperament of the calm and tough *flegmaticus* was influenced by excess phlegm, while the worry and gloominess of the *melancholicus* were due to a surfeit of black bile. Finally, the energy of the *cholericus* was due to too much choler or yellow bile in his or her system. Thus, Galen believed that one's personality was closely related to one's physical make-up (Galenica, 1996).

The introduction of the idea that temperaments could have an effect on the physical being of the individual was an early indication of what was to come in our present days with concepts such as 'Type A' and 'Type B' personalities, with 'Type A' behavior often suspected to be related to stress in the 1980's (Robbins, 1993).

Another psychosomatic element of Galen's view on disease is exemplified by an occasion on which he is known to have diagnosed the state of a young woman, apparently ill but with no physical sign, as being caused by a hidden love interest (Mesulam & Perry, 1972, as cited in Brown, 1993).

Galen's belief in the influence of strong emotions on physical health, would gain universal acceptance and would not diminish in importance in the medieval, renaissance and early modern medical history. For the next 15 centuries, Galen's views would continue to dominate medicine.

The Dark and Middle ages

Between the 2nd and the 4th centuries AD, the Roman Empire declined and ultimately fell. During this time, hunger, pestilence and war meant that there were few places scholars could go and feel safe. There was also a need for a place where the sick and wounded could go to seek treatment. The Church of Rome was the one institution left that had the power to offer and assure asylum to these people (Mayeaux, 1989). The monks who were known as 'practical men' felt that there was no need for theoretical medicine since God governed all of man's life. If some cure worked then it was repeated.

St. Benedict, born 480 AD and Cassiodorus, born ten years later, were known to have encouraged monastic medicine. The study of mainly the teachings of Hippocrates and Galen were re-emphasized. In the parts of Europe which were not under the control of the Christian church, the more primitive forms of magico-spiritual medicine had become popular once more and would remain so until all of Europe would be finally christianized (Mayeaux, 1989).

By the 9th century, under Charlemagne's Carolingian empire, which comprised what is today France and Germany, medicine, under the name of physics, was taught again. The reasons behind the reintroduction of the teaching of medicine, at the end of the dark ages, are unclear. Nevertheless, it led to the eventual divorce of medicine from magic and to some extent from astronomy. In the 12th century priests gradually become less prevalent in medicine. By the 13th and 14th centuries, a university degree was required to practice medicine (Mayeaux, 1989).

The Renaissance

By the 16th century, Paracelsus (1493-1541), who largely rejected the teachings of Galen, promoted the power of nature and the imagination in curing the body and the mind. According to Van Urk, Duin and Sutcliffe, (1992), Paracelsus' view was that "The patient had to be treated as a whole; diet, surroundings, the behavior of the doctor and caretakers, all these and more could have a profound effect on recovery." They also point out that he had a theory of the universe based on supernatural sylphs, nymphs and gnomes. He also thought that toothache could be transferred to a tree and that rubbing a weapon with a special ointment would cure the wound it had caused.

Despite these rather strange ideas, Paracelsus provided us with an early view of a more holistic medicine that took into account the relationship between people and their environment.

Earlier, French philosopher Jean Gerson, in 1500, had written of "six basic passions", consisting of three good emotions, love, lust and desire and three bad emotions, sorrow, hatred and anxiety. He was followed 38 years later by Spanish philosopher Juan Luis Vives (1492-1540) who added to Gerson's good emotions, good will, veneration, sympathy or pity, joy and pleasure. His negative emotions were displeasure, contempt, anger, hatred, envy, jealousy, indignation, vengeance and cruelty. His last group included sadness, tearfulness, fear, hope, shame and arrogance (Stone, 1997).

The 17th century: the Enlightenment

The Humoral theories introduced by Hippocrates and Galen were still prevailing in the 17th century. Humoral diagnosis, in fact, would remain in vogue until the middle of the 19th century. Burton (1621), for example, thought that the rational soul was seated in the brain and that it received sensations and controlled movement, via the action of the fluid 'animal spirit'. Talking about melancholy, he suggested that:

...as the body works upon the mind by his bad humors, troubling the spirits, sending gross fumes into the brain, and so per consequens the faculties of it, with fear, sorrow, &c., which are ordinary symptoms of this disease [melancholy]: so on the other side, the mind most effectually works upon the body, producing by his passions and perturbations miraculous alterations, as melancholy, despair, cruel diseases, and sometimes death itself.

At the same time organ theories, such as those which postulated that the uterus caused hysteria, were still promoted. Shorter (1992) reported that Sadler (1636) and Harvey (1651), following Hippocrates and Galen, both thought that an "ill affected" womb would affect the heart, liver and brain or even, the whole body. This was despite the fact that earlier, Charles LePois (1618), had written a treatise in which he had advanced that hysteria had nothing to do with the uterus and that the condition could be found in men as well as women (Stone, 1997).

Descartes: mind and body interactionism

Between the publications in 1641, of *Meditationes, de prima philosophia*, and in 1649, of *les passions de l'ame,* Rene Descartes set the foundations of what was to be known as mind/body interactionism. His systematic account of the relationship between body and mind would have an enormous influence on the subsequent discourse on psychosomatic medicine:

In Descartes' conception, the rational soul, an entity distinct from the body and making contact with the body at the pineal gland, might or might not become aware of the differential outflow of animal spirits brought about through the rearrangement of the interfibrillar spaces. When such awareness did occur, however, the result was conscious sensation—body affecting mind. In turn, in voluntary action, the soul might itself initiate a differential outflow of animal spirits. Mind, in other words, could also affect body (Wozniak, 1992).

47

The mind/body debate, resulting from Descartes's proposition, has centered ever since, on how to resolve the impasse stemming from the difficulty in explaining how the non-physical mind interacts with the physical world. This physical world necessarily includes our brain and body. If the laws of causality require cause and effect to be of a similar nature, a non physical mind cannot affect a physical body, nor can the body affect the mind.

The body as a machine

In the scientific realm, the 17th century marked the beginning of important discoveries in biology and chemistry. Aided by the use of the newly discovered microscope, these disciplines started to develop new theories. Some of the theories would lead to the increasing belief that the body was a machine and that it could be understood in terms of mechanics and chemistry. An important ingredient, it was thought, was the belief in the existence of a "vital force" which could be balanced either chemically or by increasing or decreasing stimuli (Van Urk, Duin & Sutcliffe, 1992). On the mechanical side of the equation, Kugglemann (1992) reported that in 1693, Robert Hooke had began testing amongst other things human hair, bones and sinews for their strength and elasticity and that in 1734, this was followed by experiments on blood pressure by Hale.

This an important episode in the history of the 'stress' concept. This view of the body as a machine, as well as the testing of the strength and elasticity of human tissues view, would continue well into the 18th and 19th century and would logically lead to a discourse of wear and tear. In fact Selye, the 'creator' of stress would later describe stress as being "essentially the rate of all the wear and tear caused by life" (Selye, 1956).

It was reasoned that if the body were like a machine and machines are subjected to wear and tear, then so too would be the body. Later claims that the concept of 'stress' had been based on an engineering metaphor may not have been entirely accurate. The researchers of the 17th and later centuries wanted to test these stresses and strains on the body because they believed them to be physical, not just metaphorical. Just as engineers were testing various materials to find how much load they could take before reaching breaking point, medical scientists were asking the same question about the human body.

Another aspect of a machine is that it requires some sort of energy to make it function. If the energy is low or runs out, then the machine does not function as well or stops. In the human body, this energy was thought to be produced by the nervous system.

As this theory and practice developed, the ground became prepared for the emergence of the main two medical themes that were to dominate most of the 18th and 19th centuries: Overstrain of the heart and depletion of nervous energy. In fact, in 1668, Willis, in his *Pathologia cerebri* (brain pathology) had already preempted the move when he had classified hysteria and hypocondriasis as being disorders of the nerves (Stone, 1997).

The passions, vapors and nerves

At the time of the development of the Hippocratic Corpus, many of the writers had felt that the passions caused disease. Galen, later on, wrote that passions such as grief, anger, lust and fear were amongst the causes of disease (Ackernecht, 1982). The 18th century would see a return of the passions as an explanation for some conditions. Nerves, hysteria and hypercondria, the male equivalent of hysteria, were considered organic diseases despite the lack of any physical tissue damage (Shorter, 1997).

John Purcell (1702) began to speak of "vapors" and their accompanying hysteric fits that he suggested were improperly named "fits of the mother", 'mother being another name for 'uterus'. In *The English Malady* (1733), speaking of anxiety and melancholy, Cheyne claimed that it was mainly the highly intelligent who were 'troubled with Vapors and Lowness of Spirits', a view still held by many doctors today. In that same book, he pronounced that a third of all diseases were of nervous origin.

49

Boehaave (1742) was mainly interested in melancholy which he felt was due to the "dissipation" of the most mobile parts of the blood and the thickening of the "black, fat and earthy residue". Violent exercise of the mind, joy or sorrow, frightful accidents, love, solitude and fear could also be responsible for the condition (as cited in Brown, 1993). His sentiments were echoed by Whytt (1714-1766) who in discussing the causes and cures of nervous hypochondriac and hysteric diseases, emphasized the role of "great grief, anger, terror and other passions" in reacting to "doleful or moving stories, horrible or unexpected sights" as possible causes of these diseases (Whytt, 1764, in Brown, 1993).

In Switzerland, Tissot (1769) seemed to promote a two-way interaction between body and mind when he declared that a given particular state of the body should produce a corresponding exertion of the soul and that the mind should have a similar effect on the body.

Others such as Sydenham (1624-89) had varying explanations. Whilst agreeing that hysteria was the result of a sudden fit of passion, such as anger, grief or terror, he added, "This 'great commotion of the mind' would result in 'irregular motions of the animal spirits'" which themselves were already a factor in hysteria (Veigh, 1965, in Brown, 1993).

For Cadogan, in 1772, "indolence, intemperance and vexation" were the three main reasons for chronic diseases. He argued that each person was "the real author of all or most of his own miseries". To the "indulgence, excesses or mistaken habits of life", he added the suffering of "ill-conducted passion", all of which individuals brought on themselves

Cadogan's views are reminiscent of those expressed by Cheyne, who had attributed the fall of the Roman empire to advances in learning and the knowledge of the sciences which, eventually, led the Romans to sink "into *Effeminacy, Luxury* and *Diseased*". The uniqueness of their point of view was that the patient was responsible for their diseases but also that unhealthy living could contribute to those diseases. Healthy living, for Cadogan was not merely confined to the physical aspect of life, it also involved its moral and emotional aspects.

Around the same time, in 1763 Pierre Pomme introduced the notion of 'vapors' in France. He believed that the nervous vapors, which arose from the uterus, could derange all the functions of the brain. By 1787, Daquin described how the women of Chambery, then an Italian Duchy, were increasingly suffering from the nervous vapors. In 1774, in Germany, Jacob Isenflamm claimed that hysteria, the women's nervous disease and hypochondria, the male version of the disease were almost identical and that each sex could catch the other (Shorter, 1992).

Cullen (1710-90) introduced the term 'neurosis' and went further than Cheyne, in proposing that in some ways all diseases were nervous diseases. Neurosis was defined in terms of any disturbance of any of the functions of the nervous system, with special emphasis on sensation and motion (Bynum, 1993). Cullen also tried to introduce a new dynamic disorder which he called "versania" but it never became popular as a diagnosis. With regard to hysteria, which he listed under the "Spasmodic Affect", he, like many of his contemporaries, thought it was triggered by "passions of the mind and by every considerable emotion" (Cullen, 1807, in Brown, 1993).

An interesting contribution was that of Sheidemantel, in 1787, who in his major work, *Ledenschafen als Heilmittel* (The Passions as Curative Agents), proposed that joy and laughter revitalized the vascular system and in doing so could cure illnesses like diarrhea, colic, women's disorders and lung ailments. Hate, envy, jealousy and arrogance, alternatively, were not only of no use in therapy; they could be the source of harmful effects in the mind and body (Stone, 1997). Some of his views were shared by Falconer in his publication the following year of his treatise *The Influence of the Passions on the Disorders of the Body* (Shorter, 1992).

The end of the century marked the arrival of few new concepts or notions that were to have an impact in later centuries. In the late 1790's Pinel had introduced the notion of 'heredity' in the debate about physical and mental health. He commented that heredity was one of the sources of mental illness, the other being intolerable passions of fear, hatred, elation or sadness.

John Ferriar (1761-1815) coined the term "hysterical conversion", to be also known as "sympathy" in the 19th century. The new term was meant to describe a condition in which another, sometimes distant organ, would react in sympathy with an affected organ (Stone, 1997). Freud would eventually revive the term in the 20th century, in his attempt to explain hysterical paralysis (Stone, 1985).

German and French physicians were also showing some interest in the effects of the stomach on the brain. There were also concerns that the pace of life was getting faster and was having an increasing effect on people's lives (Shorter, 1992).

The nervous century

In the 19th century the term 'nerves' would increasingly be used instead of 'insanity' and would also become a euphemism for psychosis (Shorter, 1997). Shorter (1997) has found that middle class patients believed that their 'nervous' problems were due to overwork while the lower class patients would attribute them to humoral imbalance. Doctors, for their part, believed them to be mainly genetic. This not only resulted in an understandable confusion but it also put a great deal of pressure on physicians to tell patients what they wanted to hear. Ultimately, this type of deception assisted the propagation of the idea that nerves were responsible for most problems.[4] The publication by Trotter (1807) of *A View of the Nervous Temperament* set the tone for the century. Eleven years later, Heinroth was to introduce the term 'psychosomatic' to articulate his objection to Cartesian dualism. In his Treatise on the *Disturbance of Mental Life (1818)*, following the views of Spinoza (1632-1677), he contended that the mind and body

---

[4] Shorter has suggested that the same sort of deception "occurs today when doctor tell patients they are suffering from stress" (1997).

were two aspects of the same entity, that entity being God. The acceptance of this position, known as the double aspect theory, is vital to his suggestion that harmony between body and soul are important in ensuring good health. However, there are many who would disagree that the double aspect theory resolves the Cartesian impasse.

Besides its contribution to psychosomatic medicine, the treatise also contained Heinroth's theory of mind that bears striking similarity to the psychoanalytic theory later developed by Freud. Whilst it was to be another century before psychosomatic medicine was to really have an impact in medical discourse, Heinroth's contribution has proven to be remarkable. Despite the fact that the philosophical position that underpins psychosomatic medicine has still not been universally accepted, the discipline has grown quite dramatically in the last two centuries.

As the 19th century progressed, many physicians started to blame psychological factors for organic diseases such as hyperthyroidism, angina pectoris and asthma (Trousseau, 1801-67), heart disease, peptic ulcer and diabetes (Wunderlich, 1815-77) (Ackerknecht, 1982). Other new names were invented to describe various conditions. Dupau (1819) thought of 'nervous erithism' to describe a condition which he thought was less serious than melancholia and had symptoms like irritability, emotional instability and depression. Its occurrence was mainly blamed on luxury or to be more precise its consequences.

In 1832, Brigham wrote his *Remarks on the Influence of Mental Cultivation upon Health.* His work reflected the concern of the time about the increasing complexity of modern life. There was growing fear that the human nervous system was ill equipped for life in the modern world and that as a result insanity was growing (Wosniak, 1992). It was felt that the pace of modern life was having a greater impact on the higher classes of societies. This prompted Riadore(1835) to remark that 'nervous affections', more common in the rich, would make their life so miserable that it would end up being comparable to that of the 'poor and laborious'.

Rosenberg (1992) remarked that the medical texts of the first third of the century still reflected some of the ideas developed towards the end of the preceding century. In 1825, Hatfield was still promoting the view that there was sympathy not only between the brain and stomach but also the stomach and uterus. Whenever a moral or physical cause had an effect on the brain, the stomach would be sympathetically affected whereas the uterus would be affected either directly from the brain or through the stomach. Ultimately, other organs would also be implicated (Rosenberg, 1992).

In 1836, Hungerford, following Scheidemantel, suggested that "Sorrow diminishes the energy of the nervous system, lessens the force of the circulation, impedes the secretions and induces organic diseases.... Joy is a powerful & Azhausting (sic) stimulus to the nervous system" (Rosenberg, 1992).

Around 1840, Eduard Beneke added to Heinroth's psychosomatic perspective by proposing that abnormal ideas could become symbolized and transformed into bodily reactions (Stone, 1997).

Meanwhile, the interest shown regarding the strength of the body was continuing. Flögel (1845) thought that immoderate, long continued bodily effort, "especially in the muscles of respiration" would harm the heart, whilst Bishop (1846) was testing the physical properties of bones with regard to density, hardness, elasticity and tenacity.

Later Haughton (1868), examining the relation of food to work done by the body, would describe the body in newly acquired engineering language. He would compare the muscles and the brain to the piston, beam and flywheel of the steam engine, the steam being provided "by the products of the food conveyed by the blood".

By the middle of the century Bouchout, in *De l'etat nerveux aigu et chronique, ou nevrosisme, appele nevropathie* [The acute and chronic nervous state, neuroticism, called neuropathy] described a condition which could be regarded as a forerunner to Baird's neurasthenia (Allbut, 1909). Interestingly, the term *'nevrose'*, which he created, was still commonly used in France until very recently. In 1852, Laehr, was the first to offer the explanation that a chemical imbalance in the brain, would result in mental disorder (Shorter, 1997).

The increasing pace of life was becoming more of a concern and this was highlighted by Greg (1853), a political scientist, who was talking about the severity of the struggle for existence in England in an age of "high excitement". He commented that people lived too fast and that all who worked, overworked. His remedy for such a life was for people to "have simple habits and more moderate and rational desires...sounder views of the objects of life and a juster estimate of true enjoyment". He urged English people to be content to live more humbly and be satisfied with less and "to lay aside their luxurious, wasteful and showy mode of life."

The milieu interieur

In 1859, one of France's most respected physicians, Claude Bernard, enunciated his concept of a *'milieu interieur'* or internal environment. The concept would eventually be refined and presented in the series of lectures in 1878 when he proposed that the body maintained its constant internal environment by continual compensatory reactions. He was convinced that the "fixity" of the *milieu interieur* necessary for free and independent life was possible and that all the vital mechanisms shared the common goal of preserving the conditions of life in the internal environment. His theory would later be extended by Walter Cannon and would form the basis for theories in psychosomatic medicine and, significantly, for the concept of 'stress'.

The end of hysteria

The same year, Briquet's monograph, *Traite de l'hysterie* (1859), dealt a fatal blow to the old idea that hysteria could be cured by marriage. It reported that a fifth of cases happened even before puberty and that there was little difference between the number of unmarried or married women who suffered hysteria. As LePois had done 250 years earlier, he suggested that men could also develop the condition. Hysteria, renamed the 'Briquet syndrome' consisted of multiple, vague or exaggerated complaints for which no physical cause was evident. These complaints were usually of a gastrointestinal or sexual nature (Stone, 1997). One of the reasons the popularity of the syndrome did not persist was the arrival on the scene of what was to be a prevalent and fairly enduring concept- neurasthenia.

Neurasthenia

In 1869, Beard 'discovered' neurasthenia, literally meaning 'weakness of the nerves'. Its many symptoms were caused, according to Beard, by dephosphorisation of the nervous system. Its symptoms included insomnia, fear of responsibility, desire for stimulants and narcotics, morbid self-consciousness and above all paralysis of the will. Beard attributed the disease to the peculiar tensions of industrial culture.

Neurasthenia would enjoy enormous popularity and was still used as a diagnosis until the 1920's. In fact, the term is still used in many Asian countries and in the former Soviet Union to denote a condition similar to what is now usually labelled as 'chronic fatigue' in the West (Martensen, 1994; Pichot, 1994).

In China today, 'brain neurasthenia' is believed to be brought on by excessive studying by students, the condition resulting in dizziness, poor concentration and insomnia (Stone, 1997).

Mind-body interaction

At the same time, Richardson (1869) emphasized the influence of mental action on physical disease. He thought a man could lose his mind by the failure of his blood. He reasoned that 'some horror' which came upon the man through his mind would represent an action "direct of the mind on matter, reversing the physics of the body and creating disease". Reminiscent of Cheyne (1733), he also believed that, with increasing intelligence, certain physical social evils would be less controllable and ultimately result in the degradation of the physical powers of "our most powerful men". Physical ailments such as diabetes, paralysis of the limbs, "affection" of the kidneys and "disorganization" of the heart caused by mental strain, were more likely to occur in the "professional class of men". Strain from sudden shock could strike the "least emotional person" and potentially give rise to diabetes. This moved him to say, "Diabetes from sudden mental shock is a true type, a pure type, of a physical malady of mental origin". Other diseases of nervous origin included chronic eruption of the skin, cancer, epilepsy and insanity itself.

The onset of these diseases was made possible by some preceding "hereditary or acquired" chronic exhaustion, which could be intensified by the slightest nervous shock. For him, cancer was primarily a disease of the nervous system. Ultimately, he thought that while the "uneducated, cloddish population" were the breeders of "abstract insanity", the "educated, ambitious, over-straining, untiring, mental workers" were the "breeders and intensifiers of the some of the worst forms of physical maladies."

The pace of life

By the last third of the century, there was an increasing concern with the body's ability to cope with the faster pace of life. There was some fear that the interaction of physical and mental work would prove too much. Farquaharson (1870), writing on the influence of athletic sports on health, noted that "the undue development of intellectual vigor, on the one hand, is well known to have a weakening and even destructive influence on a feeble frame, whilst on the other, muscular superiority often attends mental deficiency". The brainworker, he thought, would have no vital energy to spare with "his mind, exhausted by toiling in intellectual grooves" as his muscles "relax by disuse." He recommended a balance between mind and body obtained by the due adjustment of intelligent exercise to progressive mental work.

The strength of the heart

An article in Medical News (1873), entitled *Heart disease from over-exertion* debated the merits of sporting exercise. It remarked that only unfit or feeble persons undertaking sudden and severe exertion, without previous training, were more likely to be affected. Fears about the relative strength of the heart, led to more physicians attempting to find ways to measure that strength. Buchanan (1870) published his paper *On The Force of The Human heart*, and used physics to measure the amount of work done by the heart in various situations. Allbut (1872), at the same time was addressing the possibility that over-exertion caused the stretching of the chambers of the heart. He would note that even though a sudden shock could rupture a heart valve, this would never happen if the valve were healthy.

This preoccupation with the heart probably helps to understand why DaCosta (1871) gave the name 'irritable heart' to a form of cardiac malady common amongst soldiers during the American civil war. He pointed out that the 'affection' (sic) was not confined to troops engaged in warfare and that, in fact, it was also found in soldiers in peacetime. Nervous disorders were amongst the symptoms usually "manifesting themselves by headache, giddiness and disturbed sleep." He expressed some concerns that 'irritable heart' may, in some cases, lead to hypertrophy of the heart.

In England, Treadwell (1872) thought that excessive bodily labor was the cause of many of these cardiac diseases. Until then, cardiac disease had been regarded as arising from rheumatism in the young and nephritic troubles, rheumatism and atheroma in the old. He reported that a British government committee which investigated heart disease among soldiers between 1861 and 1863, had found that one in seven had become invalids as a result of cardiac disease and this, he noted, was in time of peace. This led him to conclude that the main cause of the problem in soldiers must have been overwork.

Wilks (1875) was not entirely convinced that overwork was really a problem. Most people, he stated, regardless of their profession felt that they were suffering from overwork. Since people were already convinced that their nerves were exhausted, they were only interested to hear the same from their physician. The real problem, he thought, was to be found in the hurried life style and diet of the time.

Wilks was still strongly influenced by the dominant view of his time about the human body, describing it as "a formidable machine with its force-producing machine". Such a machine could only do an amount of work proportionate to its power but, unlike other machines, its strength could only be maintained by use, "as assuredly it rusts and decays by disuse."

Nervous energy

Allbut (1878), for his part, was telling his contemporaries that "the reign of the brain and nerves" was taking its place supplanting "the reign of bone and muscle". "Brain forcing", as he called mental exertion, was "terribly mischievous. It urges genius into precocious fruitage, it drains the springs of nervous force, it excites high tension without giving volume to fortify it and by enforcing control, it breaks the spirit."

Alford (1881), despite having fully endorsed neurasthenia, introduced some ideas of his own in the nervous debate. He felt that the people who were lapsing into dipsomania were generally of a highly nervous, sensitive, lively temperament. Another of his suggestions was that the nervous system was exhausted by indulgences and late and irregular hours or even 'indolence and *ennui*' [boredom], all these factors being modified, not only, by the circumstances of society but also atmospheric and climatic conditions [5]. He noted that deficiency in nerve power would often result in various fears such as "fear of places, fear of society, dread of being alone, apprehension of various kinds; causeless but real and distressing fear of everything and anything", in other words phobias.

---

[5] Some current theories suggest that certain depressive states are caused by seasonal changes.

He also believed that neurasthenia was to the nervous system what anemia is to the blood and that it was associated with periodic mental depression, insomnia, general nervousness, tremors, mental irritability, hallucinations, delusions, moral decline and in some cases trances. Furthermore, excessive drinking, he thought, resulted from psychological causes such as long, continued painful emotions, either of fear or of joy, bad company, exhausting indulgences or "the mysterious effect of mind over the body."

There was also some criticism from Clark (1883) who thought that nervous exhaustion was an indefinite expression because it was often used in a lax way. "Its characteristics and the indications of its presence are by no means uniform." He felt that it was more or less general depression of vital energy, depending on a failure in the supply of nerve influence. "The battery is exhausted, the electricity is but feebly generated", he remarked. Cancer and consumption could develop especially when the nervous exhaustion was due to moral rather than physical causes. He doubted, however, that a particular form of nervous exhaustion, collapse of brain energy from overwork, ever existed *per se*, "so long as the ordinary rules of hygiene are not set in defiance." "Close rooms, neglect of exercise, encroachment on the hours of rest" as well as irregular meals and the use of alcohol, together with the 'moral influence of anxiety' were contributing unhealthy factors capable of bringing nervous exhaustion, he concluded. Clearly evident in these remarks was the same moral overtone that had been present in much of the discussions about health. Where the ancients believed that disease was dispensed by the gods, as punishment for inappropriate behavior, modern physicians thought that immoral behavior would make the patient somewhat responsible for their diseases.

Attack on neurasthenia

Three years later, Clark (1986) in another article titled *Some Observations Concerning What Is Called*

Neurasthenia, launched an even more forceful attack on the concept of 'neurasthenia'. He remarked that:

> The state or assemblage of related and unrelated symptoms to which this name has been more or less fully recognized and described by ever competent writer…for what good purpose, then, this term been has proposed, accepted, and employed I am unable to discover; and regarding it as at once vicious, inaccurate, and therapeutically misleading, I purpose submitting it to a brief critical examination.

What he had to say could apply to many of the so called mental diseases, often diagnosed by our present day psychiatrists and psychologists, but more important to this book, it could very be well said about stress today. With regard to the validity of 'neurasthenia' as a scientific concept, he declared:

> Now this theory may be accurate or inaccurate; it may be good or bad; it may help or hinder the growth or use of knowledge; but in any case the employment of it in naming and the introduction of it into a term whereby a given group of phenomena is hereafter to be known, violates a fundamental canon in the framing of a scientific nomenclature, and is in the order of science, an unpardonable sin.

He continued his attack forcefully, adding:

> When the symptoms set forth as characteristic of neurasthenia are carefully examined, it will be seen that they constitute an assemblage of incoherent indications of disorder borrowed more or less freely from inchoate forms of insanity; and from almost every disease of the nervous system; that they are not characteristics of any definite disorder; that divisions of them belong to disorders the most diverse; that no common laws of treatment can be safely applied to them; and that published with some parade as coherent and conclusive evidences of a state of 'nervous debility,' they exhibit defects of observing, reflecting, and critical powers unpardonable in those who court or claim the attention of the profession.

What is remarkable about Clark's views is that he shows an ability to distance himself from the prevailing mass acceptance of neurasthenia but, at the same time, he clearly does not realize that his criticism of neurasthenia can apply just as much to his own views about nerves. His suggestion that the proper grouping of all the symptoms should be under the "justifiable name of mere and shere (sic) nervousness" shows that his acceptance of the concept of 'nerves' blurs his otherwise sharp observations.

This should not, however, detract from the fact that his criticism of neurasthenia is correct and very relevant to the way we still eagerly invent new names to cover a group of symptoms that may or may not be related. Stress, schizophrenia, ADHD and chronic fatigue syndrome are all examples of this. Today's researchers could do worse than reflect on Clark's remarks suggesting that neurasthenia was unscientific, inaccurate and misleading and included a "mob of incoherent symptoms borrowed from the most diverse disorders...framed into an incoherent whole.

Worry and mental strain

As the end of the century approached, the attention turned towards the importance of work in staying physically and mentally healthy. At the same time, the notions of 'worry' and 'mental strain' would increasingly be found in discussion about the evils of life at high pressure. In England, Kesteven (1884), in his book *Work and Worry, From a Medical Point of View*, contrasted work and worry. He described work as consisting of tasks, neither distasteful nor unpleasant, which needed to be done. Worry, on the other hand, he defined as "all work which is done against the grain." In addition to this were the "thousand and one petty vexations to which every man, not a lunatic, is liable" and could even be the consequence of an "uneasy conscience." He stated that worry was "the devil himself" and that when "the mind or nervous system" was worried, "its powers" were absorbed in meeting that worry.

Robson (1886), discussing the wear and tear of London life, offered the view that "The human body was a machine so constructed that work is a necessity for its continued existence and well-being" but "...if the vital machine cannot be supplied with a due amount of fuel and moreover, fails to utilize that which is supplied, mental and bodily collapse cannot be far distant". The resulting symptoms, grouped under the old term 'hypocondriasis' would put people within the 'borderlands of insanity'. At the same time, he warned that "...anxiety, excitement and disappointment consequent upon struggles for power, influence and wealth" could result in mental strain.

In America, Weir Mitchell (1887), well known for his cures of neurasthenia, emphasized that wear resulted from use whereas tear came from abuse. Like his colleagues in England, he was concerned that anxiety, worry or 'excessive haste' began to work, as it were, "with a dangerous amount of friction" and could be blamed for the increase of neuralgia in crowded towns. Interestingly, he classified apoplexy, palsy, epilepsy, St. Vitus's dance and lockjaw or tetanus as nervous maladies. Concerned with the amount of mental strain found in students, he proposed that teachers were the cause of overwork and over worry.

An article in *The spectator* (1894) summed up the mood of the time as well as the growing impatience, felt by some, about the popularity and the growing frivolous use of nervous diagnosis. It commented about the seemingly "prevailing weakness of modern nerves, due to the growing evils of life under high pressure." and claimed that "the wear and tear of the conditions under which we live are playing havoc, not only with our muscular, but also with our mental tissues."

The article quoted Professor Erb, a German doctor of great reputation, who had blamed half the woes and suffering of modern life on neurasthenia. The writer of the article begged to differ, suggesting that telephones, telegraphs and railways were some of the causes of the problem. Other problems included attending to too many interests, worries from either work or money, as well as anxieties or domestic troubles. All this, the article contended, resulted in the belief that the nerves of modern man were often put to a heavier strain than nature had intended but ultimately it suggested, cowardice was the real problem, causing people to hold back from the "rough fight of everyday life". The author concluded that "The more a man talks of his nerves, the more he is likely to suffer from them... Between popular folly and the indulgent doubts of doctors, nervous disorders are making far greater strides among us than the stress of modern life would really justify."

As for women, he noted that they no longer had hysterics and fits, so prevalent in the 18th century, probably because such things had become unpopular. His recommendation was that doctors would be well advised "to invent another name for the genuine case of nervous break-down through overwork and mental worry."

Allbut (1895) contributed to the moral tone of the time when he added these comments to the growing list of things being blamed for nervous debility, hysteria and neurasthenia:

> ...the strife of business, the hunger for riches, the lust of vulgar minds for coarse and instant pleasures, the decay of those controlling ethics handed down from statelier and more steadfast generations-surely, at any rate, these maladies and these causes of maladies are more rife than in the day of our fathers... what was "liver" fifty years ago has become 'nerves' today....One of the features of nervous disease is restlessness, quakishness and craving for sympathy; and that the intellectual acuteness of many of these sufferers, the swift transmission of news by the press, and the facility of modern locomotion all favor the neurotic traffic.

Unlike Clark, he favored neurasthenia over the "so-called diseases of the nervous system, a vast, vague and most heterogeneous body, two thirds of which may not primarily consist of diseases of nervous matter at all." Furthermore, he did not think that nerves should be blamed for excitability. He rightly stated "I do not know what 'over-excitable' nerves are; I have never seen such things; excitability is their business." The problem, he thought, was more likely to be found in under excitement. Thrills, tensions, susceptibilities, sentimentalities, moodiness, fretfulness, were likely indicators of under sensitive nerves. As for the 'city man', he poisoned his nerves and blood with champagne, "stodged" his stomach with rich food three times a day and fed his mind with vulgar shows.

By the end of the century, Sigmund Freud, with Josef Bruer would publish *Studies in Hysteria*, in 1895. A year later, he would use the term 'psychoanalysis' for the first time

(Stone, 1997). At the same time in America, Lough, Solomons and Stein (1896) were investigating motor automatism and concluded that a large number of intelligent acts in normal people are automatic and outside the field of consciousness and that hysteria was a disease of attention.

The 20ᵗʰ century

This was going to be the century of science and technology, with the excitement of new discoveries tempered by the ever increasing pace of life. 'Nerves' would still dominate medical discourse for the first half of the century. Neurasthenia would slowly be replaced by psychoanalytic explanation but two World Wars would add their toll to what would seem, for many, to be an increasingly complex world.

The rise of psychoanalysis

Janet (1903) introduced the word 'subconscious' into his treatment of hysterical patients. His therapy would involve attempts to bring the patient's subconscious thoughts to the fore. Neuroses, according to him, consisted of two groups: hysteria and psychasthenia. Psychasthenia, also known sometimes as 'Janet's disease', was a condition characterized by stages of pathologic fear or anxiety, obsessions, fixed ideas, feelings of inadequacy, self-accusation and feelings of strangeness and depersonalization. His dynamic psychiatry which came earlier than Freud's would in fact influence Freud, as well as Carl Jung, Alfred Adler and Eugen Bleuler.

Meanwhile, the term 'stress' would increasingly be found in discourse about human existence. Not only was it still used to describe hardship and various adverse circumstances, it began to be used in the engineering sense of "stresses and strains", with stress resulting in strain. Sometimes it was used literally; at other times the use was metaphorical. Anderson (1905), for instance, in an article investigating strain as a factor in cardioaortic lesions, suggested that the effect of strain, resulting from "mechanical stress" had been studied in soldiers, athletes or "others who by reason of occupation or practice are subjected to severe sudden exertion or prolonged over-exertion at a time when their general health was good and their heart normal." He felt that mechanical stress in the form of exertion was capable of causing structural damage to a cardiovascular system which when sound was capable of handling severe forms of such stress.

The emergence of psychology and psychiatry

At the beginning of the century, practitioners of the new disciplines of psychology and psychiatry began to publish papers on mental health. Until then the debate had been mainly conducted by physicians. Norton Prince (1905), in an article discussing some of the present problems of abnormal psychology, considered the influence of mind on body, hysteria and modifications of character in diseased conditions. Dana (1907) later posited that hysteria unmistakably could be recognized by objective symptoms alone and that it could be differentiated from other types of neuroses even though hysterical episodes were thought to occur in all psychoneuroses. These other psychoneuroses included psychasthenia, phrenasthenia, neurasthenia and abortive types of major psychoses. It is not clear what phrenasthenia was, but as far as hysteria was concerned, Dana thought that it was a morbid condition in which emotional states controlled the body and that it was a chronic defect. Jones (1907) was also comparing hysterical fits with other types of fits. He stated that he had no difficulty in differentiating them from epileptic fits. However, he did not share Dana's views about hysterical fits or about additional types of neuroses. He could find no justification for the establishment of other psychoneuroses apart from hysteria and psychasthenia.

Irritable heart and neurasthenia

Meanwhile, Allbut (1910) was still interested in 'irritable heart'. He described how the machinery of the circulation of the heart could adapt to "stresses which in various degrees we all have to encounter". He was mainly referring to exercise or physical effort when he was talking about the "excessive stresses whether of effort or of endurance". He believed that functional diseases of the heart were frequently attributable to the sympathy of the heart "with eccentric disorders of multifarious origin, bodily and mental." His concern was mainly with the tone and elasticity of the arteries and the role of physical stress on these arteries. In another article the year before, he spoke of stress in a more metaphorical way when he stated that "neurasthenia was indeed often the product of the stresses upon the functions of the mind." He suggested that neurasthenia was not just the product of his time. Like insanity and epilepsy, it had always existed. In fact, he commented that it had been known before as 'spinal irritation'. He felt functional nervous disorder, had been "confusedly and fancifully" described by eighteenth and nineteenth centuries writers.

In an additional section to Albutt's article, Hoarsely, discussed 'traumatic neurasthenia' which, he stated, was then also known as 'nerve shock', 'nerve weakness', 'nervous exhaustion', 'concussion of the spine', 'spinal irritation', 'strain of the spine', 'railways spine' and other terms [6]. The treatment he recommended was the same as that required for severe concussion. This must raise the question as to whether all the above terms were necessary.

Osler (1910), was more concerned about the effect high pressure in modern life had on the heart. He thought that it was responsible for the growing number of people suffering from *angina pectoris*. To illustrate his point he described the Jewish businessmen in his study, in the following manner:

> Living an intense life, absorbed in his work, devoted to his pleasures, passionately devoted to his home, the nervous energy of the Jew is taxed to the uttermost, and his system subjected to that stress and strain which seems to be a basic factor of so many case of angina pectoris.

Hard work alone was not the cause of *angina pectoris*. Another factor was needed, he thought, and that factor was

---

[6] This multiplicity of names over different periods is quite common in the history of psychosomatic conditions.

worry. In fact, he differentiated between three types of *angina pectoris*: The mildest type, which he called *"les formes frustes"*, was mild and chronic and, he believed, caused by emotions. Cannon (1911) was also interested in emotion but was not so quick to blame the faster pace of life. In an experiment in which he injected epinephrine to rabbits, he concluded:

> ...the temptation is strong to suggest that some phases of these pathologic states are associated with the strenuous and exciting character of modern life acting through the adrenal glands, this suggestion, however, must be put to experimental test.

In fact, Cannon would never be convinced. Hans Selye (1956) would report later that Cannon whom he greatly admired, gave him "some excellent reasons... why it would seem unlikely that a general adaptation syndrome (the original name given to the stress theory) could exist". This, however, has not stopped many writers in the field from suggesting that Cannon was one of the originators of the stress theory or to guess, as Goldstein did (1995), what his stress theory would have been, had he ever had one.

In the next few years Freud, in his introductory lectures in 1916-17, would promote the notion that hysterical symptoms were the symbolic representation of unconscious conflicts. He would reintroduce the term 'hysterical conversion'. The diagnosis would become popular during the First World War, when soldiers would sometimes display paralysis, muscular contracture, loss of sight, speech and hearing with no apparent organic bases (Stone, 1985, as cited in Brown, 1993). The notion of 'conversion' was to remain very popular until the end of the 1940's but by the eighties, the American Psychiatric Association's Diagnostic and Statistical Manual of Mental Disorders, 3rd Ed (DSMIII) noted that the by then renamed 'conversion disorder' "apparently common several decades ago...is now rarely encountered" [7] (1987).

---

[7] Note that the possibility that a previously diagnosed 'condition' may have never existed is rarely entertained in psychological discourse.

The first World War

The advent of the First World War had also rekindled the interest shown during the American civil war about the way men, as soldiers, coped and reacted to the physical and emotional vicissitudes of war. The various explanations given for their adverse reactions reflect the persistence with hysteria as diagnosis, the gradual death of neurasthenia, the relatively short reign of psychasthenia and the growing influence of psychoanalytic thoughts. Muirhead (1916), for instance, was of the opinion that some "class of persons...by constitution and by their previous life experience" was unfit for military service. These people were generally "gentle, often mentally brilliant creatures, for whom the rough and tumble of life, whether in war or in peace", was "a too ingenial setting." He was convinced that they could not compete with their "less sensitive, stronger-nerved competitors" [8]. Of all the diagnoses that were available at the time, he thought that the condition they were more likely to suffer from was "neurasthenia verging toward melancholia."

Abrahams (1917) felt the term 'soldier's heart' had been abused to the point that he thought we should regret that it had even been invented. He insisted that it should not be used in relation to a large variety of symptoms:

> ... which are evident in men who happen to be temporarily khaki clad and most which have nothing whatsoever to do with the heart, nor, for that matter, with military service.

In a statement that could easily be applied to most of the concepts discussed so far and just as equally to 'stress', he noted that "a large variety of different conditions have been at various times described as if they were all the same thing." To make his point he suggested that cases were either blamed on 'strained heart', 'athlete heart', 'toxemia', indigestion due to bad teeth, the condition of the thyroid gland, excessive cigarette smoking or even deficiency of butter salts in the blood.

---

[8] This notion of 'strong nerved' individuals is not unlike the concept of 'hardiness' present in current discussions about the ability to cope with stress.

Rivers (1918) had also something to say about the various diagnostic labels of the time. He was not entirely happy with using the term 'hysteria' because it was still perceived to be a condition more likely to affect women. He preferred the term 'functional'. He commented on the fact that the term 'neurasthenia' "...was becoming every year of less value". Additionally he felt that it had lost the last remnants of the scientific value it once possessed. 'Psychasthenia', he thought had been used in medical textbooks in a very unsatisfactory sense. The term had been used for cases of obsession, phobia and compulsion with no sign of mental exhaustion which he thought was the main symptom of this condition. However, he was in some agreement with the usefulness of 'conversion neurosis', introduced by Freud, in which paralysis or other afflictions were supposed to be the manifestation of underlying unconscious tendencies. It must be noted at this point that even though Rivers talked about the stresses of warfare, like his contemporaries and many to come after him, he never defined stress.

Solomon (1917) shared Rivers' views. He felt that there should be a definite meaning of terms in psychology. He thought 'neurasthenia', 'hysteria', 'consciousness' and 'subconsciousness' needed a clearer, truer, better definition or delineation. He also suggested that the use of the same terms, with the same ideas or concepts in mind, would lead to less disagreement, less misunderstanding, more harmony, more good will, more rapid progress and more scientific and accurate observations and thinking.

The birth of homeostasis

Between 1929 and 1939, expanding on Claude Bernard's earlier description of a *milieu interieur,* Cannon developed a theory of a balanced body that became known as 'homeostasis'. In *Stresses and strains of homeostasis* (1935), he proposed that the organs and tissues were set in a 'fluid matrix' covered by a 'lifeless' layer of skin. In this article, he discussed purely physical stresses such as "cold, lack of oxygen, low blood sugar, loss of blood". Each of these stresses could produce a 'breaking strain' and with greater stress, "the strain on the organism may become too great, even though the compensatory sympatho-adrenal apparatus is working at it utmost. Then the fluid matrix becomes altered." His view therefore was that the body would react up to a point without disturbing the fluid matrix. Once stress was excessive, it would induce a breaking strain in the homeostatic mechanisms. He pointed out that "exercise is clearly too complex and awkward a method of measuring the critical stress." He also proposed that we would need to learn "how steady are the steady states and where critical stress is found not only in normal individuals, but also in individuals at various developmental epochs and during various disorders." He finally admitted that he had not been able to bring a well-tried method of assessing the degree of homeostatic adjustments.

In a later book Cannon, (1939) would describe the physiological responses involved in rage and fear and would label those reactions "flight or fight". This notion would ultimately come to play an important part in the stress discourse. Talks of "alarm setting off" and "mobilisation of resources" to ward off unpleasant stimuli would lead some theorists to reduce stress to 'flight or fight' while others would suggest that stress was caused by a left over of this primitive phenomenon (Tache, 1986). The concept of 'homeostasis', like that of a *milieu interieur*, its predecessor 70 years earlier, would make the introduction of stress possible. For an adaptive response (stress) to be needed, there had to be some sort of disturbance caused to the body. Without homeostasis, the concept of 'stress' would not be necessary. Cannon's work would also eventually result in the notion of a 'body with a predetermined purpose' supplanting the former prevailing view of the 'body as a machine'.

Psychasthenia and other conditions

In the early part of the century, psychasthenia was still enjoying its short-lived popularity. However, like neurasthenia before it, its days were numbered. Nevertheless, Woolley (1929) studied 87 patients diagnosed with obsessive ruminative tension states and psychasthenia. Their conditions were investigated in terms of their sex, psychological type, clinical personality type and body type. He reported a definite correlation between obsessive ruminative tension states and paraergastic reaction sets in the fields of sex, body type and psychological type. In Germany, Heller (1930), thought that psychasthenia was responsible for children not being able to speak even though they comprehended language. Cremieux (1930), summarizing the opinions on neuroses of the time, stated that he considered neuropathy as an organic disease of the instinctive-affective life, distinguishing it from psychopathy in that the patient was aware of his morbidity. The main neuroses of the time were according to him, simple hyper-emotionalism, anxiety, hypochondria, cenesthopathy, psychasthenia, neurasthenia and hysteria. In declaring that neuroses were now considered as psychobiological states, from the perspective of both psychology and biology, he reflected the beginning of a psychosomatic approach to medicine.

The early years of psychosomatic medicine

The early 1930's saw the beginning of psychosomatic medicine as a discipline. Two notions would dominate in its early days: 'psychogenesis' and 'holism'. The concept of 'psychogenesis' implies the belief that psychological factors can cause disease, whereas that of holism suggests that because of the unity between mind and body, the sick person should be treated as a whole. An early influence was Swiss psychiatrist Adolf Meyer (1866-1950). He is considered the father of psychobiology, a science that viewed people as having a complex interaction between their psyche and their biology. One of his followers, Helen Dunbar, was instrumental in the establishment of psychosomatic medicine. The publication in 1935 of her book, *Emotions and bodily changes: A survey of literature on psychosomatic relationship: 1910-1933*, was the basis of one aspect of the discipline, the other, promoted by Franz Alexander (1950) was derived from psychoanalysis. By the 1950's there would be a gradual decline of the psychoanalytical approach (Lipowski, 1986a).

The beginning of tension and stress

The concept of 'nervous tension' seemed to have been introduced in the first quarter of the 20th century. In a study investigating gastric secretion, Farr, Leuders and Bond (1925) suggested that it was strongly influenced by emotions or increased nervous tension. Emotions and nerves were alternatively blamed for the tension. Bagby (1927) favored emotional tension. He blamed high levels of such tension for a compulsion of hand biting. McCowan and Quastel (1931), after finding a relationship between emotional tension and blood sugar levels, suggested that it had implications for psychotic patients. For Oedegaard (1932), emotional tension was synonymous with marital unhappiness. Others were proposing their own types of tension. Frank (1928) believed that physiological tensions had to be managed to ensure a healthy development of personality, whereas, Brown (1928) thought that psychic tension was of importance.

Tension was also blamed on the pace of modern life as evidenced by a book by Jacobson, titled *You Must Relax, A Practical Method of Reducing the Strains of Modern Living* (1934). The label of 'nervous tension', not to be confused with the 'nerves' of the 19th century, was increasingly used to explain the occurrence of some medical conditions. Beam (1938), for instance, declared that high nervous tension and sedentary habits, created by modern civilization, were responsible for irritable colon. He argued that gastrointestinal upsets were occurring in varying degrees in persons under great nervous or emotional strain, when such strain would upset the equilibrium of the autonomic system. Tensions had to be released to regain that equilibrium (White, 1932). Such release was also necessary to dispel the harmful organic effects of tension (Rombouts, 1934) and to free the organism of painful tension (Gutierrez-Noriega, 1940). Inhibited emotional tensions were thought to be highly correlated to blood pressure fluctuation (Alexander, 1939).

Nervous and emotional tension would offer an alternative diagnosis to psychoanalysis and its 'hysterical conversion' for a while. At the same time, neurasthenia, psychasthenia and hysteria, would gradually disappear. The publication of a letter to *Nature* in 1936 of *A Syndrome Produced by Diverse Nocuous Agents*, did not arouse much interest. However, it was the modest beginning of what would be eventually known as the concept of 'stress'. In fact, it would be another 20 years before Selye would popularize the concept in his book, *"The Stress of Life"*, and another 20 years before the concept would appear in the popular press in the form of stress quiz (*New York Times*, 1976).

The second World War

The advent of the Second World War refocused attention towards war neuroses. Attempts were made once again to label these neuroses. Moersch (1942) was concerned that new terms used during this war, such as 'battle syndrome' and 'battle fatigue' would, like their predecessors, fall into disrepute through faulty usage. Wittkower & Spillane (1944) looking at some of these predecessors, thought that studying the effects of the First World War on soldiers may be useful. They found that states of depression, anxiety and hysterical syndromes were more likely to be found in predisposed individuals and were brought on by emotional tension. They remarked that "...a survey of the literature on neuroses in war time was complicated by the varying terminology of the classifications used in various countries by various authors." They suggested that there was no fundamental difference between peace and wartime neuroses.

Grinkler and Spiegel (1945), in their psychoanalytic account of the mental disorders experienced by airmen during World War II, discussed stress but never really defined it. They nevertheless developed a 'stress tolerance test' which attempted to measure the emotional strength of pilots.

After the war, the psychoanalytical explanations, that until then had largely ignored the social environment, became intertwined with talk of 'nervous tension' and 'stress'. However, whilst stress was increasingly being discussed, it was still not defined. It was mainly used to indicate hardship and adverse elements in the environment. The interest, meanwhile, was still focused on life in the military. Shaskan (1946), for example, promoted the use of group therapy in military settings and revealed that the latitude of verbal expression allowed to the patient served to relieve the psychoneurotic of his anxieties as well as nervous tension. The same year, Menninger (1946) estimated that more that 50% of people visiting doctors were doing so primarily because of emotional difficulties resulting from some type of psychoneurotic reaction to the problems of their lives. He suggested that the "...strenuous existence of the Army precipitated further neurotic expressions." He remarked that people resorted to the use of neurotic defenses when under special stress of the environment. These defenses could also be used sometimes when the stress was entirely internal.

More tension

During the war the concept of 'tension' had sometimes been re-labeled as 'war nerves' (Cory, 1944) but Bennett (1945) did not think that war nerves were much different than peace nerves but were merely aggravated by war. The best way to soothe the nerves was thought to be with music. Music was found to improve feelings towards co-workers, to help deal with monotonous tasks when tired and to help forget worries (Kerr, 1942).

Harms & Soniat (1952), who focused on the causes of fatigue, proposed that 80% of patients who complained about fatigue were psychoneurotic. They thought that fatigue could result from either debilitating illness, in which constitutional make-up and reaction to illness played a role or emotional disorders, the latter being due to lack of motivation, nervous tension or anxiety. They also made some distinctions between fatigue in depressed patients, which they labeled 'the business man's syndrome' and hysterical attacks of fatigue or fatigue due to chronic inhibitions of ego-function.

Stress

The concept of 'stress' as formulated by Hans Selye was being met with growing acceptance by some members of the scientific community. Selye in collaboration with Fortier (1950), was still talking about a General Adaptation Syndrome, which was described as the 'response of the body to stress'. The theory was recognized as having important implications for psychosomatic medicine (Le Vay, 1952). In a later article, Selye described his theory as a theoretical attempt to develop a unifying concept for health and disease in the light of the general adaptation syndrome (Selye, 1954).

Around the same time, Neel (1955) was investigating the relationship between job attitudes and feelings of nervous tension. He concluded that a combination of both individual and situational factors contributed to poor mental health in industry. He proposed that mental heath programs should be designed to give more consideration to situational factors such as supervisory practices, physical working conditions, job satisfaction and attitudes toward company policies. Whilst the title of his paper was *Nervous stress in the industrial situation*, he was still talking about workers experiencing nervous tension rather than stress.

The following year, Selye (1956) published *The Stress of Life*, a popular version of his views on stress. The book was the first occasion in which his general adaptation theory had been replaced by a theory of stress. In the book, he described how the transformation took place. He would compare his 'discovery' (really an 'invention'), with little modesty, to the discovery of America by Columbus.

For the next few years, 'nervous tension' and 'pressure' remained popular concepts used interchangeably with the concept of 'stress'. The veritable explosion of the popularity of the 'stress' concept, which was to follow, can be traced back to its introduction in the mass media. The stress quiz, published in the *New York Times*, in 1976, seems to be the first instance of a major newspaper article on stress, in the USA. In Australia, it would be another 6 years, before *the Sydney Morning Herald* (Williams, 1982) would publish an article *Stress: one thing that is booming* which involved an interview with the proprietor of a pharmacy who was doing boom trade in medication during an economic recession.

Summing up

Some lessons can be drawn from the last few hundred years. One is that alongside biological medicine, there has always been some kind of additional explanation of disease, be it magical, spiritual, astrological or psychosomatic. The popularity of psychosomatic medicine has increased despite the fact that the mind/body question is yet to be conclusively answered. It seems that some researchers have completely avoided the philosophical impasse and relied instead on a seemingly commonsensical view. They have done so by either ignoring the problem or by evoking the authority of a god or other mystical phenomena. There are certainly limitations to scientific discourse but to rely purely on common sense is not without problem. There are, of course, some dangers in introducing mystical elements under the pretext that empirical science is too limited. Many of the explanations offered in early history were based on assumptions rather than scientific evidence. It took, after all, the scientific work of Briquet (1859), on the role of the uterus in hysteria, to rid medicine of a belief that had been held for 23 centuries.

Another lesson of history concerns the problem facing psychosomatic medicine. While the psychosomatic school has been critical of biological reductionism, in attempting to prove biologically that the mind can affect the body, it would, if it were to succeed, ultimately have created its own reductionism. It would have reduced the effects of the mind to its biological reactions. Moreover, by eagerly embracing the concept of 'stress', as it has, it is implicitly reducing all events, physical and psychological, to biological reactions. In the final analysis, the dilemma facing the psychosomatic school is that it can either offer an alternative reductionism or increasingly find itself returning to the magical, spiritual and astrological past of early history on which science was supposed to improve.

Also, it appears that at different times in history, people have accepted whatever labels or explanations were given for diseases. In fact, at times, they seemed to have been happy to comply with the symptoms that were expected of them. It has been quite common throughout history to find that the introduction of a new phenomenon has been followed by a rapid increase in the number of cases being diagnosed. Patients usually start to 'feel' some of the symptoms and doctors start to 'see' more of the disease. Its previous absence as a condition has usually been easily rationalized by stating that it was always present, but since we had not discovered it, we were ignorant of its existence and therefore incapable of noticing it. Ultimately the disappearance of such phenomena is explained in terms of cures and eradication of the underlying problems rather than admitting that the condition may never have really existed.

This may be explained by the fact that people have imagination and feelings. As a result what we label as psychosomatic diseases may not really be so. There is, after all, a distinction between 'being sick' and 'feeling sick'. Sometimes we can experience both, sometimes one and at other times neither. For example, in early forms of cancer or HIV, patients feel quite healthy, yet they have a disease. In other instances, people may feel unwell, when in fact, they are really free of disease. Psychosomatic diseases may just be 'feeling' diseases rather than 'being' diseases. Similarly, with stress it is more a case of 'feeling stressed' rather than 'being stressed'. If there are 'diseases' of imagination, it is no wonder some of them appear to be cured by that same imagination.

Finally, the preceding chapters have illustrated how different themes have dominated various periods of Western medical and social history. Retrospectively, some of the labels may appear naïve but they all seem to have attempted to explain some aspects of the relationship that people have with their environment. In this context, stress may just be another in a long line of pretenders, following from the vapors, the nerves, hysteria, hypochondria, conversion, neurasthenia, psychasthenia and nervous tension. Like these concepts, it may also be serving some social purpose. As Martensen (1994) has astutely observed:

Neurasthenia was one of those wonderful 19th-century diagnostic entities that promised something for almost everyone involved. A disease with loads of symptoms and little, well, finally no, organic pathology, it satisfied a number of the conditions any nosologic category must meet if it is to be broadly applied. During its heyday, which lasted from the 1870s to the turn of the century, the diagnosis of neurasthenia provided patients with a scientifically (and, hence, I would argue, socially) legitimate explanation of their inability to perform their expected roles.

The same thing may be said about stress now.

LINGUISTIC CONSIDERATIONS

In this chapter the concept of 'stress' will be investigated in relation to several linguistic aspects: definitions, abstraction, metaphorical language and interchange of words or synonyms. The various definitions quoted are offered in contrast to those given by popular writers quoted in the first chapter. While they exhibit some similarities, they also show that the wide differences of opinion held by particular writers are also present amongst 'experts' and scientists. These definitions I argue, indicate more than just a divergence of opinions; they represent descriptions of different phenomena. The variety of opinion is made further possible by the abstract nature of the concept of 'stress'.

Abstract concepts are discussed with more specific reference to broad concepts. Their varying levels of vagueness, subjectivity and the resulting definitional difficulties make it possible to have different points of view about what is supposedly the same phenomenon. Metaphorical language, interchange of words, reification and personification can add to any discourse by giving explanations that may at first appear coherent but may ultimately prove not to be so.

Definitional difficulties

The vagueness and subjectivity of broad abstract concepts make it difficult for agreement to be reached about what is being discussed. This is evidenced by the fact that often in discussions about various broad abstract concepts, a more precise definition is given of what will be discussed. This definition may not be acceptable to all but it serves to focus or contextualize what is being discussed. For instance, someone discussing the environment would need to not only explain what type of environment is being discussed but also what specific aspects will be covered.

An agreement about the definition of broad abstract concepts is rendered difficult when the assumptions that underpin the various definitions are not compatible. When this happens a common definition will always prove to be problematic. Agreement can also be a problem when the concept has many forms. 'Conflict', for instance can denote a war, an internal dilemma, a difficulty with someone etc… To what extent any of these is truly 'conflict' is often difficult to assess. It may also be difficult to assess what constitutes a 'massacre'. To some it may be the nature of the killing, to others it may the number of people killed. Nevertheless, with either definition, problems remain in determining what sort of killing or how many dead bodies warrant the use of the term 'massacre'.

As for 'stress', the many forms of the concept, the many types or many explanations make it difficult to decide which, if any, best explains the phenomena the concept is meant to describe.

Definitions of stress

Researchers from various disciplines such as psychology, psychiatry, medicine, biology, neurology, endocrinology, immunology also with views from different theoretical perspectives have attempted to define 'stress'. The following definitions demonstrate their different points of view:

Stress to us is a very general term that means somewhat different though related things at different levels of analysis…Each of the levels of stress analysis is partially independent in that it refers to different conditions, concepts, and processes (Lazarus & Launier, 1978).

Stress is 'perception.' It is the demands that are imposed upon us because there are too many alternatives. Stress is caused by being conscientious and hardworking (Selye, 1979).

Somewhere between the stressor and its effects lies the subjective, phenomenological experience of stress itself… such experience lies outside the realm of objective inquiry. Accordingly, behaviors classified as stress effects can also be categorized as the effects of anxiety, the effects of conflict, etc. Insofar as expression of emotion, performance deterioration or symptom manifestations are concerned, stress is interchangeable with these other concepts (Breznitz & Goldberger, 1982).

82

Psychological stress requires a judgment that environmental and/or internal demands exceed the individual's resources for managing them (Holroyd & Lazarus, 1982).

There is general agreement that stress refers to a response of the organism to a noxious or threatening condition (Pearlin, 1982).

...stress is a familiar concept to us since it is an inescapable part of life. We feel we know what stress is because we experience it in its various forms in everyday life. We recognize it when we are faced with the prospect of having to pay an overdue bill, have an argument with another motorist, become frustrated with the boss, anticipate surgery at the dentist, or await a driving test. We speak of stress in general terms because it incorporates so many areas of our lives (Dobson, 1983).

Stress seems to refer to things that people are exposed to, that they are under (experience?), but in general it seems to be characteristic of situations (Mandler, 1984).

Stress is a cerebral reaction of a particular individual to a stimulus event (Skinner, 1985, in Goldstein, 1995).

Stress is part of a complex and dynamic system of transaction between the person and his environment (Cox, 1985).

Stress may be viewed as the body's response to any real or imagined event perceived as requiring some adaptive response and/or producing strain (Eliot, 1988).

Stress has sometimes been described as an increase in catecholamine levels, a change in adrenal weight, or as a score on a life event scale or subjective reaction index (Steinberg & Ritzmann, 1990).

Stress can be defined as an underload or overload of matter, energy or information input to, or output from, a living system (Steinberg & Ritzmann, 1990).

Stress is part of an adaptive biological system, where a state is created when a central processor registers an informational discrepancy (Levine & Ursin, 1991, in Goldstein, 19950.

In essence, stress can be considered as any factor, acting internally or externally, that makes it difficult to adapt and that induces increased effort on the part of the person to maintain a state of equilibrium both internally and with the external environment (Humphrey, 1992).

Stress, a term borrowed from physics by W. Cannon and H. Selye and set to mean the mutual actions of forces that take place across any section of the body is a state of *threatened homeostasis* (Stratakis & Chrousos, 1995).

The term 'stress' may be used in two ways in psychiatry: it may be used to identify events or circumstances that are perceived adversely ('stressors') or to describe the state induced by such events or circumstances (the 'stress reaction') (Glue, Nut & Coupland, 1993).

Stress is a subset of emotion (Lazarus, 1993).

Stress is a term for certain types of experiences, as well as the body's responses to such experiences. The term generally refers to challenges, real or implied, to the homeostatic regulatory process of the organism (McEwen & Mendelson, 1993).

The process of coping with life's pressures and problems and the negative feelings this can generate (Thompson, Murphy and Stradling, 1994).

Stress is caused by a multitude of demands (stressors), such as an inadequate fit between what we need and what we are capable of, and what our environment offers and what it demands of us (Levi, 1996).

Stress is a useless term for pragmatic researchers, because it represents different things to different people, reality is different for each of us, and most importantly, often cannot be measured with any significant degree of accuracy (Rosch, 1996).

Psychosocial stress refers to the socially derived, conditioned, and situated psychological processes that stimulate any or all of the many manifestations of dysphoric affect falling under the rubric of subjective distress (Kaplan, 1996).

Stress is the external pressures and tension the internal pressures (Saunders, 1997).

The sum of biological and psychological disturbances caused by any aggression on the organism (Larousse French dictionary, 1971).

As these sample views show, definitions of stress have been a source of disagreement and confusion. Many agree that the field of stress research has been plagued by difficulties in defining the concept (Breznitz & Goldberger, 1982; Burtchfield, 1979; Derogatis & Coons, 1993; Dobson, 1983; Haan, 1982; Hinkle, 1987; Humphrey, 1992; Kasl & Cobb, 1982; Laux & Vossel, 1982; Mason,

1975; Mulhall, 1996; Norman & Malla, 1993; Newton 1989; Ursin & Olff, 1993).

Cox (1985) best summarised the situation when he stated that:

> The concept of 'stress' is elusive because it is poorly defined. There is no single agreed definition in existence. It is a concept which is familiar to both layman and professional alike. It is understood by all when used in a general context but by very few when a more precise account is required and this seems to be the central problem.

Goldstein (1995) has lamented that:

> ...most researchers have not defined stress before delving into its endocrinological, physiological and psychological effects. Some have skirted the issue by defining stress empirically -but actually circularly- by those effects. This approach...has left the impression that stress can be anything to anyone and that it can contribute to virtually any disease.

Similar sentiments have led Ellis & Thompson (1983) to declare that "Stress, in addition to being itself and the result of itself, is also the cause of itself". Another scientist, Soderberg (1967, in Newton, 1989), had already commented that stress was "the most grandly imprecise term in the dictionary of science." Others have felt that in its current form, the term 'stress' had been considerably trivialized and lost an important part of its meaning (Fontaine & Salah, 1991) or that it "...is something which is not naturally occurring but is a manufactured concept which has now become a 'social fact'" (Pollock, 1988).

The *Oxford English Dictionary* shows that the first recorded use of the term 'stress' was in 1303 by English poet Robert Brunne, referring to hardship and adversity. In addition, it offers explanations for 27 other meanings. Amongst them, is a psychological or biological definition which describes stress as "An adverse circumstance that disturbs, or is likely to disturb, the normal physiological functioning of an individual; such circumstances collectively. Also, the disturbed state that results". It situates this particular usage of the term as being first used in *Endocrinology* XXXI, in 1942, in relation to physical stress in an animal experiment. The term 'stressor' on the other hand, is credited to Hans Selye in 1950.

Stress: an abstract concept

The different understandings of what constitutes stress arise from the fact that 'stress' is ultimately an abstract concept with no precise point of reference in the physical world. Because we cannot see, hear, touch, feel or smell stress, it is always going to be difficult to imagine what stress could be like, let alone define it. This is not to say that all abstract concepts are as hard to define as 'stress'. When an abstract concept describes a simple event or situation, an agreement and/or a definition can usually be obtained. However, this is not the case with 'stress', which has been used in an attempt to explain everything in general and nothing in particular. A major problem with the concept of 'stress' is that it has been used to replace existing concepts as well as to provide an explanation for novel phenomena. All the various conditions encompassed by the concept of 'stress' may appear at first to share much in common but after closer scrutiny they can be seen to exhibit more differences than similarities.

Many of the definitions offered earlier have assumed the existence of stress but the stress they describe is only compatible to the model of stress their authors presuppose. This contributes to the difficulty of finding a universal definition or even of proving the existence of stress itself. At best, what might be shown is that if stress existed, what is being observed could be caused or associated with that stress. Claims of the discovery of 'stress hormones', for instance, really cannot be justified since the existence of a 'stress hormone' necessarily depends on the existence of stress in the first place. As was indicated in the previous chapter the concepts of 'vapors', 'nerves', 'hysteria', 'hypochondria', 'hysterical conversion', 'neurasthenia', 'psychasthenia' and 'nervous tension' eventually disappeared. The diagnosis of stress may eventually meet with the same fate only to be replaced by some newer and more exciting label. This is similar to what has happened with 'depression'. At first, it used to be called nervous breakdown, then depression, manic-depression, bipolar disorder and finally for those without the manic episode, unipolar disorder. One might argue that these are only words and that it does not matter which term is used but this would be grossly underestimating the social nature and effect of language.

Abstract concepts: assumptions and implications

Concepts, abstract or concrete, are distinct from the words that represent them. Concrete concepts can usually be explained in terms of characteristics or attributes. For instance, the concept of 'chair' involves legs, a backrest and something made up of a solid substance capable of supporting the weight of a person. It also denotes its purpose: something which can be sat on. The absence of a backrest, for instance, results in the concept of 'stool' being used instead of that of 'chair'. Abstract concepts differ in that they do not have physical observable characteristics. They have nothing tangible than can be pointed to or observed. Instead, they rely on assumptions about the aspect of the world they are attempting to describe, but these assumptions may vary greatly between individuals.

The concept of 'politeness', for example, relies on the assumption that certain behaviors are indicative of someone who is polite. Since 'politeness' itself cannot be directly observed, it is not possible to ascertain which particular behavior embodies the true characteristics of 'politeness'. The concept may be understood by someone to be the absence of rude or swear words, to someone else it may be exemplified by asking permission to do something, to another person it may be to properly address people or it may even be all of these things.

These understandings of the concept may also be affected by various situations. Circumstances may produce a broadening or narrowing of what the concept means. Nevertheless, whatever we assume to constitute 'politeness' will have a bearing on how we behave in situations where we feel 'politeness' is required. This is an important point. It shows that the acceptance of

87

assumptions about a particular concept has specific consequences for the way we deal with a particular aspect of life. These assumptions, however, may eventually prove to be correct or incorrect.

An incorrect assumption often made about abstract concepts is that if a word exists, then what it describes must exist. While there appears to be some justification for this, a closer examination is warranted. A concept may be created in an attempt to describe and explain a certain situation or relationship but its usefulness depends on the validity of the assumptions it makes. The concept of 'hysteria', as described by Hippocrates, came for instance, with the assumption that the uterus traveled to the brain. The basis for the introduction of this concept was that women exhibited some symptoms or unwelcome behaviors which necessitated an explanation. The situation existed, as did the symptoms and the behavior. But the assumptions about the nature of the situation which the concept of 'hysteria' tried to describe, however, would eventually be shown to be incorrect.

The acceptance of Hippocrates' concept of 'hysteria' meant that solutions to the problem would have had to include a remedy for the wandering uterus. Proposing early marriage seemed a reasonable attempt to deal with the problem. The sexual part of marriage and childbirth could presumably have had a settling effect on the uterus. Yet, our current medical knowledge makes it evident that this would have made no difference to the problem of hysteria. All it might have done is lower the marrying age for women.

An acceptance of the validity of the concept of 'stress' invariably has implications for the way we deal with what we perceive to be happening. For instance, if we thought that 'stress' was something we did to ourselves, we would say that we were 'stressing'. However, when we say that we are 'stressed', we implicitly accept that stress is something being done to us or that something external to us is responsible for our state. This notion of an 'external stress' is reinforced by comments urging us to deal with stress, to cope with it and to combat it. Its often alleged inevitability, somehow, seems to partly take away our responsibility for its occurrence. We could not be responsible for something that will happen anyway, regardless of how we feel or act. This makes the concept very appealing in a social world seemingly full of 'demands'.

A perceived inability to fulfil those 'demands' may result in a sense of failure. However, this feeling of failure can be avoided if these 'demands' are part of an inevitable stress. It would appear that all that is left then, is to deal with stress, to cope and lament its existence. The notion of 'coping' ironically brings the blame back on the 'stressee'. Unfortunately, inappropriate coping can also create a sense of failure. The individual is responsible after all for being 'stressed' and may even end up being 'stressed' about being 'stressed'.

Vagueness of broad abstract concepts

Concepts such as 'love', 'pride', 'intelligence', 'politeness', 'reliability', 'justice', 'honesty' are just a few examples of abstract concepts. Abstract concepts play a very important role in shaping social life. Not only are our social institutions built on them, so are our lives. Many of these concepts are used in explanations for many physical, psychological and social situations. There are great advantages that can be gained from the economy of words produced by the use of broad single word concepts. While this parsimony is encouraged and sometimes desirable in the case of ordinary everyday discourse, it can become a source of frustration when an attempt is made to analyze and explain the various phenomena embraced by such concepts.

The vagueness of these concepts is evident when they are describing a large body of experiences or situations. Concepts like 'environment', 'justice', 'love' or 'stress', for example, cover many possible situations. 'Environment' can involve many aspects of the physical, psychological and social world. Similarly, the concept of 'justice' can be applied to many social situations, as can that of 'love'.

Alternatively, concepts such as 'idea', 'thirst', 'hunger', 'happy' and 'sad' are generally relatively easier to grasp. The reason for this is that they tend to be associated with more specific phenomena. Even though one can have many 'ideas', experience 'thirst' or 'hunger' several times a day and can be 'happy' and 'sad' many times and about different situations, there is usually a reasonable amount of agreement about these definitions. This distinction between broad and what may be termed 'specific' abstract concepts is not always evident or easily recognizable.

Goldstein (1995), for instance, seemed unaware of this distinction when he reasoned that stress, despite its many problems, was still "a useful conceptual abbreviation". He arrived at this conclusion by comparing the concept of 'stress' with that of 'hunger'. It may be, however, difficult for Goldstein to argue that most people are faced with the same confusion about hunger as they are about stress. There would be very few, if any, publications attempting to conceptualize and explain hunger but there have been hundreds of thousands of books and articles written about stress. Additionally, there are many more definitions of stress than there are of hunger and few people would have difficulties explaining what hunger is.

The vagueness of broad concepts can also be a source of confusion. 'Environment' can be used to describe many factors, yet because of its vagueness it really describes none. The concept of 'environment' often needs to be subdivided into more specific concepts, such as 'work environment', 'school environment', 'cellular environment', etc....This can lead to misleading uses of the concept.

Some psychologists have advanced that there is an interaction between genes and social events because in molecular biology language genes are described as being expressed in the environment. These psychologists have based their reasoning, unfortunately, on a confusion between the molecular environment of cells, enzymes, nucleic acids and so on and the social environment of people and events. These 'environments', however, are vastly different and cannot be interchanged.

The vagueness surrounding the concept of 'stress' makes it possible for statements which suggest that most events in life are 'stressors', to go unchallenged. Yet if we accept that most events in life are 'stressors', then life itself must also be mostly 'stressful' for all of us. This is despite the common observation that events can vary greatly for many people in term of their impact, quality, quantity and importance.

The confusion is even greater when the impact of stress is discussed. We are told by many 'experts' that stress could kill us but that if we approach it with the right attitude it will not. We are also told that it can be good for us and that we actually need some stress. Too much stress and we are 'stressed'; not enough and we are still 'stressed'. Just enough and we can supposedly perform at our best. Yet according to Selye, we cannot, however, contemplate a life without stress. "Total elimination of stress...would be equivalent to death" (Selye, 1976). If this is true, then not only could stress kill us, but no stress could also do it. Whatever happens we appear to be doomed. Ultimately, it seems that virtually anything can be said about stress.

Further, like other broad concepts discussed earlier, 'stress' is largely reductionist. Many physical, psychological and social life events are reduced to stress. In theories suggesting that cognitive appraisal is the ultimate determinant of stress, the appraisal is reduced to stress. In physical stress studies, it is physiological responses that are synonymous to stress.

Interestingly, at the same time as the concept has been used to include anything and everything, more and more types of stress have been created to try to accommodate its multiplicity. As is the case with 'environment', we now have 'work stress', 'techno-stress', 'chronic stress', 'mild stress', 'post traumatic stress', 'emotional stress', 'biological stress', 'vacation stress', 'exam stress' and many more. This apparent contradiction may be the best indication yet that the concept, while useful in providing the desired economy of words for everyday discourse, is in difficulty as a universal scientific explanation.

This does not seem to have been recognized by some researchers who persistently try to fit more and more things under the label. One of them (Pearlin, 1982) has declared that:

It is the very nature of stress that it can be so many things, and we should not try to reduce the multidimensionality of this phenomenon by arbitrarily declaring that stress is only one thing or another. It is much more productive, I believe, to recognize the diffuse character of the stress phenomenon and to bend our efforts to understanding how its multiple manifestations are interconnected.

Pearlin's statement is an interesting case of reification, a phenomenon that is discussed in more detail in the next paragraph. Not only does he speak of stress as having a nature, he also proposes that it is not merely a thing but, in fact, many things. A closer inspection of the statement reveals more confusion. It seems that Pearlin cannot really decide whether stress is many things, a thing with multiple dimensions or a thing which manifests itself in different ways that are in some manner connected.

Reification

With no physical point of reference, it is often left to our imagination and creativity to decide what the abstract world is made of. When a word has been around for a long time, it is more likely to be taken for granted. Few people, for example doubt the existence of 'love'. When this happens we are more likely to be misled into thinking that what it describes exists as a material reality. This can result in reification, which is the tendency to treat abstract concepts as if they were real and turn them into things. In other words, to reify is to 'thingify' (Condon, 1966). The process has also been called hypostatization. The fallacy of hypostatization occurs when we regard an abstraction as if it were something concrete (and go on, sometimes, to ascribe human-like properties to it). We hypostatize when we say such things as "the state can do no wrong", "nature decrees what is right" and so forth. These are fallacies, for neither the state nor nature is capable of thought, intention or design (Engel, 1995). Our use of 'ordinary language' also encourages reification. When describing a number of abstractions, we often say "things such as love and happiness...", although these are not things.

We often use abstract concepts, in the form of labels, to try to understand various aspects of human behavior. This certainly has helped in creating a dialogue between scientists but one of the disadvantages of labeling is that it can limit our powers of observation, in that it can result in us missing, discounting or misinterpreting anything that does not fit the model that corresponds to our label (Condon, 1966). For some, the choice is confusing as evidenced by Saunders's (1997) comment that "stress is as much a mind-set as it is a physical reality." Describing stress as a physical reality has had a negative impact on the study of stress according to Lipowski (1986b). He deplored that:

> ...the concept of stress has often been unduly reified, that is to say, considered to be a clearly definable environmental noxious agent, like a poison or a pathogenic microorganism, for example, one that may 'cause' disease. Such a simplistic, if regrettably popular notion has served to detract from the value of the concept and to encourage use of such vague terms as 'stress diseases'.

The point made by Lipowski is quite pertinent. Therefore, it is rather puzzling how, later in the article, he labels catecholamines, corticosteroids and adrenocorticotropin as 'stress hormones' (Lipowski, 1986c)- terms possibly just as vague as 'stress diseases'.

Personification

Not only is there a tendency to reify abstract concepts, there is also a tendency to personify many of them. This results in ascribing illegitimate agency to abstract concepts. The problem of false agency is not limited to abstract concepts. We also personify concrete concepts. We can say, for instance, "this wall annoys me", even though it is impossible for an inanimate object like a wall to do so. If we needed to identify what our problem truly was, we would have to reconsider and speak more accurately and rephrase the sentence as "I am annoyed by the wall". Viewing the problem in these terms would be more likely to lead to an appropriate resolution. Directing our efforts towards understanding why we are getting annoyed would seem to offer better hope of a solution than trying to find out what the wall has done to annoy us. This example may seem rather simplistic and obvious but it is less so when we try to explain why "this person annoys me". There are probably instances when we blame others for our annoyance, when it is due to their mere presence.

This sort of error does not only occur in everyday discourse, it is also found in science, social or otherwise. In the study of 'stress', agency has often been given to the brain, the body or events. For instance, in the next chapter it is shown that Tache (1986) personified the body when he suggested that the 'primordial' man in us is aroused whenever the body analyses any 'perception' as a threat.

The use of metaphors

The use of metaphors has a place in the scientific domain, insofar as it helps us to proceed from the familiar to the unfamiliar. Sometimes, however, the metaphor, after many years of popular usage, can become accepted as a reality. When this happens, the term is no longer considered a metaphor but a new definition of the word and it carries with it some of its implications. An example of this is when patients are diagnosed with a loss of short-term memory. Although countless brain operations have failed to reveal such a thing in the brain, the patient feels that the condition can only be physical as the notion of a loss usually implies an original existence or presence. Russell (1921) has noted that vocabulary, by promoting the hypostatization of pseudo entities, encourages false beliefs concerning the contents of the world.

In the discourse about stress we hear of pressure, work overload, demands and structural constraints and coping mechanisms. On the biological side, we are told about an immune system, giving the impression that a whole, well defined system exists. There is also talk of a stress alarm system, yet to be discovered after a 60 year search. This multitude of metaphors and additional abstract concepts increases the complexity of what is being discussed. When this happens, as it has with stress, the abstraction is further complicated by the introduction, in explanations, of even more abstractions, each one interpreted subjectively and elastically by the audience. Ultimately, the confusion, often enhanced by the introduction of new unfamiliar terms which need to be learned and understood, can become greater than it was to begin with.

At other times, problems and confusion can arise through the metaphorical nature of explanations. Metaphorical explanation can result in giving a totally wrong impression of what is taking place. Sapolsky (1994) provides a good example of this. In attempting to describe the stress reaction, he explains that when we worry, *"we turn on* physiological responses". *"We* so often *activate* a physiological system meant for acute physical emergencies, but *we* turn it up for months on end". "When *we activate* the stress-response out of fear of something that turns out to be real, *we congratulate ourselves* that this cognitive skill allows us to *mobilize* our defenses early". "If you are faced with a physical stressor and *you* cannot appropriately *turn on* the stress response, you are in big trouble." But "if *you repeatedly turn on* the stress-response or if *you cannot appropriately turn off* the stress response at the end of a 'stressful' event, the stress response can eventually become nearly as damaging as some stressors themselves". [italic added].

Readers could be excused if, after reading this, they felt guilty about being so silly that they would keep doing these things to themselves. But more to the point, implied in Sapolsky's statements is the notion that the stress process is a conscious inadequate handling of some sort of unified response system.

Synonyms and interchange of words

Language contains synonyms. They are used to describe either different degrees or nuances of the same things or things that are closely related without being similar. There are numerous terms that have been used in the stress discourse, with some writers in the field suggesting that stress can be interchanged with many other terms without losing the meaning of what is being said. Some commentators seem to have had some problems in differentiating between stress and other concepts when studying physiological responses. Pairings have included anxiety (Glue, Nut & Coupland, 1993), unpleasant emotional arousal (Dimsdale & Moss, 1980), strong emotional states (Bohus & Koolhaas, 1993), anger and hostility (Chesney & Rosenman, 1985) and emotional suppression (Steptoe, 1993).

The various perspectives from which researchers have approached the problem have added to the confusion. As the concept of 'stress' came into vogue, many investigators who had been working with a concept which was felt to be related to stress, substituted the word 'stress' and continued with their previous line of investigation. This resulted in concepts such as 'anxiety', 'conflict', 'frustration', 'emotional disturbance', 'trauma', 'alienation' and 'anomie' being described as 'stress' (Cofer & Appley, 1964). What has also complicated matters somewhat has been that often the same terms have been suggested as being a *cause* of stress. Frustration, worries, fears, anxiety have also been said to be the *result* of stress. It seems that all these terms could *be* 'stress', *cause* it and *result* from it; which would mean that stress causes stress which in turn causes more stress. A literal cascade of stress.

The real meaning of 'distress'

An interesting case of word interchange or confusion, by Hans Selye has been with 'distress'. Selye proposed that there were two types of stress: good stress and bad stress. He introduced the terms 'eustress' for good stress and 'distress' for bad stress. 'Eustress' was a new term but 'distress' already existed. Whenever he used these terms, he would always carefully explain that 'eustress' was made up of the Greek prefix 'eu' meaning good and 'stress' (Selye, 1956, 1976). However, on these occasions, he never explained how he arrived at 'distress'. A possible explanation may be that 'distress' could never mean bad stress. Even if we allow that dropping the 's' in 'disstress' would make the word more elegant and more in accordance with grammatical convention, we are still left with the problem that 'dis' does not mean bad. It is the Latin prefix for 'no', as in 'disharmony' or 'dishonesty', indicating that 'distress' should properly mean 'no stress'. To be accurate, Selye should have used the Greek prefix 'dys' meaning "bad" and describe bad stress as 'dystress'.

The confusion resulting from the use of 'distress'

It is unclear why Selye used the term 'distress' to denote bad stress instead of the more appropriate 'dystress'. After all, there are numerous examples in his writings that Selye had a good knowledge of Greek and Latin. It seems reasonable to suggest that he would have known the difference between the different prefixes. Many doctors, in their studies, become acquainted with the various uses of these prefixes, as they are present in many disease names. The only thing that can be ascertained, however, is that it has created a great deal of confusion. At times the term 'distress' appears to have been exploited, wittingly or unwittingly, by many in the field of stress research. Many like Goldstein (1995) have re-labeled psychological stress as 'distress' or 'emotional distress'. At other times, the word 'distress' has been used in different contexts and in doing so has confused potential readers. Selye's 'carelessness' with the use of 'distress' is not to be underestimated because of the connection of 'distress' with emotions. When we are distressed, it denotes some sort of affective state, usually of a negative nature. When Goldstein (1995), for instance, suggested that stress was physical and distress psychological, this seemed reasonably coherent. It would have been different, however, had he used the term 'dystress' because most people understand 'distress' to means some emotional disturbance, not bad stress. To say, therefore, that stress is physical and bad stress is psychological does not seem so coherent after all. This ambiguity has meant that many writers have been able, like Goldstein, to use the term 'distress' without having to face the incoherence of their explanation.

Incidentally, it is notable that the term 'eustress' is only occasionally found in scientific literature or in lay discourse. Moreover, of greater importance, there never seems to be any suggestion that we ever experience 'emotional eustress', even though it is obvious by Selye's definition that 'eustress' can only be encountered in psychological situations. 'Eustress' has never really taken off as concept and is in fact absent in most dictionaries. This may have been due to the fact that a notion of 'good stress' was not appealing to most people. Yet, more simply it might have been that the concept was not sufficiently coherent to be accepted by most people.

Language in the social context

The way we are introduced to the world has much to do with the way we ultimately make sense of it. On many occasions, words are learnt within the context of a conversation. When this is the case, the situational circumstances in which the concept is first heard may have a bearing on the ultimate understanding of what it means.

In everyday language, there are many examples of objectification and personification, so that being told that 'stress kills' seems a real possibility. Much of the information we are provided with about the world, much of it being overheard, forms a large part of our culture. Each culture has its own unique concepts. Some of these concepts can sometimes be translated; at other times, only an approximation can be offered. An example pertinent to the concept of 'stress' is the Japanese concept of 'karoshi', meaning 'death from overwork.' In the words of its creator Tetsunojo Uehata it is a

> ...condition in which psychologically unsound work processes are allowed to continue in a way that disrupts the worker's normal work and life rhythms, leading to a buildup of fatigue in the body and a chronic condition of overwork accompanied by a worsening of pre-existent high blood pressure and a hardening of the arteries and finally resulting in a fatal breakdown (Impoco, 1991).

Impoco (1991) explained that when the 'corporate warrior' dies the Japanese Ministry of Labor only recognize 'karoshi' if the victim can be shown to have worked continuously for 24 hours or for 16 hours a day for seven days leading up to the death. He also reported that a recent poll conducted by an insurance company revealed that 40% of its employees feared that overwork may kill them.

While 'karoshi' may seem to be remarkably similar to the Western concept of 'stress', there are some differences. For instance, the notion of 'harmony' is prevalent in Japanese culture. Furthermore, the belief that a pre-existing condition is needed together with the connection to work ' differentiate 'karoshi' from our broader concept of 'stress'.

This example serves to illustrate how a given culture can provide a particular explanation about an aspect of the world. Once we are socialized into a specific culture, questioning will be generally done from the 'inside' of a culture. In some ways, it could be said (metaphorically) that our culture puts an accent on our ability to see the world in terms other than those of the society we belong to. What is 'stress' to Westerners may be 'karoshi' to Japanese. The two concepts may be related but they also reflect different assumptions about similar problems. In both cases, the concepts may not offer an entirely satisfactory explanation but their acceptance is made possible by the cultural and linguistic contexts in which they are used.

For the Japanese worker, 'karoshi' seems to fit easily with the notion of 'warrior'. For Westerners, something like stress or some of its predecessors, may provide a relief from our constant difficulties in making sense of what we call our lives. If social life, an abstract concept itself, is full of 'stress' then there is little we can do about it. If it is a disease or it is caused by modern life and is an integral part of that life, it is not our fault. Since there is no physical point of reference for stress, no one can suggest that we are not suffering from it. In fact, the more we believe it exists, the more we can feel it. We can even feel sick when we are not sometimes, for we have imagination.

To complicate matters, experts, who are also part of our society and supposedly more knowledgeable about these things than we are, tell us that we are more than justified to believe that we are 'stressed'. It is nice to know that we were not imagining it. It then matters less that explanations are confused, reified or distorted by personalization. In our everyday language, economy of words often takes precedence over accurate explanations.

Summing up

This linguistic investigation of the concept of 'stress' has shown that there have been many definitions of stress proposed by various researchers. As a result a definition of stress, acceptable to most, has not emerged. The reason advanced for this is that 'stress' is an abstract concept. Abstract concepts have been described as such because of their lack of physical representation. These concepts are based on assumptions and have implications that flow from the acceptance of these assumptions. Furthermore, some abstract concepts are vaguer than others and this is especially true of 'broad' abstract concepts. Such concepts are also more difficult to define, subjectively understood and more likely to be redefined to fit particular arguments. The confusion between concrete and abstract concepts is made possible from the way we learn and use language within a society. Reification, personalization and the use of metaphors or metaphorical language are often responsible for the attribution of false agencies. Together with the use of synonyms, they can lead to inadequate explanations of phenomena under consideration.

The way we learn and use language also has an impact on the way we understand the social world. It not only makes it possible to accept the imperfect 'fit' of certain concepts with the world, it also makes it difficult to differentiate between concrete and abstract concepts. For most lay people, habitual everyday language reflects reality despite all its flaws. The scientist, on the other hand, cannot afford to underestimate the vagaries of abstraction because they will often lead him towards a false explanation. All the factors I have discussed in this chapter have combined to make an improbable concept like 'stress' acceptable to many people.

THEORIES AND THEORETICAL
ASPECTS

Over the last 50 years, the concept of 'stress' has been of interest to scientists from many different backgrounds. Sociologists, psychologists, neurologists, immunologists, endocrinologists and even molecular biologists, among others, have attempted to offer possible explanations of what stress is. Attempts to define and understand stress by such diverse groups have meant that interest has been focused in areas such as life events, personality, hardiness, coping mechanisms, physiological effects, cognitive evaluation, as well as psychological and physical causes of stress. The various perspectives from which they have approached the problem seem to have added to the confusion.

Some investigators seem to have automatically presumed that work in areas remotely related to stress was in fact about stress. Dobson (1983), for instance, has credited Dunbar (1935) and Alexander (1950) with psychosomatic models of stress when their work had been primarily concerned with the role of emotional factors in disease.

Other writers seem to believe that 'stress' has been with us for a long time. Rosch (1996), for instance, quotes an anthropologist who at the turn of the century had attributed the absence of cancer amongst Hunza natives with them being "endowed with a nervous system of notable stability." He automatically assumed this was a sign that they were 'resistant to stress'. Others have surprisingly proposed that "Psychogenic stress was mentioned by Epicurus, who suggested that coping with emotional stressors was a way to improve the 'quality of life'" [9] (Johnston, Kamilaris, Chrousos, & Gold, 1992). Going even further back, Saunders (1997) tells us that stress may have been "...around as long as humans have been around

---

[9] It was mentioned in the chapter on the linguistic aspects of stress that the term 'stressor' had been introduced by Selye in 1950.

the planet... and...wasn't given a name until this century. Human beings have been feeling its effects without knowing why."

This contradicts Albrecht (1979) who has warned, like a number of his colleagues have, that stress was "...a strange new epidemic which has found its way into the lives of people in highly industrialized nations of the world. It has been steadily growing, affecting more and more people with ever more serious consequences."

The chapter on the historical perspective of the 'stress' concept has, amongst other things, already demonstrated the relative novelty of the stress concept. There is still a need, however, to determine when the first theory of stress did emerge. This is important because there has been some confusion as to when this did occur. In their attempt to demonstrate that stress had been around for a long time, some writers, whilst acknowledging the various uses of the term 'stress', seem to have overlooked the fact that each use had its own specific definition. It is proposed that the use of the word 'stress' was, at various times in history, used to denote mainly hardship and difficulties. At other times, it has been used as an engineering metaphor, to convey a notion of 'pressure'. It is only relatively recently that it has been used in the sense that we know today.

Various scientists, e.g. William Osler (Dobson, 1983), Walter Cannon, Harold Wolff and Helen Dunbar (Kuglemann 1992), have been incorrectly credited with the creation of the modern concept of 'stress'. Despite this, there seems to be a general agreement that Hans Selye was responsible for the 'invention' or 'discovery' of stress. He, in fact, made such claim in his book *The Stress of Life*. Before Selye, words like 'eustress' and 'stressors' as well as expressions like being 'stressed' or 'stressing out' were never encountered. That they are commonly used today bears testimony to his legacy.

Hans Selye's theory

Here is a revolutionary new concept of mental and physical illness, explained by its discoverer. This startling new theory of disease may be the most important and far-reaching idea in the history of medicine. It has often been compared with the contributions of Pasteur, Ehrlich and Freud. Hans Selye has been acclaimed throughout the world by scientists, physicians, and psychologists for his brilliant exposition of the stress theory. Here, in language easily understood by the general reader, the man who has been called 'the Einstein of medicine' explains his modern concept.

This rather grandiose claim on the book jacket of *The Stress of Life* (1956) was to mark the official arrival in the public arena of the 'stress' concept.

However, it all began in the early 1930's with Selye's observation, as a medical student, that most patients when sick seemed to share symptoms quite apart from their disease. He theorized that those symptoms must be part of a 'syndrome of just being sick'. Later, having unsuccessfully tried to discover a new sex hormone, in desperation he injected mice with formalin and found that they developed an acute reaction. He followed this up with hundreds of animal experiments using diverse distressful stimuli, which ultimately led to his theory of a 'General Adaptation Syndrome' (GAS). This culminated with the publication in *Nature* in 1936 of a short article called *A Syndrome Produced by Diverse Nocuous Agents*.

In his experiments involving reactions to extreme heat or cold, loud noise, blinding light, immobilization in a 'spread-eagle' position or exhausting physical conditions, he found that mice responded to these various conditions in a similar fashion. "The changes observed appeared to be a consequence of marked stimulation of the pituitary-adrenal cortex axis resulting in the production of large amounts of glucocorticoids" (Selye, 1946, as cited in Rosch, 1984).

Selye labeled this the 'alarm reaction', the first step in the three stages of the GAS, the others being 'resistance', followed by, when the stress was persistent, 'exhaustion'. During the resistance phase, he hypothesized, the increased resistance to the 'stressor' resulted in a decreased resistance to other stimuli and could end up in a depletion of 'adaptation energy'. Later, according to Selye, after much opposition from the scientific community, he added the concept of 'stress' to his syndrome describing it as "the non-specific response of the body to any demand upon it" (Selye, 1956). This, however, marked a change from the stance he had adopted in a previous publication in which he had described the General Adaptation Syndrome as a response of the body to stress (Selye & Fortier, 1950).

Selye's definitions of stress

In attempting to explain what stress was, Selye acknowledged that the term 'stress' had been used too loosely and that there had been so many differing definitions that it may be useful to state first what it was not. This is what he had to say:

1- Stress is not nervous tension.

2- Stress is not an emergency discharge of hormones from the adrenal medulla.

3- Stress is not anything that causes a secretion, by the adrenal cortex, or its hormones, the corticoids. ACTH. The adrenal-stimulating pituitary hormone can discharge corticoids without producing any evidence of stress.

4- Stress is not the nonspecific result of damage. Normal activities - a game of tennis or even a passionate kiss - can produce considerable stress without causing conspicuous damage.

5- Stress is not a deviation from homeostasis, the steady state of the body. Any biologic function (the perception of sound or light, the contraction of the muscle) causes marked deviations from the normal resting state in the active organs.

6- Stress is not anything that causes an alarm reaction. It is the stressor that does that, not stress itself.

7- Stress is not identical with the alarm reaction or the GAS, as a whole. These reactions are characterized by certain measurable organ changes which are caused by stress and hence could not themselves be stress.

8- Stress is not a nonspecific reaction **(It affects specific organs).**

9- Stress is not a specific reaction. (It can be caused by virtually any agent) (Selye, 1956).

Selye (1956) recognized that the concept may be perceived to be somewhat confusing, vague, hard to define and that perhaps it was not sufficiently clear to serve as the object of scientific analysis, but he protested:

> But what is vague? The abortive attempts at a definition are but surely not stress itself. It has a very clear tangible form. Countless people have actually suffered or benefited from it. Stress is very real and concrete indeed (p.54).

This is in direct contradiction to his earlier statements that stress was an abstract concept. He then stated, "Of course, the concept of stress is an abstraction"(p.40) and "It is important to keep in mind that stress is an abstraction; it has no independent existence"(p.43). He also asked, "But how does one dissect an abstract concept?" (p.48) and "Could the abstraction of stress furnish us with such common hold by which to grasp all the manifestation of the GAS?" (p.4).

Perhaps this definition of 'stress' may clarify his views:

> Stress is the state manifested by a specific syndrome which consists of all the nonspecifically induced changes within a biologic system.

This definition still seemed too vague but Selye argued that stress had its own characteristic form and composition though no particular cause. If the elements of its form could only be seen by the visible changes it created, it seems these changes would be difficult to recognize. After all, he had also explained that "reactions which tend to repair wear and tear are not strictly stress but rather responses to stress." A further difficulty was presented when he recognized that "In practice, it is rarely (if ever) possible to distinguish between damage and repair." Also, if, as he explained elsewhere stress was a non observable condition, it seems that we could not only never know what it was but that it would even be impossible to recognize its effect with any confidence. Selye seemed aware of this and attempted to provide a solution to this problem, by explaining that:

You have to observe a great many living beings exposed to a variety of agents before you can see the shape and [sic] stress as such. Those changes which are specifically induced by only one or the other agent must first be rejected; if you then take what is left- that which is nonspecifically induced by many agents- you have unveiled the picture of stress itself. This picture is the GAS. Once this is established, you can recognize stress no matter where it turns up; indeed, you can even measure it by the intensity of the GAS.- manifestations which it produces.

Under this explanation, 'stress' seemed to be the common effects that all 'stressors' possess, once each of their specific effects had been discounted. Moreover, if the picture of stress is also the picture of GAS, it appears to indicate that stress and GAS are one and the same. But they can't be. On the previous page, Selye had stated that stress could not be the GAS, since stress caused it. He also claimed that stress was a 'specific syndrome'. So, if the syndrome of stress caused the GAS, itself a syndrome, then it would mean that we have a cascade of syndromes, with the stress syndrome creating the GAS. Ultimately we are still left to wonder whether GAS and stress describe the same thing or whether stress causes GAS. If it is the latter, then we cannot possibly distinguish between a stress response and a GAS response.

Selye never appeared to provide an adequate explanation of the respective roles of stress and GAS. Instead the concept of 'stress' seems to have been belatedly added to the GAS. Eventually, the 'GAS' concept just disappeared from discussions. It is unclear why this was so, but while its disappearance removed some confusion from the theory, it also made the theory less coherent. GAS was after all the fundamental element of the original theory.

Another confusion relates to the suggestion that physical activities such as a game of tennis or a passionate kiss can cause considerable stress without any conspicuous damage. If there is no damage, there is nothing for anyone to observe, therefore there is no means of recognizing the presence of stress. It is also difficult to imagine how a game of tennis or a kiss could result in a state being labeled as 'stress' if no damage occurred, when such damage is the only indication that 'stress' is experienced.

Other aspects

There are more difficulties with other aspects of the concept of 'stress' as described by Selye. The following sections investigate and discuss some of these difficulties.

'Stressors'

Selye seemed to have developed the concept of 'stressor' as a means to eradicate the confusion that had existed with the various understandings of what constituted 'stress'. Selye was partly to blame for the confusion by settling on the term 'stress' for his theory in the first place. Stress, in engineering terms, described what Selye would later call a 'stressor', whereas 'strain', the effect of stress, was what he termed 'stress'. The title of his book, *The Stress of Life,* was confusing by Selye's definition. Had he been consistent, he would have called it *The Stressors of Life.* This is unless, of course, he meant to say that life itself was a 'stressor'. "A stressor is naturally that which produces stress" was the simple definition he offered for his new concept.

Later, as the focus of research would shift towards psychological stress, psychologists such as Lazarus (1966) proposed that the presence, absence, or amount of stress in various situations depended on the individual's appraisal. Selye, however, was still trying to explain the differences by advancing that an agent was "more or less a stressor in proportion to the degree of its ability to produce stress, that is non specific changes." (1956). Not only had Selye shifted from his previously unambiguous position of a 'stressor' being "that which produces stress", he was proposing something rather unlikely. It is difficult to imagine how something could be labeled a 'stressor' which implied an ability to have a certain effect (produce 'stress') and only have that ability to a certain extent, especially when that something has been also labeled 'an agent'.

For example, a killer cannot be more or less a killer and his or her victim could not be more or less dead. The way

Selye arrived at this, it appears, was by suggesting, as he had done previously, that specificity was always a matter of degree. This seems a rather contradictory proposition. It does not seem possible that something or anyone can be specific to a certain degree. One would have thought that the very concept of 'specificity' was meant to exclude the vagaries of variable degrees. Eventually, he appeared to abandon this puzzling position and revert back to his original position when he suggested later that "a stressor is an agent that produces stress at anytime" (Selye, 1976) and that all life events, physical, chemical and psychological, caused some stress (Tache & Selye, 1985).

Psychological 'stressors'

In its original form, Selye's theory was essentially a physical stress theory since it dealt mainly with the effects of physical factors such as cold, heat, etc.... Despite brief references to psychological factors, the evidence for justification of the concept of 'stress' was derived exclusively from experiments on animals. It seems, however, that as the interest in the field began to focus more on the psychological aspects of stress, Selye attempted to generalize many of his findings about physical factors to psychological factors. Selye (1982) obviously embraced the concept of 'psychological stress' with great enthusiasm as evidenced by his following comments:

> Stressors, it should be noted, are not exclusively physical in nature. Emotions - love, hate, joy, anger, challenge, and fear-, as well as thoughts call forth the changes characteristic of the stress syndrome. In fact, psychological arousal is one of the most frequent activators.

Selye added that these emotional responses could be prevented by suitable counseling or psycho-pharmacological measures (drugs and counseling) or by the individual not appreciating them as stress. He also made the valid point that under deep anesthesia " a person cannot be placed under the stress of the most irritable boss, spouse or financial calamity" (Selye, 1980).

In order to cope with psychological stress, he suggested we could remove 'stressors' from our lives by seeking relaxation or diversion from life's demands. This in some ways, contradicted an earlier suggestion he had made that we should not try to eliminate stress. He argued that a total elimination of "the demands made upon any part of the body, including the cardiovascular, respiratory and nervous system would be equivalent to death" (Selye, 1976).

He had also contended that stress was a 'perception'. "It is the demands that are imposed upon us because there are far too many alternatives, too many choices" (Selye, 1979). Stress, he added, was caused by conscientiousness and hardworking. He believed that stress was with us to stay and that all we could do (besides removing it) was to try to cope with it. His recommendation for effective coping was to "enjoy a maximum eustress and a minimum distress."

Selye's various pronouncements render the task of understanding where he stood with regard to psychological stress somewhat difficult. Selye, it appears, was prepared to accept most definitions of stress that were offered. This may have been caused by his obvious pride at the amount of research his concept had generated. Commenting on the fact that everyone at the time seemed to be talking about stress, he remarked that few people had defined the concept the same way or even bothered in some cases, to define it at all. He recognized that to some, stress was equated with frustration or emotional tension, concentration problems, chemical events, muscular tension and that the list could be extended to just about every human experience or activity. Yet, instead of recognizing the problems this could cause, he concluded: "Somewhat, ironically, there is a grain of truth in every formulation of stress because of demands upon our adaptability to evoke the stress phenomenon"(Selye, 1980). It did not appear to disturb him that some of these formulations were describing distinctly different phenomena, some of them being totally unrelated.

At the same time, Selye was trying to redefine stress as being "the nonspecific (that is common) result of any demand upon the body, be it mental or somatic." This formulation Selye (1980) told us, was:

...based on objective indicators such as bodily and chemical changes which appear after any demand, that has brought the subject (so popular now that it is often referred to as 'stressology') out of the stage of vague cocktail party chitchat into the domain of science.

We are nonetheless left to ponder, what in fact constitutes a demand and whether it has to be real or perceived. We also have to contemplate how the mere precedence of a demand to the appearance of bodily and chemical changes somehow launches the concept of 'stress' into the respectability of the scientific domain. Moreover, on this occasion Selye seemed to have abandoned the notion of non-specificity. It seems that he no longer felt there was a need to differentiate between the specific and non-specific effects of these demands.

Even if all the confusion and contradictions encountered so far are ignored, the biggest problem facing Selye in trying to include psychological 'stressors' in this theory was that if such 'stressors' existed, they would vary substantially from physical 'stressors', in many respects. He was correct, if we were to accept the validity of the 'stress' concept, in suggesting that physical stress depended largely on the 'stressor'.

Taking cold as an example, the intensity of the cold will affect the responses of the body. If the temperature is so low as to threaten life, then few things can be done by the organism. One response would be to seek a warmer environment. If this were not possible, then there would be little else that could be done. In the case of a human being, more clothing could be worn but there would still be a point at which exposure to a temperature, too low to allow life, would result in injury and ultimately the death of the organism. In this instance, the body's reaction to a sufficiently low temperature, is purely due to a physical action of atmospheric conditions on the body.

In the case of psychological stress, no law of physics or chemistry stipulates that a demand, or any situation for that matter, can evoke a direct alteration of the physiology of the body. Therefore, to suggest as Selye did that all life events, physical and psychological, can cause stress, cannot be justified. Leaving aside for a moment that the term 'stress' may not even be useful to explain physical events, Selye's explanations of stress make far more sense from a biological rather than psychological point of view. With psychological stress, mediating agents need to be found to convert the abstraction of psychological life events to the concrete physiological responses of the body. These mediating agents, in the form of alarm signals, had been proposed by Selye as elements of the stress response.

The alarm signals

Early in his writings, Selye had recognized that "our ignorance about the nature of these alarm signals is one of the most serious handicaps in the study of stress" (1956). The situation had not changed 20 years later when he declared "As yet, nothing is known about the chemical nature of the first mediator; ... Identification of the first mediator appears to be one of the most fundamental tasks of future stress research" (Selye, 1976). He seemed to suggest that these alarm signals and especially the initial one, could be a case of 'flight or fight', in contradiction to his earlier proposal that "Stress is not an emergency discharge of hormones from the adrenal medulla" (1956). Nevertheless, there seemed to be a hint of "flight or fight" when Selye (1976) described the "evocative agent" of disease:

> Here, we are dealing with the curious phenomenon that an essentially useful defensive reaction, developed in the course of evolution for protection (e.g., emotional arousal in preparation for fight, immunologic and inflammatory responses to foreign intruders), can be the major cause of disease, if the defense is inappropriate under the circumstances. It is true that, in the course of evolution, most of the inappropriate defense reactions have gradually been eliminated as only the fittest survived; but evolution is still in progress - we are not yet perfect.

Later, Tache and Selye (1985) were more to the point when they explained that when confronted with an objective stimulus, the body assessed the responses, strategies and coping mechanisms needed to ensure survival. The reactions pertaining to the fight were described as physical, metabolic or 'catotoxic' activity, those of flight were explained in terms of physical withdrawal from the situation or reactions such as daydreaming and mental suppression of ideas or events, amongst other things.

Tache (1986) took the point even further and left no doubt about his views, stating that in each one of us "lies dormant a primeval man who in certain situations, aroused and imperiously takes command of the personality.". The use of the "ancient solution" of 'flight or fight', he continued, was inadequate to modern problems. He was also telling us that we are relying too much on 'flight or fight', renamed an 'alarm reaction' for the occasion. This alarm reaction, he felt, was taught and then "sets and develops into a habit, a way of life". The 'primordial' man in us is aroused whenever the body (one would have thought the mind) analyses any 'perception' (event?) as a threat.

He continued "One cannot but decry the use and abuse of this ancient blind mechanism to exact a better or longer performance from other human beings." The ancient way of doing things was not useful, he concluded: "this biological vestige is mobilized in circumstances where it need not be."

It seems doubtful that he was proposing a literal use of the 'flight or fight' response. People do have not have hair standing on their back, stand snarling, with their whole being ready to either strike or escape, whenever they are faced with various challenging situations, like the death of a spouse or losing a job. They are more likely to feel a sense of despair. The reflex of 'flight or fight' seems mainly to arise, for human at least, in times of startling danger or fear. On these occasions it still seems to be useful.

The problem of identifying an alarm system did not seem to be a concern for Ursin and Olff (1993). They thought Moruzzi and Magoun (1949) had already found it. Naming it "the most important contribution to our understanding of the total stress response", they explained that Selye never included it in his model because of his concentration on the adrenocortical axis. They arrived at this conclusion by crediting Morruzzi and Magoun with the discovery of a general activation or alarm system in the brain. They defined it as "the process in the central nervous system (CNS) which raises the activity of CNS.", from one level to another and keeps it at the higher level. General activation, they further explained, was characterized by the subjective feeling of wakefulness versus drowsiness. In other words, for Ursin and Olff, the system which allowed people to wake up from their sleep was the alarm system.

They did express the view, however, that their discussion of the stages and levels of activation, with regard to defense and coping, was only tentative and that more research was needed and that until the results from such a research were available, the exact psychological and physiological mechanisms at play during the 'stressful' encounter would remain obscure.

Nevertheless, despite Ursin and Olff's belief, the search for an alarm response has remained an area of difficulty for theories of stress. Later, Selye (1982) had felt that there had been considerable progress in the analysis of the mediation of stress reactions by hormones. However, he acknowledged that identifying the carrier of the first alarm signal, responsible for the call for adaptation, had still not been achieved. But he rationalized that the problem was not fatal and that "whatever the nature of the first mediator, however, its existence is assured by its effects, which have been observed and measured." This, it seems, is another instance of circularity by Selye: he claims that even though we don't know what the first mediator is (it is also possible that there may not even be one at all), we know it exists because its effects had been observed. However, it is unlikely that we could ever be certain that these effects belonged to any mediator if we had no way of matching mediator and effects.

Further, the lack of evidence about the nature of an initial mediator renders claims about the occurrence of stress purely speculative. The mere fact that an event or situation, which is subsequently labeled a 'stressor', occurs before or close to a set of biological reactions labeled 'stress' or 'stress reactions', cannot be used as hard evidence to support the existence of stress. This would be like attempting to explain the occurrence of planes flying into the distance by suggesting that they do so because of a barking dog. The evidence appears quite overwhelming that the dog has succeeded in chasing each plane away, given that each departure follows a bout of barking.

Adaptation

If the stress response could not be understood in terms of what triggered it, it may be more useful to concentrate on the reason for the response. Adaptation was offered by Selye as the main determinant of the stress response but he felt that the process came at a cost. Selye contended that the stress process involved the consumption of 'adaptation energy', which he defined, like other concepts, in a circular manner. "Adaptation energy" said Selye was, "that which is consumed during continued adaptive work." He differentiated it from caloric energy and candidly admitted "but it is only a name and we still have no precise concept of what this energy might be. Further research along these lines would seem to hold great promise..." (Selye, 1956).

Unfortunately, 43 years later the promise has still not been fulfilled. He further speculated that the amount of adaptation energy varied from individual to individual. This variation was determined at birth by the genetic background, namely the parents. Each individual could draw upon 'inborn capital', "thriftily for a long but monotonously uneventful existence or he can spend it lavishly in the course of a stressful, intense, but perhaps more colorful and exciting life. In any case, there is just so much of it and he must budget accordingly" (Selye, 1956).[10]

Selye's understanding had been deduced from experiments in which he had exposed rats to increasingly lower temperatures. He was convinced that the rats could be

---

[10] The reference to the long uneventful existence contradicts Selye's later view that boredom could also induce stress and that some stress was needed to function adequately.

trained to adapt to lower temperatures and that after they had learned to live in the cold they could go on resisting low temperature forever. This did not turn out to be the case. Similar experiments, this time involving intense muscular exercise and injection of toxic drugs, both over long periods of time, resulted in similar failures to adapt. This, however, did not necessarily prove as Selye thought, that these failures were due to a limited supply of adaptation energy. It may just have been evidence that the body can only take so much of these types of unfavorable biological conditions.

For example, preventing an animal or a person from breathing (a physical stress, according to Selye and others) is not so much a case of reducing their adaptation energy but rather one of making it impossible for the organism to absorb enough oxygen to sustain life. If an adaptation to a lack of oxygen existed, it would be very short (around 3 minutes) and as such it would seem very unlikely to deplete what is claimed to be a lifetime reserve of adaptation. It may seem reasonable to deduce that the death of an organism is proof of a lack of adaptation, in the sense that the organism did not sufficiently adapt to the situation to survive. To deduce from this that the depletion of a yet unknown 'adaptation energy' has taken place seems hardly justifiable. To be so would require evidence that adaptation is only possible with the assistance of some sort of energy. This evidence has not as yet been found.

Conditioning factors

In trying to understand variation in adaptation in individuals' responses, Selye hypothesized about the factors that could play a part in such a variation. Selye often mentioned conditioning factors. He used the term 'conditioning' in the Pavlovian sense but he also used it in relation to any factor that would affect the body's predisposition to stress and stress responses. He thought that genetic make up, age, sex, hormones or drugs treatment and exposure to environmental factors like pollution and social influences, were some of the factors

115

that could explain how and why it was that various people react differently to the same 'stressor' (Selye, 1976).

He also felt that innate defects, under-stress or over-stress, as well as psychological mismanagement could cause the adaptive response to breakdown (Selye, 1982). He confessed to be a great admirer of the research on 'type A' personality which he believed to be of genetic origin. However, he explained that the situation was not hopeless for people like himself suffering the 'stigma' of having a 'type A' personality. The solution was simple and it was to convert distress into 'eustress'. Not only did he not elaborate on how this could be done, he also failed to explain the mechanism by which conditioning factors would affect the stress response.

Disease

The concept of 'adaptation energy' discussed earlier also led Selye to his belief that most stress-induced diseases were in fact diseases of adaptation. These diseases, he commented, were "...consequences of the body's inability to meet these agents in adequate adaptive reactions, that is by a perfect GAS"(Selye, 1956). In other words, the imperfections of the GAS played the major role in disease. If this were true, then it would not have been correct to say that diseases were stress-induced. They would have been more accurately described as GAS-induced. Yet when Selye (1980) later wrote of stress diseases he commented:

> Some maladies are almost completely due to our appreciation of their stressful effect. High blood pressure, heart accidents, mental breakdowns, migraines and insomnia... Most likely, the vast majority of all maladies for which the patient seeks medical attention are predominantly due to stress - particularly to psychogenic stress, which is the basis of psychosomatic medicine.

His reference to 'psychogenic stress' indicated that he had changed his position, believing that stress, not the GAS, was playing a major role in disease. However, this position, has been the object of criticism. An historian of psychosomatic medicine has stated that "...the psychogenic connotation of the term 'psychosomatic' should be dropped as it reflects historically interesting, but no longer tenable views on causation of disease. The term 'psychosomatic' must not be used to imply causality, the sense of something 'psychic' causing something 'somatic' " (Lipowski, 1986a).

Eustress and distress

A notion of disease causing 'stress' seems to be incompatible with a notion of 'beneficial stress'. Yet, Selye believed that stress could actually be good for people. As a result, he coined the term 'eustress', meaning good stress and suggested that stress could sometimes be useful to the body. Alternatively, distress was the bad stress. Repeated exposure to distress would lead to diseases of adaptation (Selye, 1974). He also considered that some 'strong stressors' such as physical exercise, hydrotherapy, electroshock and insulin shock might be beneficial in some situations. It is uncertain whether we should take this to mean that under a definition emphasizing usefulness, electroshock and insulin shock would somehow be forms of 'eustress'.

Overall, Selye has been vague on the subject of 'eustress' or good stress. In another attempt to justify 'eustress', he explained that it could be differentiated from 'distress' merely by the absence of tissue damage or by the fact that life had not been shortened (premature death?). Under this definition, the goodness or badness of stress could only be determined retrospectively and the person experiencing the stress would be unable to determine its nature until it was too late. There may also be some difficulties assessing what would constitute a shortened life since it would require a knowledge of how long that life would have been otherwise.

In another instance, Selye suggested that 'eustress' was "the satisfactory feeling that comes from the accomplishment of tasks we consider worth while" (Selye, 1976). Generally, however, his advice was to try to turn the 'distress' of fatigue and failure into the 'eustress' of success and fulfilment. It is still rather challenging to try to imagine how something he often described as being so

117

harmful could suddenly be turned into something pleasant. If it were achievable, this would indicate that the goodness or badness of stress is dependent on either the imagination, the willingness or the perception of the person experiencing the stress. Under this model, the recipient of stress becomes responsible for its nature.

Strangely, according to Selye (1986), even 'eustress' could sometimes be harmful. Even though eustress "is by definition agreeable", Selye continues "if sudden and very intense, it can kill instantly, presumably, as a result of cardiac fibrillation." It now seems that the intensity rather than the goodness/ badness could be the key factor in determining how harmful stress could be. Selye came to this conclusion apparently because:

> ...as time went by and more refined technology became available, it was noted that even happy circumstances, such as great pleasure, joy or success, and healthy muscular exercise also trigger the same stereotyped stress response...which is closely connected with Cannon's emergency 'flight or fight' reaction.

What is obvious from this statement is that good stress has the same effect as bad stress. This, however, contradicts some of Selye's previous descriptions of 'eustress'. In an earlier discussion on the subject, he had proposed that "we must remember that everything depends not upon what actually happens to us but upon how we appreciate the events" (Selye, 1980). On this occasion he was talking about converting bad stress to good stress. He was saying that its nature was perceiver-dependent.

If an event needs our appreciation to become a good 'stressor' or indeed a 'stressor' at all, then it is not the event which is the 'stressor'. In the absence of a feeling of being 'stressed' there is no stress; but if we feel 'stressed' and we welcome the event then we have made the stress good stress rather than bad stress. So it seems that under this particular pronouncement we not only determine what is to become stress, we are also responsible for its goodness or badness. Yet this would not be possible if, as Selye stated earlier, all events cause stress.

Even if we were to ignore the contradictions in the various explanations given by Selye we are still left with the fact that the concept of 'eustress' appears to be limited to psychological stress. It is unlikely that it could readily be applied to physical stress and/or to animals. We do not know enough about animal cognition to deduce that they would be able to translate what are often painful or distressful experiences into something pleasant. Taking into account all the criteria implied by Selye's definitions of the concept, it seems very unlikely that animals ever benefit from exhaustive exercise, oxygen deprivation or 'spread eagle' immobilization. Just as remote is the possibility that animals could experience "the satisfactory feeling that comes from the accomplishment of tasks we consider worthwhile"(1976).

There is probably even less chance that animals would be capable of turning an extremely distressful situation into a sensation of fulfilment or of appreciating the event in a more positive way. In fact, the concept appears not to have been used in studies of physical stress or in reference to animals. This may be indicative of its lack of usefulness in these situations. With regard to people, it does not seem realistic to suggest that, say, a person being suffocated (lack of oxygen) would respond differently depending on how they felt about it. It is highly unlikely that many people could interpret such a situation pleasantly.

Non-specificity

An important facet of Selye's theory has been the notion of 'non-specificity'. Selye's brief explanation of the notion was that stress and stress responses were non-specific, for they can be brought on regardless of the nature of the 'stressor'. The response consists of a stereotyped pattern involving an enlargement of the adrenal glands, involution of the thymus gland and peptic ulceration of the stomach. As discussed earlier, the non-specific responses that are left after the specific responses of particular 'stressors' have been eliminated is what is supposed to constitute stress.

This doctrine of non-specificity has been disputed by Goldstein (1995) who has remarked that as research is

119

discovering more systems that seem to participate in stress responses, it has become increasingly unclear whether after removing these specific reactions any truly non-specific reaction would eventually remain. Mason (1971) earlier had found that in response to different 'stressors', there could be an increase or a decrease in the activity of the pituitary-adrenocortical system. In other instances, the system would remain unaffected. Mason hypothesized that the reason Selye found similar neuroendocrine reactions in his various experiments might have been due to the fact they all involved a distress response to the various 'stressors'. It is unclear whether Mason meant the term 'distress' to refer to an emotional response or bad stress. Either way, it does not seem to provide a satisfactory explanation.

Selye (1977) appeared to change his mind about non-specificity, possibly as a result of Mason's findings. He argued later that:

> Each stressor or stress producing agent, however, also elicits specific effects, depending upon its specific properties or characteristics, and these specific actions will in turn modify the nonspecific (stress) response of the organism.

He now appeared to suggest that the specific effects of the 'stressor' had an effect on the stress response. If that were the case, it would be difficult to assess the presence of stress since it would not be possible to distinguish between the various effects. Furthermore, if the response could now be caused by specific effects, Selye did not explain how this would affect the stress response. In his original explanation the stress response was what was left after the specific responses were discounted since they were not supposed to be part of the stress response. So it appears that we are left again, as with many of Selye's various explanations, with contradiction followed by confusion.

Stress as the wear and tear of life

Selye had an alternative explanation of what stress could possibly be. In the Preface to the original edition of *The Stress of Life*, Selye described stress as being "…essentially the rate of all the wear and tear caused by life". This definition is at odds with his other stated view of stress as a residue left after specific effects. It is not entirely clear what Selye meant by 'life'. He might have been trying to say that life itself was the 'stressor' or that the mere fact of being alive was itself 'stressful'. Another possible explanation could have been that all the events that form what we call life were responsible for such wear and tear. In all these various possibilities, 'life' can be described as either a biological state or as a combination of psychological and physical events. In either case, stress becomes a vague notion of 'wear and tear' which can just as easily be attributed to aging. This is in fact what Selye himself would later propose when he stated that the General Adaptation Syndrome appeared to be irreversible and accumulated to constitute the signs of aging (Selye, 1975).

Summing up

A consideration of Selye's various pronouncements, regarding stress, reveals many inconsistencies, contradictions, changes of mind and, in the end, confusion. The theory, however, has yielded much influence, as exemplified by the hundreds of thousands publications that have followed. One of the major difficulties with the theory has been that it has been based primarily on experiments introducing physical variables deemed to cause stress. Most of the research has been conducted using animals. Many of the findings, whether valid or not, have subsequently been generalized not only to psychological events but also to humans.

Looking back at the progression of Selye's theory, it is littered with changes of mind and contradictions. At first the GAS was the center piece of his theory. The first mention of stress was as a cause of the GAS. Gradually, following rather messy attempts at explaining the relationship between the GAS and stress, the GAS disappears for his writings. By then, stress has become not the cause but the state.. In an attempt to eliminate the confusion he had created, he invented the concept of 'stressor' which he circularly described as 'that which stresses'. This resulted in two versions of stress: the engineering one in which stress caused strain and Selye's in which 'stressors' caused stress. In everyday parlance, however, it has often been a case of stress causing stress.

Additionally, stress was at first defined as a non-specific response but by 1977, he claims that the specific effect of an individual 'stressor' can modify the non-specific response. It is hard not to conclude that ultimately, Selye did not have any idea of what stress was.

Finally, when some of the solutions proposed by Selye to master stress are considered they should raise some concerns as to his understanding of the social and psychological aspects of life. [11]

---

[11] In his later writings Selye suggested that 'altruistic egoism' was the answer to stress. After all, he contended, all living creatures are and must be selfish but cannot be so 'recklessly'. People, he recommended, cannot only think of themselves as this creates too many enemies. People should no longer feel guilty about being selfish and accept the situation. They should try to satisfy the "natural egotistic tendency to hoard capital for security" but this capital should be stocked in the form of personal satisfaction, love and good will, as we "learn to be useful to others." *Love thy neighbour as thyself* was not possible, he told us, what was needed was do "earn thy neighbour's love". This, he was certain, "...will best assure homeostasis and resistance to stressors throughout life..." (Selye, 1976).

OTHER THEORIES AND CONCEPTS

In the space available here, it is not possible to cover all the variations of stress theories that have been proposed. It may be more useful, at this point, to discuss the main theories that have followed Selye's introduction of the concept, with an emphasis on psychological theories of stress, given that psychological stress has constituted the main area of research in the last three decades.

Life events

A major consequence of Selye's belief that all life events were 'stressors' was the creation of the Holmes Rahe scale (1967). Spurred on by a belief that four fifths of all those who had experienced major life changes during a year could expect to have a serious illness during the next 2 years, Holmes, with his colleague, Rahe, developed a readjustment scale (Dobson, 1983). The intention of the scale was to give a score to a variety of life changes and calculate how a numerical total would match up with subsequent medical conditions. Top of list was the death of the spouse with a score of 100, divorce was second with 73, marital separation was next with 65, whereas a jail term, or the death of close family scored 63. At the bottom of the scale were things like minor law violations with 11, vacation 13, change of eating habit and change in number of family gatherings 15. The scale was subsequently tested with various subjects and it was found that 80% of people with a score around 150 developed serious illnesses, depression or heart attacks, compared with 33% of those whose score was below 150 (Dobson, 1983). Generally, it was accepted that a score between 50 and 100 indicates a low stress life, between 100 and 200 a moderate stress life, over 200 but less than 300 a highly 'stressful' life and that a total over 300 an extremely highly 'stressful' life.

Holmes (1979) estimated that over a thousand studies involving the social readjustment scale had been published. At first the scale was used predominantly with white middle class adults. In the 70's, the literature of 'stressful' life events grew at a rapid rate. By 1982, Perkins reported that the scale had now been used in a variety of populations differing from the original group with regard to race, ethnic composition and nationality. He claimed that the results obtained left no doubt that there was a significant relationship with the experience of stress and the development of various conditions. He listed the following conditions: tuberculosis, diabetes, arthritis, cancer, heart disease, depression, schizophrenia, neurosis, accidents, athletic injuries and poor academic performance as being possible consequences of accumulated life changes. Despite these apparently impressive results, Perkins was concerned that many of these results were supported by a very small correlation between stress and the conditions, typically .30 or less, accounting for under 10 % of variance (Perkins, 1982).

Problems with life events or change scales

Perkins' concerns were justified, as there are several problems with this sort of scale. For instance, many of the scales have asked subjects to recall some events and it is clear that important and high scoring events may be easily recalled but some less important events may not be remembered. Alternatively, some events may be purposely left out because they may involve something the respondent prefers not to divulge or because he/she does not think they are relevant. Also, the significance of other events may be exaggerated.

A second area of concern resides with the types of changes that are listed in the scales. There is no doubt that they are, in the main, socially significant. However, it may be simplistic to assume that everyone would react in the same predictable manner to all of them or would always do so at various times. It seems that the authors of the scale not only assumed the existence of stress, they also expected the items within the scale to be 'stressors'. In doing so, they automatically deduced that the source of stress was external to the individual and was situated in unpleasant as well as pleasant circumstances.

Furthermore, the mere fact that these changes were presented as being part of a measurement of stress could conceivably influence many people to think these changes must be contributors to stress. This could have helped create the belief that stress was out there in the environment and that it was an integral part of everyday life. Yet, this may not always be the case. Consider the case of the loss of a spouse, which scores so highly in the scale and is often a source of anecdotes of partners dying soon after of a broken heart. The amount of upset (or stress) experienced could vary, depending on the length of the relationship, the age of either spouse, the pain and suffering experienced in a preceding illness and/or its duration. Additionally, the status of the relationship prior to the death (loving, hating, indifference, domestic violence), the resulting financial situation, the dependence or independence of the surviving partner and probably many other factors of varying importance could have a bearing on the grieving process.

While it is true that many changes are important socially, their importance will also depend on each individual's circumstances. Events, circumstances and the changes that occur are neutral; people give them psychological and social meaning and make them pleasant, unpleasant or indifferent. Moreover, events do not cause anything, let alone stress or disease. For this, they would need some sort of agency, which they do not possess. Changes and various life events, themselves do not have a cumulative 'stressful' effect. The sense of overwhelming unhappiness and the sometimes accompanying feeling that life might not be worth living, are no more than the cumulative effect of strong and also sometimes vague feelings towards various events. This should not be taken to mean that feelings therefore must be the source of stress. Feelings are no more capable of agency than the events, changes and circumstances which make their presence possible.

Another problem with the scales has been with single individual events. These events may have a low score in the scale or may not even be allowed for. Yet a particular person may react very strongly to such an event and as a result end up feeling more 'stressed' than would have been the case with an accumulated score deemed to produce a high stress level.

The scales have also essentially focused on the notion of change rather than that of desirability. Vinokur and Selzer (1975) investigated subjects' perception of the desirability and undesirability of change events in relation to stress and found that only undesirable events were substantially correlated with stress and also required greater adjustments than the desirable ones. This applied equally to single and combined events. They added, however, that it was not clear from their evidence whether the negative experience of the event or the resulting negative outcome was the most important factor in producing the stress. They gave two examples to illustrate their point. The first was an instance of someone losing a wife who had suffered a prolonged terminal illness. This was a case of an undesirable experience being followed by a desirable experience. This second example was about someone having an affair, a desirable experience, followed by a pregnancy, an undesirable experience. They also thought that two more dimensions could be crucial in the whole process, namely the presence or absence of anticipation of what was to take place and a feeling of control over the event.

The scales also appear to have many biases. Some of the items may be more applicable to some sections of society while other events that are important to certain people may be missing from the scales. According to the scale, a single non-working male gay student is potentially less likely to be affected as he cannot lose his spouse, separate or divorce, experience marital reconciliation or have a son or daughter leaving home. He is unlikely to marry, to get pregnant, to be fired from work or to have had problems with in-laws or a boss.[12] On the other hand, there is no provision in the scale for the effects of discrimination or for the non-acceptance of sexuality by parents, two items likely be relevant to many gay people.

---

[12] These are events in Holmes and Rahe's life event scale

As another example of the inadequacy of the scale, consider the case of a married man whose wife left him because of difficulties in conceiving a child, then divorced him only to remarry him and fall pregnant to him and all this in a reasonably short period of time. This would score 273 on the scale, a score which would qualify the man for being labeled as 'very highly stressed'. Yet this man might be expected to be reasonably happy with the eventual outcome. These two examples illustrate the point that when individuals assess events in their lives, they may be more concerned about the contextual importance of the event than they are about the mere accumulation of socially important events. Another limitation of the scale may also be that some people have many less roles and are involved in less situations than others. It could be possibly argued that they have, according to the scale, less chance to become 'stressed'. The scale does not allow for the fact that this might be counteracted by a greater focus on a fewer events.

Finally, the scales may have a problem with internal validity since most of the items in the scales are independent of each other. Ultimately, the stress scales have proven to be too crude a measure of stress. The arguments that have been offered against them are only a sample of their limitations. Many factors are at play in the evaluation of events and circumstances suspected to be a potential source of stress. The resulting feelings or emotions that are felt can never be adequately captured by the 'life-events' scales.

The transactional model: appraisal and coping

The problems with the life change approach should have highlighted the fact that any serious study of psychological stress would need to involve other factors. This combined with the fact that not everyone reacts the same way to the same events, has led to theories involving the concept of 'appraisal'. It has been argued that if people appraised an event differently they would, in turn, react differently. Whilst most of the credit for the inclusion of appraisal into the debate about stress has been given to Lazarus (1966), earlier work by Arnold (1960) had already addressed the issue. The difference was that Arnold applied her theory to emotions whereas Lazarus' concern was with stress. Arnold had suggested that "...to arouse an emotion, the object must be appraised as affecting me in some way, affecting me personally as an individual with my particular experience and my particular aim." Holroyd and Lazarus (1982) would later define appraisal as "...the evaluative process that imbues a situational encounter with meaning for the person." They elaborated that something important had to be at stake or in jeopardy. The situation would not be appraised as 'stressful' if it were deemed to be irrelevant, minor or pleasant. The judgment of an event as a threat would precede it, whereas that of harm or loss would occur after the event. They also advanced that the perception of something as a challenge would involve the combined judgments of what was at stake and that some sense of mastery was required.

The latter hinted at another use of appraisal and this had to do with the assessment of the resources available to the person to deal with the negative evaluation. This assessment usually results in an attempt at coping with the event. Coping is the other element of what has been described as the transactional model of stress. According to this approach, stress occurs when individuals feel that demands tax or exceed their resources (Lazarus & Cohen, 1977). Under this model, stress begins with the initial cognitive appraisal that some response is needed to reduce perceived physical or psychological problems. The second appraisal results in the realization that an effective response is not readily available. In some cases, the best possible response is given and that, in turn, leads to a further revaluation and so on. The cognitive appraisal and coping responses as well as their subsequent reappraisals are what constitute the transaction.

The definition of stress, in this model has emphasized the relationship between people and their characteristics on the one hand and the environment and its nature on the other (Lazarus & Folkman, 1984). Lazarus and Cohen (1977) have distinguished three types of stress stimuli, as distinct from 'stressors': major changes affecting many people, major changes affecting one or few people and daily hassles. The first involves situations such as war, imprisonment or uprooting. Their duration could be short or long but their effects may last a long time. Individual major changes on the other hand are more like those described by Holmes and Rahe (1967) and include death of loved one, losing a job, divorce, etc. Daily hassles, finally, are less dramatic minor events that occur in the course of everyday life and that can potentially frustrate, annoy or anger. These may be arguments, traffic delays, feeling lonely, too much work and many more.

There have been some subtle variations of the transactional model. McGrath (1970) has described stress as a substantial imbalance between demand and response capability, under conditions where failure to meet demand has important consequences. Cox (1985) has also advanced that stress was "a perceptual phenomenon arising from a comparison between demand on the person and his ability to cope" and that any imbalance is this mechanism in situations of importance result in a stress response. Coping in this model included the physical as well as the psychological. For another investigator, stress has been a negative experience associated with threat, harm or demand, such an experience requiring some sort of adjustment (Baum, 1990).

Common to these theories is the notion of 'demand'. The 'demands' are not always real, they are often perceived or imagined. The term 'demands' is usually used in a metaphorical way but it is used so frequently that it seems that many people believe that 'demands' are real rather than perceived. Believing that 'demands' are real is not the worst aspect of the problem. Instead, the additional belief that these 'demands' need to be fulfilled seems to be the source of most of the trouble. The absence of such a belief would no doubt eliminate the need to perform or cope and as such would make it very difficult to recognize a situation as 'stressful'. We often speak of the 'demands' of modern life or the 'demands' of a job when neither modern life nor a job has the capacity to demand. The only 'demands' that exist are those that we make on ourselves and these are strongly linked to expectations that we have about ourselves and about our place in the social world.

Nevertheless, the various transactional models have seemed to make more sense than the stimulus response model offered by Selye or the life changes approach, but the coping aspect of the package has been difficult to study. The difficulty inherent in the psychological aspect of stress has been that human studies have been limited in scope because of ethical concerns. As stress is deemed to be unpleasant and uncomfortable, it is not ethical to induce stress in people. The research in the field has been mainly limited to developing taxonomies of coping behaviors (Cameron & Meichenbaum, 1982). A taxonomy designed by Lazarus and Launier (1978) differentiated between coping resources and strategies. Cameron and Meichenbaum (1982) have emphasized the importance of accurate appraisal. Despite their acceptance that " life is fraught with ambiguity", they have argued that "the quality of human transactions with the environment will depend in the first instance upon the adequacy of the person's interpretations of experience. Successful coping efforts presuppose interpretations that minimize distortion and blind spots".

However, this statement is not without problems. Implying that some interpretations are more adequate than others, immediately raises not only the question of evaluation but also who can best perform that evaluation. It is also feasible that a judgment about the adequacy of an interpretation may only be possible retrospectively. Furthermore, it would seem that distortions and blind spots and many other sorts of biases are the stuff of which individual perceptions are made of. The concept of 'interpretation' usually implies a deviation from an absolute position or from an objective fact. The various interpretations given to events are only possible because of the diverse social meanings particular events have for each individual. The broad range of socially acceptable positions makes human diversity and its varying perspectives possible. Any attempt to impose a particular position, even in the name of effectiveness, might create more problems than it solves.

Problems with the transactional model

The notion of 'coping' brings with it many other problems. Coping denotes some amount of success with a situation. Conversely, an inability to cope brings thoughts of failure, loss of control and sometimes despair. Under the transactional model, an individual who perceives an event as 'stressful' or as a 'stressor' is expected to cope. Cameron and Michenbraum (1982) believed that "effective coping requires that a person not only perceive the world clearly but respond in ways that defuse threat." They also suggested that "some behaviors are so universally required in our society that the absence of adequate response skills is likely to be debilitating and to constitute a source of considerable stress, as defined in transactional terms." But the fact that the authors have not contemplated the possibility that stress may not exist may represent an inability on *their* part to see the world clearly. If this were the case, it could have been due to one of these distortions or black spots they had referred to.

Another concern, however, is with their belief in the universality of some behaviors. They appear to have confused universality with either social acceptance or with prevalence (mainstream behavior). They appear not to have considered that perhaps some people lacking these behaviors might not care enough about not possessing or exhibiting them to be considerably 'stressed'.

Hardiness

The concept of 'coping' has also led to the introduction of a concept of 'hardiness'. Some researchers who had believed not only in stress but also in its inevitability seemed to have decided, after observing that some people did not react 'stressfully' when most people did, that these people were somehow more hardy - i.e. more resistant to stress (Manning, Williams & Wolfe, 1988). Sapolsky (1994) emphasized the point when he recommended "From the same stressful sorts of lives, identify who emerges in the best shape. Figure out what is special about those people and then determine how everyone else can become more like that." It may not have occurred to these researchers that perhaps some people did not get 'stressed' simply because stress *per se* did not exist.

If stress existed as an independent entity and it was as Selye proposed, part of life, then no one could escape it and coping would be the only possible strategy available. Instead, these researchers decided that the 'hardy' types might have possessed something that their 'weaker' counterparts lacked. They speculated that teaching the 'weak' types the coping mechanisms used by the 'hardy' types would help them improve their ability to cope with stress. This is despite the fact that in Manning *et al*'s study, 'hardiness' "...not only failed to function as a stress moderator- i.e. to reduce the negative effects of stress, but appeared instead to enhance stress" (Kobasa-Ouellet, 1993).

Kobasa-Ouellet has been a pioneer in this area of research. She recalled that her choice of business executives in earlier research in 1979 was justified "because a case needed to be made strongly that not everyone falls sick under stress (1993). Her other agenda was that she "intended to capture people's attention and direct it toward a less pessimistic and more useful view of stress." However she concluded that she had to admit that she "...has not been able to recommend *the* final, perfect hardiness scale." and in fact devoted the last section of her article to the question "is hardiness really the personality construct to study?"

An exploration into 'hardiness' inevitably did lead to inquiries about what sort of personality types would be more or less prone to feel or get 'stressed'. Unfortunately, many personality-type constructs rely on stereotypes and on a belief that personality is public and constant and as such can be measured with some accuracy. While it is possible that some people fit into some of the many models that have been proposed, this could be coincidental rather than a confirmation of the accuracy of such models. On the other hand, to say that some people are more likely to feel 'stressed' because of the way they look at the world in general may be more accurate. This is, however, a different proposition which may be difficult to assess with personality questionnaires.

An additional problem with the notion of 'appraisal' is that if an event depends on a judgement that the event is 'stressful' for stress to be present, it reduces stress to a perception.[13] Moreover, if being 'stressed' depends on interpretation, this would mean that the interpretation causes stress. If this were so, then there is no such thing as a 'stressful' event or even a potential 'stressful' event. An event can never realize its potential. Only agents can realize their potential. A potential killer, for instance, will only become a fully-fledged killer if he or she decides to realize his/her potential. The potential victim can beg or plead but ultimately the decision and therefore the agency, would reside with the person who has the potential to kill. Furthermore, while it may be possible to say that an event evokes a feeling of stress, this is quite different to suggesting that an interpretation of that event causes stress. Moreover, 'feeling' and 'being' are two different things. We can be something without feeling that we are and we can feel that we are something without being it.

In conclusion, the transactional model does not offer new evidence that there is such a thing as stress. In fact, if it is accepted that stress is perceiver dependent, the notion of 'stressor' can only be applied to the perceiver. The consequence of this is that whatever stress may be, it can only be self-inflicted. If what we experience is stress, then we are still left with the task of finding a mediator for stress.

Often in the literature, it has been proposed, directly or indirectly, that emotions are responsible for stress (Cox, 1985; Selye, 1982). The physiological aspects of these emotions are often offered as the means by which stress enters the physical domain of the body. If this were the case, it is difficult to see the usefulness of a concept of 'stress'. These various emotions may be all we are

---

[13] Promoting a notion that stress is a 'perception' surely implies that stress *per se* does not exist and is simply a figment of our imagination.

experiencing. If this is so, we do not need stress as a 'middle man'. This is what Lazarus (1991; 1993) has suggested in a roundabout way. After over 25 years of involvement in the study of stress, he has now turned back to emotions, stating "Although stress and coping are still important, social scientists have began to realize that these concepts are part of a larger rubric - the emotions" (1991).

Lazarus has in fact gone full circle. Having originally adapted Arnold's (1960) notion of 'appraisal' in emotions to stress, he proposed in a later publication, that we should think of stress as a subset of emotions. Emotions, he then believed, were far more useful in understanding what the person went through, as each emotion was often distinct enough and represented a different experience (Lazarus, 1993).

The information processing and arousal model

The work of Morruzzi and Magoun (1949) on simulation of the reticular system was discussed earlier. They noted that the stimulation of the reticular formation led to the cessation of electrical activity characteristic of drowsiness and sleep. Further work by Lindsley (1952) confirmed their findings when he discovered that cats with lesions in the reticular formation would remain permanently asleep. The work of these scientists resulted in Hebb (1955) developing a theory dealing with the relationship between arousal and information processing. He theorized that the relationship was that of an inverted U-shape function, indicating that low and high levels of arousal would have a detrimental effect on information processing and therefore performance by individuals. This theory has also been labeled an 'emotional arousal theory' (Dobson, 1983).

Levi (1972) sought to apply Hebb's model to stress and argued that low and high levels of arousal were likely to produce stress. His position appeared to be an attempt to confirm some of the claims made about stress by Selye. Selye has stated that life would be nearly impossible to live without stress but that too much stress was harmful. Had Levi been successful in his attempt, he may have been able

134

to show that we need not too much or too little but in fact, just the right amount of stress (or arousal). If we were to accept this view, it would become easier to believe that stress was not only necessary but also that it may, in some situations, be desirable and therefore be good for us. While all these ideas may appear intuitively right, there have been criticisms of this view. Some researchers have offered evidence that stress is not proportionally related to the level of arousal and that stress and arousal are in fact independent (Mackay, Cox, Burrows and Lazzarini, 1978, as cited in Cox, 1985). They have claimed that other factors could be involved.

They appeared, however, to have missed an important flaw in Hebb's theory and subsequently in Levi's theory, namely that arousal may have nothing to do with performance or stress. To be awake, drowsing or asleep does have something to do with performance. There is little doubt that our movements and our thinking are not always at an optimum and adequate level when we are not properly awake. There are, however, problems with making the same claim with regard to arousal and particularly, high arousal. High arousal is not the same as a highly awake state. This is an important distinction because the study by Morruzzi and Magoun, as well as that by Lindsley, dealt specifically with the reticular system and its effect on awake, drowsy and sleeping states, but not with arousal. By re-labeling the awake state as 'arousal', Hebb and Levi have departed from the findings of the original research and cannot therefore claim empirical support for their model.

Hebb and Levi could only claim that support by retaining the notion of 'wakefulness' but this would have posed a problem for their model since 'highly awake' is not a legitimate state. Unlike arousal which can be high or low, wakefulness can only be that, neither high nor low. If one is not fully awake, one is drowsy but once awake, there are no more levels of wakefulness that can be attained. On the other hand, it is possible to be highly aroused or even too aroused.

If they are to be faithful to the work of both Morruzzi and Magoun and Lindsley, Hebb and Levi can only propose two states: drowsiness and wakefulness. With regard to Hebb's theory, the only state during which performance can be adversely affected is drowsiness or at least various degrees of drowsiness. In order for Levi's theory to prove that we need some stress but not too much, we would need to replace 'wakefulness' with 'alertness'. Then the next move would be to proceed from alert to alarm. These two moves at first seem unproblematic, since in ordinary discussions we often associate the notion of 'being awake' with that of 'being alert'. However, being awake implies that we are in a position to notice whatever comes to our attention but being in a state of alert may denote a state of readiness for emergency. If this path were to be followed, little would be needed to go to the last link: 'flight or fight'. Moving from synonym to synonym (or concepts appearing similar), the notion of 'alarm' Selye was seeking, could be created.

This may have been the path followed by Ursin and Olff (1993) when they suggested that the stress alarm system had been found by Morruzzi and Magoun (1949). Agreeing with Ursin and Olff may give the illusion that the search for a mediator between events and stress has ended. But this can only be true if we are prepared to accept that ultimately 'flight or fight' and 'wakefulness' are one and the same.

When the role of 'awakedness' is considered in relation to stress, it does not appear to play an important role with the notable exception that one probably needs to be awake to appraise an event. In fact, being drowsy may be more helpful in coping with perceived stress. Many people seem to rely on sedatives, alcohol or other drowsiness producing substances to alleviate such stress.

The engineering model

This model is best exemplified by the work of Wheaton (1996). Critical of the 'life- events' inventory, he pointed out that many researchers use 'stress reasoning' but do not refer to stress specifically, while others refer to life difficulties, life problems, life situations, daily hassles and strain, but never speak directly of stress. His motivation to provide an alternative to the 'life events' approach was apparently fueled by the belief that stress, as defined by Selye, was not the problem of social scientists. His view was that "one cannot use the biological stress model as a basis for derivation of any particular psychosocial stress model." An exception to his rejection of Selye's model was his acceptance of the term 'stressor'. He thought that these 'stressors' had never been defined adequately and that this should be the first task of any theory. His own definition of 'stressors' was:

...conditions of threat, demands, or structural constraints that, by the very fact of their occurrence or existence, call into question the operating integrity of the organism.

He recognized that his definition was abstract and "not entirely helpful" but that it respected the true generality of the stress domain.

Wheaton developed his engineering model after reading an article by a metallurgist on stress. An earlier event, the collapse of a bridge in Connecticut in 1984, also had an impact on his eventual model of stress. The bridge apparently had collapsed without "the slightest provocation by an 'event'. No high winds, no unusual rate of traffic that day, nothing." This, he explained, made him realize that the 'life-events' model had missed a very important point, namely that disease and distress could occur without a precipitating observable event. The critical structural limit of the bridge had been reached, he reasoned, by being subjected to the stress of unobservable rust. He further advanced that stress and 'stressors' did not appear to be distinct phases in the engineering model and that "...they both refer to the external force, pressure, threat to the body." This led him to the conclusion that "...this immediately makes this model more amenable to translation into the psychosocial model."

Wheaton (1996) believed that his model offered greater flexibility and was better suited to psychosocial stress than Selye's model since it allowed for enhancement and deterioration in coping capacity. Furthermore, the engineering model permitted the distinction among types of 'stressors', rather than imagining them as a single class. This, he claimed, was important considering that different types of 'stressors' would require different models of effective coping. However, he pointed out that not all physical forces would act as 'stressors'; they needed to be applied at excessive levels to do so. He also suggested that there were many benefits to his model. It introduced a stimulus-focused type of response as opposed to the difficult-to-measure internalized process popular in social sciences. Since the 'stressor' was, in fact, stress, there was no need to measure its effects, even though some might be present, to understand its impact. The elastic limit of the material could be measured holistically as a characteristic rather than part of the object. The model allowed both normative and excessive levels of stress. It made it possible to account for positive as well as negative coping capacities in responses to the 'stressors' and allowed "for heterogeneity in the type of stressors, distinguishing between discrete and continuous form of stress."

The main thrust of Wheaton's model could be found in his definition of 'stressors'. He suggested that of the three conditions mentioned earlier, threat, demands and structural constraints, the first two were mostly used in research. Structural constraints were "the disjunction between goals and means" and were "essential to understanding that stressors arise from and are embedded in location in a social structure." A 'stressor', furthermore, represents a problem that requires a resolution and will result in damage if unattended. It must also be 'identity relevant', that is the pressure it exerts "…derives its power from the fact that it has the potential to threaten or alter current identities. However, an awareness of its potential damage is not a necessary condition of that stressor having negative consequences."

Many other points were raised by Wheaton but their importance would diminish in the light of some of the major problems with his concept of 'stress'.

Problems with the engineering model

Wheaton's professed motivation for the theory is probably its first serious problem. The main aims of the theory were to improve on the weaknesses of both Selye's biological model and that of the 'life events' model. There is no doubt both models are flawed, but not for the reasons Wheaton has proposed. Their main flaw relates to the generality of the 'stress' concept. Their attempt to include most elements, physical and psychological (Selye) or most good or bad changing life circumstances ('life events') have resulted in some incoherence, due mainly to their ignoring the factors responsible for the individuality of responses to various so-called 'stressors'. Wheaton's model has not addressed this issue. In trying to maintain the generality of the stress domain with his definition, he was not able to take into account the perception or appraisal of the individual, thus leaving unanswered the question of differing responses by individuals. He actually went a step further, arguing that:

> In order to save the definition from a requirement of perception, appraisal, or cognition, we must be able to specify stressors that are free of awareness or articulation as 'problems' by the individuals they may affect, while including articulated problems as well.

This may be what happens when one tries to generalize from stress on a bridge to stress on an individual. His comment that "...the bridge, in effect, does not feel its rust." seems to speak for itself. A bridge possesses neither the mind nor the ability to feel. It appears that the only way Wheaton can match the bridge and people is by personifying the bridge and this is exactly what he has done.

While on the question of appraisal, there remains a need to investigate what constitutes threats, demands and structural constraints. Threats and demands both need to be perceived as such. Perception, it would seem, requires some form of cognitive evaluation. For example, imagine a man coming towards another man with a gun. It is possible that the man without the gun may not feel he was facing a threat, if he did not know what a gun was or what damage a gun could do, if he thought the gun was not loaded, or the gun was not a real gun, or if he believed that the other person was only joking or would not have the courage to shoot.

A threat can only be defined as such in terms of an evaluation that some danger or unwelcome event may follow. That sort of evaluation is to be performed by a social being with sufficient knowledge of the things that make up the world, social and physical and who can also assess their potential harm or danger. Events *per se* are no more threats than they are 'stressors': only people in the act of perception can grant them these characteristics.

The same can be said about demands, since demands do not exist independently of the person interpreting events or situations. Demands need to be recognized as such for people to yield to them. Be they job demands, societal demands or even, as Selye would propose, adaptation demands, they have to be perceived as such to constitute a 'stressor'. Should they be perceived as challenges or as means to gain experience, they would no longer be viewed as demands or 'stressors'.

Finally, with regard to structural constraints, Wheaton thought that they would help do away with the need to take into account internal (cognitive) processes involved in appraisal. However, if these structural constraints result, as Wheaton stated, from a disjunction between goals and means, that disjunction needs to be assessed. Goals and means vary from individual to individual. Moreover, the amount of disjunction must result from an evaluation of the adequacy of the means to fulfil the goals. It is difficult to contemplate how this could be done without cognitive evaluation, thereby indicating that Wheaton's 'structural constraints' are the outcome of some sort of cognitive assessment.

Interestingly, Wheaton discussed a pilot study he had conducted which had investigated the 'stressful' effect of people living away from their parents and which found that living too close or too far could have the same effect. He concluded that we couldn't rely on an objective measure like distance and that the real problem was a structural constraint. This constraint was the result of living alone, which he suggested could be quite 'stressful', as could be the desire for a living partner. This raises several points. Describing living alone as 'stressful' makes the assumption that either this event possesses such a characteristic or that everyone would feel the same way about living alone. These are the same types of assumptions that are usually made by the 'life-events' model whose limitations Wheaton was trying to avoid. It is also difficult to conceptualize of a desire as anything but an internal process, another factor he was also trying to do away with. Finally, appraisal would, it seems, have to play a part in determining what constitutes too close, too far, or even just right and whether living alone was enjoyable, unpleasant or neutral.

These are not the only contradictions in the model. Wheaton, for instance, argued that it was possible for 'under-demand' to be a stress problem but he had also said that external forces needed to be applied at a sufficiently excessive level to constitute stress. It seems problematic to imagine how under-demand, in other words insufficient demand, could ever constitute a sufficiently potent 'stressor'.

Wheaton has tried to address some of the issues that confront the field of stress research but the main weakness of his theory is to be found in its conceptualization. The rust on the bridge was observable but it had not been observed because no one had looked for it. It does not seem unreasonable to suggest that any maintenance engineer might conduct regular inspections of a metal structure to ensure that it does not rust. Most people, not just engineers, know full well that metal can rust and as a result can lose much of its strength. It would appear that Wheaton has failed to distinguish between an unobservable and an unobserved event. Ultimately, the problem with Wheaton's model is that it is a metaphorical model and in trying to make his analogy fit Wheaton ends up in a theoretical tangle.

Additionally, the collapse of the bridge had been preceded by an event and the event was the rusting of the bridge. It may have been less dramatic and may have taken more time than high winds and excessive traffic to cause the collapse but it was an event nevertheless. Finally, Wheaton did not seem to fully realize the difficulties in translating from the world of physical objects to the psychological world. People may be physical objects but unlike other objects they also have the ability to evaluate, interpret and interact with the physical and social world around them. Any theory that ignores that state of affairs is likely to provide an inadequate account of the aspects of human life it attempts to investigate.

Goldstein's homeostatic theory

In reviewing most of the biological and some of the psychological literature, Goldstein was critical of Selye's model of stress. After discussing the many limitations of the 'stress' concept, he nevertheless decided to retain it. He felt that despite its many shortcomings, it offered a "useful conceptual abbreviation" and that it was "not an inescapable burden of life, an intuitive notion, a legal term, or a justification for business schemes, but the subject of a scientific theory" (Goldstein, 1995).

He arrived at his own theory, drawing from the works of Cannon on homeostasis[14], Levine and Ursin (1991) in biology and Lazarus (1966) in psychology. Goldstein, (1995) defined stress as a condition but not a conscious experience which occurred under the following conditions:

Stress is a condition where expectations, whether genetically programmed, established by prior learning, or deduced from circumstances, do not match the current or anticipated perceptions of the internal or external environment, and this discrepancy between what is observed or sensed and what is expected or programmed elicits patterned, compensatory responses.

---

[14] He was nevertheless quite critical of some aspects of Cannon's views on homeostasis.

Goldstein added that not all intervening variables were a stress, for there had to be an effort at a compensatory response which required the organism to sense a disruption or a threat of disruption of homeostasis. This sensation was a comparative process in which the brain was thought to receive information from homeostats, with each homeostat comparing that information with a set point. A sufficiently large discrepancy from that point would provoke a response.

Unlike Selye, Goldstein did not speak of 'eustress' and 'distress' but he did distinguish between 'stress' and 'distress'. Stress did not need consciousness but distress did since it also required a perception by the organism "that homeostatic mechanisms may not suffice." For Goldstein, stress was purely biological and distress was psychobiological. However, Goldstein(1995) had some doubt about both these aspects of stress since he thought that:

Fundamental questions remain about whether psychological stress can bring on physical disease in otherwise healthy individuals and about whether physical stress contributes to psychopathology. The existence, location, regulation and pathology of psychological 'homeostats' associated with the experience of distress remain largely unknown.

His attempt to integrate biological and psychological stress has not been successful. However, at all times in his analysis, Goldstein remained candid and did not try to make the data fit his theory. Goldstein (1995), in fact, had more to say about distress, which he also called emotional distress:

Difficulties in defining, measuring, and controlling the relevant independent and dependent variables in humans have impeded research about the clinical neuroendocrine and cardiovascular consequences of emotional distress.

He concluded that many of "the assertions" presented in the book were "highly speculative and should be viewed as attempting to provide a conceptual framework rather than summarizing an accepted body of knowledge."

143

Problems with the homeostatic theory

Goldstein's definition of stress is problematic. It is unclear how expectations could be genetically programmed. If this is to be understood to be a computer analogy of the type often found in the cognitive discourse, then Goldstein does not say how that process takes place. Moreover, considering that programming could not occur spontaneously, it is not totally clear who or what could be responsible for such a programming. It would seem from Goldstein's further elaboration that the brain might be responsible for such a programming. The brain, however, is the organ used to think and probably feel but it is not the agent responsible for the thinking or the feeling. To accept the notion of 'the brain as an agent' may provide a better fit for the theory but it does not reflect reality.

Another option may be to suggest that Goldstein's wording is a problem. After all, an expectation must be a social and/or mental concept that requires consciousness. It seems doubtful that it would be possible to evaluate whether an expectation has been fulfilled or not, unless there is a consciousness of both what it was that was expected as well as of what was happening. Moreover, Goldstein's proposition, that stress occurs when expectations do not match "the current or anticipated perceptions of the internal or external environment and this discrepancy between what is observed or sensed and what is expected or programmed.", also appears problematic. Anticipation and observation require some form of consciousness. Anticipation cannot be a reflex. To anticipate, some evaluation as to what may be taking place is necessary. Anticipation also relies on an ability to extrapolate 'what will' be from 'what appears'. As for observation, it is more than just being aware. It implies notions of 'monitoring' and of 'making some sense' of the information.

In the final analysis, Goldstein's attempt to construct a theory of stress that addresses both biological and psychological elements has yet to succeed as evidenced by his recognition that we are still a long way from understanding the physiological effects of stress. With regard to the biological aspect, his explanation is fraught with many difficulties. As for the emotional distress side of the equation, his theory, by his own admission, cannot be tested. The theory may in the end, be the best evidence that stress is not such "a useful conceptual abbreviation" after all.

Work stress

In the last few decades, work stress has been a growing area of stress research. Changing work conditions brought on by more difficult economic conditions have meant that employees have had to work harder and have also felt increasingly insecure in their jobs. Under these conditions, a notion of 'stress' seems to have been widely accepted. This has resulted in a great number of publications dealing specifically with work stress. The views expressed by Albrecht (1979), in his book *Stress and The Manager. Making It Work for You*, have been selected as they are fairly representative of others in the field of work stress. The tone of the debate is quite dramatic as evidenced by the first few sentences of the book:

A strange new disease has found its way into the lives of Americans and into the lives of people in other lightly industrialized nations of the world. It has been steadily growing, affecting more and more people with ever serious consequences. It is now reaching epidemic proportions, yet it is not transmitted by any known bacterium or other microorganisms. The range of symptoms is so broad as to bewilder the casual observer and to send the typical physician back to the textbooks. The symptoms range from minor discomfort to death, from headache to heart attack, from indigestion to stroke, from fatigue to high blood pressure and organ failure, from dermatitis to bleeding ulcers.

After this, we are reassured that stress is not really a disease but "rather, a runaway condition of a normal physiological function, namely stress." Stress is further defined as a chemical process which, "we now know" in its chronic form, "…causes diseases of various sorts, complicates others." The culprit for all the stress is anxiety. Later, Albrecht confesses that "in the broad sense, this book is about wellness, -what it is, how and why we've been steadily losing it and how we can get it back.".

More evidence is advanced to suggest that "Many practising physicians have commented that fully 80% of their patients have emotionally induced disorders." and that in the last quarter of this century, "...it is becoming embarrassingly obvious to most scientists - but not especially to physicians and psychiatrists - that all disease has both psychic and pyschologic components." The problem, Albrecht thought had been the subdivision by professional practitioners along the arbitrary lines of 'mind' and 'body' which had made it impossible to study the person as a whole.[15]

In more emotive language, in a chapter entitled STRESS *IS KILLING PEOPLE*, Albrecht states that "...the list of diseases that medical researchers now recognized as being caused by stress or aggravated by stress reads like "Who's Who in American Disease" and that "Authoritative research has now linked the heart attack firmly with stress." He also mentions that " Some medical researchers believe that sudden, acute stress can actually kill a person whose health has been weakened either by prolonged stress itself or by degenerative factors such as age or circulatory disease."

Few of these claims are supported by any evidence. Despite this, Albrecht expresses little doubt when he states, "It is indeed a fact of life for twentieth-century Americans that *stress can kill.*" In a rather perplexing admission, however, he reveals that stress is also a physical and chemical process within the body and that it is entirely normal to our functioning as living creatures. It is only when it remained 'turned on' at high levels for long periods that it became a problem. When this happens, all that is left is escape. Frequent drinking, overeating (especially sweets), smoking, coffee, marijuana, drugs, tranquilisers, sleeping pills, lashing out at others, were all means of escape since they

---

[15] This statement seems to indicate a possible lack of familiarity with the mind/body debate resulting from Descartes' interactionism.

substituted a known pleasant feeling for the unpleasant feeling of stress. And if this was not enough, lack of maturity and social adjustment could combine with chronic stress and lead to antisocial behavior or even violent crime.

There was worse to come for those "stressed beyond their limits". Albrecht suggests that they may choose insanity as a means of escape. "They go crazy in order to drop out of the terrifying, unrewarding, hateful, stressful microworld in which they have been living. There is certain peace in insanity." Finally, suicide, he suggests, provided the ultimate in stress reduction.

Despite all this, one could still choose from the few forms of stress avoidance that had the potential to constructively reduce stress. Relaxation and "...re-engineering the pressure situation or simply departing physically from it for long enough periods to relax, unwind, and achieve a peaceful frame of mind.".

Albrecht draws a distinction between pressure and stress. Pressure was the situation that may be problematic and demanded some adaptation. Stress, alternatively, was a specific set of biochemical conditions within the person's body. All that was needed to overcome stress was to convert stress into pressure. One's personal history of experience and learned reactions were the key. All we had to do is not say "I am under of lot of stress lately" but say instead, "I am under a lot of pressure lately". The distinction between stress and pressure, he declares, "would also open up significant avenues for stress reduction." Albrecht also felt that we should not consider pressure or stress as being intrinsically bad or undesirable. In any case, "zero-stress" was impossible to achieve and it was impractical and unworkable to expect a no-pressure situation.

With regard to the physiological effects of stress, readers again are left in no doubt whatsoever. Albrecht declares "...we are speaking of a definite clear-cut, and well-defined electrochemical response pattern within the human body." He also suggests that "Both Cannon and Selye agreed, and other researchers have confirmed, that the human body possesses a life-saving reaction pattern - the stress response- which comes into play in a variety of pressure situations."[16] This may sound puzzling considering the earlier declared benefit of converting stress into pressure.

Later, Albrecht also hints at the 'flight and fight' reaction, stating: "Clearly the stress reaction is a coordinated chemical mobilization of the entire body to meet the requirements of life and death struggle or of rapid escape from the situation." The intensity of the reaction depended on the perception of the brain (not the person) regarding the severity of the situation. However, he points out that "the great physiological dilemma of stress" was that "we so often mobilize our bodies involuntarily for flight or fight and that we seldom carry through the process in physical terms."

The above description gives a sufficient glimpse of Albrecht's views. Unfounded, inaccurate and misleading claims, contradictions, overlapping of concepts as well as dramatic pronouncements designed to induce people to act, they are all part of the usual arsenal of many stress management books. While one would expect that most serious researchers in the field of stress would be bemused by some of the claims Albrecht made, this was not the case for Hans Selye, who prefaced the book thus:

His [Albrecht] description of the stress concept is wonderfully well-presented. Simplicity and style of prose are the telling hallmarks of this volume. The end product is a well balanced book, written with an astute understanding of the complexities of the stress mechanism and the distress factor in business today. I would not hesitate to support this book and will give it a place of prominence among recommended reading in the library and documentation service of our *International Institute of Stress*, for all those concerned with management.

Summing up

This chapter provided an overview of some of the main theories and theoretical aspects of stress. The confusion and contradictions that are present in the study of stress have

---

[16] The same stress that was killing people was now a life saving reaction.

been highlighted. What started out as a generic term for hardship and adversity changed irrevocably once Selye developed his theory and in the process 'reinvented' the term. It has been shown that most theories since Selye's have failed in their attempts to either improve on Selye's concept of 'stress' or depart from his model completely. The major problem has been and this will be discussed in more detail later, the different processes involved for what would be physical or psychological stress. Those concentrating on psychological stress have shown little interest in the problem of identifying biological markers of stress, preferring instead to rely on assumptions drawn from biological studies. There have been difficulties in defining the various factors that could be involved in psychological stress, such as appraisal, coping, personality hardiness and social events or changes, but also in finding means to measure these factors. Furthermore, attempts to establish a mind/body connection by the mere presence of 'stressful' events or 'stressful' states before disease have proved inadequate and, therefore, inconclusive.

OTHER THEORETICAL PROBLEMS

This chapter deals with some problems that do not belong under the previous rubrics but nevertheless need to be addressed. The first problem concerns the difficulty in scientifically testing the notion of 'purpose' implied in theories of stress and homeostasis. The second problem involves the differentiation between physical and psychological 'stressors', while the last problem relates to the usefulness of studies that use animals in testing for psychological stress.

The teleology of homeostasis and stress

Even if the problems that have been discussed so far are put aside, there are still other difficulties with the concept of 'stress' as a scientific concept. Theoretically, the concept rests on some assumptions which need testing. One of these assumption is the notion of a *'milieu interieur'* or 'homeostasis'. Until its introduction by Bernard in 1878, medicine had relied on the Cartesian notion of 'the body as a machine'. Under such a notion, the main goals of surgery were to repair injuries and remove diseased areas (Johnson, 1991). The body was understood to function according to chemical and physical laws and separate systems in the body were seen to be largely independent of each other. The novelty of Bernard's explanation was that he proposed that the body functioned in order to maintain a stable internal environment. This suggested for the first time that the body had a purpose or overall goal.

This theme was further adapted by Cannon (1935) who coined the term 'homeostasis' and advocated that the maintenance of that stable environment was dependent on the sympathetic nervous system. His explanation of the 'flight or fight' responses, in which the rapid activation of the homeostatic system preserves the internal environment by producing compensatory and anticipatory adjustments, is still often used as the starting point of how stress occurs. Some even see the 'flight or fight' responses as a primitive form of stress. The concept of 'stress', as described by Selye, would not be coherent without the notions of a '*milieu interieur*' and/or 'homeostasis'. Furthermore, theories that do not specifically mention homeostasis still rely on some sort of compensatory responses to explain stress. The problem with a notion of 'homeostasis' is that whilst it may appear intuitively right that people respond physiologically to their environment, there are problems with the proposition that the purpose of the body is to maintain a balance. Goldstein (1995) and Johnson (1991) point to the fact that any biological theory reliant on a notion of 'purposiveness' is in effect teleological. The theories of Bernard and, Canon as well as Darwinism rely very much on the doctrine that an overall useful or purposeful end dictates natural phenomena. Selye admitted that "It is evident that our unified concept is based upon teleological thought: the principle of purposeful causality" (1956).

The difficulty for Selye and the others mentioned above is that it is beyond the scope of science to scientifically prove this purposeful causality. When looking at the body from a wonderment perspective, it is easy to marvel at the cleverness of the body's design. However, the conditions under which the human body can adequately function are merely sufficient and necessary conditions for its survival. To suggest that the body adapts to unfavorable conditions raises an important issue, namely, whom or what may be responsible for this adaptation. There appear to be only two main choices: an external agent or the body itself. If we accept that adaptation is crucial for life to continue, choosing the latter means that the body is in effect the agent for its own health

The body as an agent of its own health

This is exactly what Sullivan (1990) has proposed. The 'wisdom of the body' evoked by Canon (1932) has been interpreted by Sullivan as 'self knowledge'. He remarked that "the self regulation of organisms entailed a form of wisdom, or self-knowledge on the part of the organism". He added that bodies, just like minds, were capable of knowledge and wisdom. Beneath the level of consciousness, the body continually monitors its internal state, aided by sensors and effectors. This view may be, however, incompatible with some aspects of Cannon's theory. Homeostatic reactions and adjustments are supposed to be merely reflexes or automatic reactions, as is the case with the "flight or fight" responses and it is doubtful that an automatic response could be construed to be indicative of knowledge or wisdom. Furthermore, the proposition that the body can 'monitor' its own state at a subconscious level is questionable.

Self knowledge and wisdom

The first point that needs to be made about Sullivan's explanation is that there is an important difference between 'self knowledge' and 'wisdom'. Knowing about oneself does not guarantee wisdom. Wisdom implies not just a notion of 'knowing' but also a notion of 'applying that knowledge in given circumstances'. *The Concise English Dictionary* (1980) describes wisdom as the "ability to make right use of knowledge". This means it also reflects an ability to determine what is best suited in these circumstances. This would require a cognitive evaluation of not only what is taking place but also of what should ideally take place. Self-knowledge would not be sufficient for self-regulation. For example, some people may know they drink too much. That knowledge alone is not enough to regulate their drinking. Furthermore, knowing that they are an alcoholic (self-knowledge) does not necessarily guarantee the wisdom that would allow them to stop drinking.

The body feedback system

The fact that sensors and effectors relay information to the brain does not necessarily constitute wisdom either. Breathing, for instance, does not require consciousness. Neither does it require self-knowledge of the respiratory system. The heart can be restarted when stopped and keep beating automatically again, but it cannot restart itself. To do so would require the heart to recognize that it has stopped and it also has the ability and volition to start itself again.

The body probably cannot monitor its own state. At best, the body might be compared to a security system. The sensors in a security system can be triggered in an automatic fashion and this results in a series of mechanisms being initiated that will alert people to the presence of a possible intruder. However, these sensors or the system they are part of, cannot identify the source of the intrusion or its intent. They cannot tell whether the person entering the premises is its owner or a trespasser. Furthermore, security systems can fail to operate properly. The same thing can happen in the human body.

In some cancers, for instance, the feedback systems within the cell fail to recognize that some cells are being reproduced at a greater rate than required. Some auto-immune diseases occur also because the sensors on immune cells wrongly identify parts of the body as foreign. Moreover, a rarer case involves the residual immune mechanism of a transplanted organ rejecting the body of the organ recipient. One might suspect that a 'wise' body could not be fooled so easily. Such a body, however, would need to do more than merely process information; it would need to analyze it, understand it and then take appropriate action. Cognition may take place in the brain but it should not be deduced, as many cognitive scientists do, that the brain is responsible for homeostasis or any other self-regulating behavior. The brain is the organ with which we think; it is not the thinker. It does not possess agency anymore than the body does. To hold the brain responsible for any self-regulating process would be a case of personification. Additionally, to locate wisdom in any part of the body would be a case of reification.

We may understand to a certain extent, how various autonomic systems operate but the question of why they operate the way they do remains beyond our reach. We face the same problem when we try to understand how thoughts originate. We may very well one day be able to fully understand the mechanics of the human brain, yet that

154

knowledge will not guarantee that we understand the origin of thoughts.

Predetermined purpose

If the body is not 'wise' and therefore not the agent of its own health but we still believe that it has a purpose, we are left with the possibility that such a purpose may be predetermined. What or whom is responsible for such a predetermination cannot be answered scientifically. This presents a real problem for theories of stress that rely on homeostasis. If homeostasis cannot be proven, then talk of purposeful physiological compensation and adjustment remains speculative. Goldstein (1995) was well aware of the problem when he noted that:

> Purposiveness, while helpful in deriving testable hypotheses, cannot constitute the essence of a rigorously scientific stress theory... A scientific theory of stress therefore should avoid including the notion of 'purposiveness' and should transcend the notion of 'compensatoriness' to include the survival advantage of adaptiveness.

It is not clear what is meant by "survival advantage of adaptiveness" and whether this totally removes the notion of 'purposiveness'. It would seem that the purpose implied in homeostasis and stress is also survival. Whether that survival is achieved by compensation or adaptation, it still constitutes a purpose. Furthermore, when Goldstein formulated his own theory of stress, he spoke of genetically programmed expectations and responses. If these expectations and responses were programmed, they must have been for a purpose. Programming can only but imply a purpose. It would be pointless for an organism to be programmed unless there was a need (a purpose) for the program. Moreover, the question of who or what is responsible for the program would still need to be answered.

Selye's attempt at resolving the issue

Selye (1956) himself clearly identified the problem and even defined teleologic thought as implying "more than mere causality. It suggests purposeful causation, i.e., intention, to achieve an end or aim." He recognized it,

155

saying "I can certainly not avoid dealing with this problem here. All my factual observations were made possible by experiments planned on the assumption that stress-responses are purposeful, homeostatic reactions.". Despite acknowledging that "Science cannot and should not attempt to embrace the purpose of the original Creator", he concluded, "but it can and constantly must examine teleologic motives in the object of creation." Selye appears to have been saying that we can't be concerned about the purpose of an agent directly but that we can be indirectly through its actions. The point apparently missed by Selye is that purposefulness cannot be scientifically proven either directly or indirectly.

The example he uses to support his argument gives us further insights into his thinking. He suggested that an automobile, a man made product, "will *give the impression* of continually looking out for its own interests; it will meet hostile influences with "intelligently planned defense reactions." He then described how the car will cool its own motor and protect its body against damage with the aid of springs and will even be capable of 'true *wound-healing*' if equipped with self-sealing tires. Even though he acknowledged that someone had to make the car, he felt that "…it leads us to the point where our teleologically constructed brain can no longer follow, for we cannot understand anything without a cause" [Italic added].

The problem with Selye's approach

Besides the obvious personification of the car and the tires, there are several flaws in Selye's reasoning here. Given that an impression is clearly not the same as a fact, we know if we understand how cars are designed that the purpose of a radiator is to cool the engine. We also know that springs have been created with the purpose of protecting a car against bumps on the road. Finally, the inventor of a self-sealing tire would have purposefully made the tire to self-repair. In all cases, we know, or at least can know that there was a purpose and what that purpose was. We can follow scientific principles of investigations to determine these facts. It is also likely that the purpose of each of these

156

creations would have been investigated and tested before they were installed in the car.

Proving the nature of the purpose

Even if we accept the fact that we cannot scientifically prove a creator, we may still want to infer that nature seems too complex to have emerged by accident but such an inference would still need to be proven. Even if we could prove a creator, we must also prove a purpose since the notion of 'creation' does not automatically involve a purpose. For example, one may create a car accident and have had no intention (purpose) of doing so. Even if a purpose could be proven, we are still left with the problem of finding out the nature of the purpose which does not necessarily follow from the proof of a purpose. All that can be done is to speculate about the nature of the purpose and this is exactly what Bernard, Canon and Selye have done with their theories.

Summing up

Despite the difficulties encountered with teleological theories, they continue to be popular. This may be because a notion of a 'purposeful body' neatly fits in with the notion of a 'purposeful life', which is implied in most beliefs about a creator. If this is so, it highlights the difficulty caused by the cohabitation of science and religion (or more broadly the belief in the existence of a creator).

Finally, the notion of 'homeostasis' appears to convey a notion of 'steady state' in a body. But there is no evidence that the body is ever truly in a steady state. It seems instead to be in a constant state of flux. We know for instance that emotional and physical activities are present most of the time in our lives. It is well accepted that they have an accompanying effect on the physiology of the body. If this is so, the body can never truly be in a steady state. High blood pressure, for example, often needs be monitored over a period of time to confirm that it is above a critical point because individual 'abnormal' readings at any given time are thought to be influenced by everyday activities and are therefore unreliable. The same rationale applies to taking a resting pulse. What seems more likely is that the body is in a constant state of flux and that as long as that flux is within an acceptable range, in terms of intensity and duration, no great deal of harm will come to the individual.

If this is what happens, this poses an additional problem for most physical and psychological stress theories. That is, most activities may not necessarily require an adaptive response. If we get excited about something we eventually calm down. If we feel fear, that fear does not last forever, or if we go for a jog, our heartbeat returns to normal after a while. The fact that chemical and physical reactions occur as a result of these situations does not necessarily prove that the steady state of the body has been disturbed. It may just be evidence that these reactions are part and parcel of being a human being and that the body in fact can sustain such reactions.

It is only when parts of the body are damaged or faulty that problems can occur. In these instances, what would not be a problem for most people, becomes one for someone who has a pre-existing condition. For instance, a penicillin injection which can be beneficial to most people at times of infection, can kill someone with an allergy to the substance. The same problem can arise with jogging. It may be beneficial to someone in good health but kill someone with a pre-existing heart condition.

Physical and psychological 'stressors'

Another area of concern for theories of stress has been the difficulty in determining what causes stress. Selye introduced the term 'stressors' after there had been some confusion about the correct use of the term 'stress'. The following discussion will investigate the problems of determining what constitutes a 'stressor'. This will begin with an attempt to identify possible differences between various alleged physical and psychological 'stressors'. This will be followed by a comparison between these two types of 'stressors'.

158

Physical 'stressors' and their characteristics

Selye investigated many types of 'stressors' in developing his theory. They included: injection of formalin, 'spread eagle' immobilization, lack of oxygen and exposure to cold and heat. Some of these had also been sources of inquiry for Cannon (1935) in his study of 'homeostasis'. These various physical factors, however, seemed to provoke quite different reactions. Selye, in fact, agreed that the responses were different. Reminiscing that at first there had been a resistance to him using the term 'stress' because it might have led to some confusion with other possible meanings of the term, he specifically commented on the need to differentiate between his usage and Cannon's. Cannon had referred to "stresses and strains" upon homeostatic mechanisms. He argued that Cannon had clearly shown that "the specific stabilizing or homeostatic reaction to lack of oxygen is quite different for that with which the body meets exposure to cold; this, in turn, is virtually the reverse of what is required to resist heat" (1956). These reactions, Selye indicated, had to be discounted since they were not part of the stress response. The residual response, once these specific effects had been eliminated, was what constituted the stress response.

Specific effects of physical 'stressors'

This position is not without problems for Selye. Leaving aside any possible role for stress in the process, it seems that the specific effects of, say lack of oxygen, extreme, cold or heat could be fatal to living creatures. Most living creatures who depend on oxygen for their survival will die when insufficient oxygen is present in their body. Short-term deprivation under certain conditions may result in brain damage. Lowering temperature below a level compatible with life for each specific organism will also result in death, with intermediate levels causing loss of body parts or damage to tissues. Alternatively, intense heat may lead initially to dehydration and possibly burning of tissues. When dehydration is prolonged death also occurs.

In all the examples given it would be uncontroversial to suggest that it was the specific reactions of the 'stressors' which ultimately led to the damage or death of the living creature. If this is true, then we are still not the wiser as to what constitutes the stress residue or what role it could play. It appears that the specific effects of each 'stressor' are sufficient to cause the damage and it is uncertain how and what a stress response would contribute to the process or even if it would contribute at all.

The search for the common non-specific effects

Another question requiring a response is whether the introduction of the 'stress' concept helps or hinders the understanding of what is taking place. Before answering the question, it may be useful to remember why attempts are usually made to improve our understanding of events in our world. By better understanding, we can deal with what is taking place in a more effective and purposeful manner. If we use this criterion to analyze the usefulness of the 'stress' concept, we are left to wonder whether we have a richer and more useful explanation since there is great difficulty in assessing what stress actually is.

This common link or residue left after the specific effects are taken into account, seems to have eluded most researchers. In fact, few if any have looked for it. There may be two possibilities as to why this has been so. Either the researchers were not aware that this was what stress was supposed to be or if they were, they might have felt that such a common link would not really further help understand the effects of the various situations labeled as 'stress'.

Common and predictable features of physical 'stressors'

One thing these physical conditions seem to have in common is that they can have an impact on living creatures, including human beings, without any input from these creatures. Another shared feature is that their effects can usually be predicted. Like the three physical 'stressors'

160

just discussed, various forms of physical exercise, viruses and some bacteria produce their effects without any conscious interference from the creature on which they have an effect. Physical exercise, after a given time, produces diverse effects to muscles, ranging from warming up to physical damage. Viruses and some bacteria have an effect on our body that cannot be avoided once they have entered our body. Moreover, each specific virus or bacterium has its own specific effects.

When these physical conditions occur, their effect is direct. There seems to be no need for a mediator to convert them to something that will produce their effects. An infection produces a response from the immune system because it is detected via feedback mechanisms, as not being compatible with the organism.

Physical 'stressors': concrete and measurable

Physical 'stressors' are called physical because they are concrete, as opposed to abstract 'stressors'. Heat, cold, lack of oxygen can be measured in a precise way. The movements of the muscles involved in physical exercise can be seen, viruses and bacteria can be observed and identified. Moreover, the effects of these 'stressors' on living creatures come into existence according to the laws of either chemistry and physics or sometimes both. Yet, at times, it appears that something else might be accompanying the effects of a particular 'stressor'. This may have been what Selye had in mind when he thought of stress as a 'syndrome of just being sick'. Selye suspected the existence of a 'general syndrome of sickness' which seemed to be superimposed on all diseases (Selye, 1956). These may have been reactions from the immune system but had this been the case, it would not be a 'stress' reaction, just an immune reaction. However, many physical events labeled as 'stressors' are not always disease producing, so the 'syndrome of just being sick' could not be applicable to them.

If we turn our attention to the other possible definition Selye seemed to have contemplated, which depicted stress as the 'wear and tear of the body', this is also of little use. If by 'wear and tear' he meant that stress was the total sum of physical, as well as psychological events, then stress becomes no more than a generic term used to describe many different physical and psychological situations. This may very well be useful in everyday descriptive conversation. In scientific discourse, however, better understanding and solutions are sought and the use of a generic term conveys the impression that these are in fact an accumulation of many varied phenomena which could just as easily come under the rubric of 'aging'. Selye, in fact, suggested that "normal life also causes some wear and tear in the machinery of the body"(1956). If this were the case, the effects of 'stressors', specific or common, would not seem that important to the overall outcome. If normal life causes wear and tear and wear and tear is stress, it means that normal life causes stress. This could imply that one way to escape stress could be to lead an abnormal life.

Usefulness of a classification of physical 'stressors'

Regardless of which definition is used, to have a classification of physical 'stressors' does not appear very useful while we have no clear understanding of what constitutes stress. All a classification would appear to provide us with would be a grouping for what are many varied conditions. Their two common factors seem to be a direct interaction with the physiology of the creature they affect and the fact that the interactions are subject to laws of chemistry and physics. If each physical 'stressor' has its own unique effects and if these effects are sufficient to create the reaction, then any generalization from one 'stressor' to another is not possible. It must be noted that in biology, where physical 'stressors' have usually been the main interest of study, stress is rarely defined and when it has been, it has more often than not been in a generic sense. In some cases, a 'stressor' is deemed to be so by the mere presence of higher levels of 'stress hormones', such as that of cortisol, as a response to a physical event. Many biologists, immunologists and virologists agree that 'stress' is probably more complex than they assume in their studies and prefer to leave its complexity to psychologists and other social scientists, as was evidenced earlier by Bonneau's comments.

Confusion between physical and psychological 'stressors'

It is interesting that one of the most common stress variables used in biological studies is immobilization. But immobilization is not really a physical 'stressor'. Keeping an animal immobilized in itself does not provoke physiological reactions, with the possible exception of an altered blood circulation. Yet it is commonly assumed that animals 'fret' when immobilized. The notion of 'fretting' would seem to indicate some sort of emotional reaction. Furthermore, there appears to be no other possible reason as to why immobilization has been labeled a 'stressor'. Therefore, immobilization should be labeled a psychological rather than a physical 'stressor'.

It appears that biologists need to approach the problem of defining 'stress' more seriously than they seem to have done. There are two reasons for this. The first is that if experiments measure the effects of implied psychological stress, a psychological and not a physical label should be given. The second is that most of the findings from physical science are often regarded, not always justifiably, as constituting harder evidence than those originating from social science. Many results based on experiments involving physical 'stressors' are often generalized to unrelated psychological situations and in doing so give the erroneous impression that an overwhelming body of evidence supports the legitimacy and validity of the 'stress' concept. Furthermore, because evidence of the effects of stress seems to have come from many diverse and respected scientific areas such as medicine, biology, psychiatry and psychology, this has helped reinforce the illusion that 'stress' is a legitimate scientific concept. The media and the general public are rarely aware that different types of 'stress' are being discussed and investigated and are left therefore with the impression that stress is a

163

genuine condition worthy of scientific research. Such a general lay acceptance has in turn led to the belief by many scientists in these various disciplines, that with so many people feeling 'stressed' there must be something out there worth investigating.

Types of psychological stress and their characteristics

The perceiver as a 'stressor'

Few analysts of the 'stress' concept would argue against the view that any assessment of psychological stress by an individual is highly subjective. What represents stress for one person may not necessarily do so for another and is therefore left to the appreciation of the individual. This appreciation will be followed by a reaction when the event or situation is not indifferent to the person. Because events and situations *per se* are neutral, they need to have some significance and importance for the person who is experiencing them for that person to feel something towards them. Events or situations alone could not cause stress. The only possible causal candidate for stress is the individual's reactions to certain events.

The role of emotions and feelings

Reactions to events are usually labeled 'feelings' or 'emotions', with the former encompassing a broader category under which the latter is usually included. Feelings are not always accompanied by a physical reaction. In some circumstances reactions may be mixed. We may be glad in some ways that something occurred but at the same time be unhappy that it did. In other circumstances we may not be able to understand how we feel. Emotions can also be confused at times. Additionally, there have been arguments as to which reactions qualify as emotions. Nevertheless, some emotions seem to elicit some definite physical reactions. Embarrassment, for instance, can be accompanied by blushing, happiness brings smiling and anger can lead to bloodshot eyes and frothing at the mouth.

Physiological effects of feelings and emotions

When various feelings and emotions have physical signs, that physical component may be strongly evident. This component, however, according to Selye's model cannot be stress, for these reactions are specific to the various agents (in this case, feelings or emotions). We are left again with the elusive residue and its possible effects. If we turn to some of the other definitions of 'stress' that were presented earlier, psychological stress is emotions (Breznitz & Goldberger, 1982) or negative feelings (Thompson, Murphy and Stradling, 1994). If this is true, we don't need the 'stress' concept at all. Mandler's (1984) view that stress refers to things that people are exposed to seems to ignore the neutrality of these things. If the stress reaction is the state induced by events or circumstances (Glue, Nut & Coupland, 1993), a subset of emotion (Lazarus, 1993), a perception (Selye, 1979) or a cerebral reaction to a particular event (Skinner, 1985, as cited in Goldstein, 1995), we are back to feelings and emotions. If it is a transaction or discrepancy between resources and perceived demands (Cox, 1985; Holroyd & Lazarus, 1982; Levi, 1996), then a reaction in the form of a feeling or an emotion takes place once the resulting evaluation has been made in negative as well as in positive terms.

Definitions of psychological stress

An examination of the literature reveals four broad possible definitions of psychological stress:

ρ Psychological stress is caused by life events.

ρ Psychological stress is the result of our direct reactions to events or reactions, subsequent to an evaluation of the circumstances surrounding events

ρ Psychological stress is emotional stress or distress.

ρ Stress is what is left after any specific effects are taken into account

Life events as psychological 'stressors'

The view that psychological stress is caused by life-events personifies these events by attributing to them a characteristic ('stressful') which they do not have and also gives them an agency that they do not possess. Furthermore, if this position were true, then everyone would react the same way to each specific event, no matter how they felt, just as they do to a certain extent with physical agents. Attempts have been made to prove that this is the case, often by proposing that most people react a certain way to a certain event. All this would have shown, however, is that certain events are of a greater importance to many social beings in a given society and as such are more likely to be reacted to in a relatively predictable way. It would not necessarily prove that these events have a universal effect on people.

Reactions as 'stressors'

If psychological stress is the result of our direct reactions to events or reactions subsequent to an evaluation of circumstances surrounding events, then stress is superfluous to the discourse. If stress is ultimately feelings or emotions, as mentioned before, we don't need the concept of 'stress'. The concept is again reduced to a convenient discursive abbreviation with no real scientific usefulness. Even if we are still tempted to scientifically study this 'generic' stress or emotion in its different forms and its effect on the body of various living organisms, what we are really investigating is whether feelings and emotions are harmful to these organisms. Next, we need to ask whether all emotions or feelings have the same effects on people or whether anger produces the same reaction as worry or sadness. We also would need to find out whether some emotions are better or worse for our health than others. We know from everyday experience that different emotions seem to have different bodily reactions. Many researchers have suggested that emotions are the source of most psychological stress. They are, in doing so, proposing that worry, anxiety, fear, anger and other emotions produce another state called 'stress', but if stress is a response and emotions are also a response (to an appraisal or evaluation), then what we have is a response bringing on another response. This is similar to Selye's proposal that the syndrome of stress produced the syndrome of general adaptation. So instead of a cascade of syndromes, we have a cascade of responses. It is unlikely that we need a mediating factor between emotions and the physical reactions that accompanies them. Again the effects of each emotion seem to be sufficient.

Emotional stress

If the stress caused by psychological 'stressors' is emotional stress, then it becomes unclear what emotional stress is. It could denote a stress caused by emotions as discussed above or it could suggest that there are different types of stress. If it implies that emotional stress is different from physical stress, then it appears that we are dealing with two separate phenomena. If we need two distinct names to clarify what is being investigated or discussed, the unitary value of the 'stress' concept is compromised.

Labeling psychological stress as 'emotional distress' also throws a different light on the problem. We have already discussed how 'distress' does not really mean 'bad' stress as Selye had intended; but some scientists such as Goldstein (1995) have made a distinction between an unconscious physical stress and the conscious emotional distress. The Concise English Dictionary (1980) definition of 'distress' is "extreme pain, that which causes suffering; calamity; misfortune". The addition of the term 'emotional' only appears to be useful in differentiating between physical and emotional aspects of distress. Additionally, if stress is unconscious and emotional distress is not, this implies that the two are distinct phenomena. Finally, if we are not conscious of stress, it is difficult to understand how we could deal with it. Dealing with a given state of affairs usually involves an awareness of that state of affairs. Conscious emotional distress, alternatively, seems to imply that emotions are always a source of distress. There is no doubt that worry, anger and envy can cause some distress but it is less clear whether this is the case with excitement and other more positive emotions. It seems unlikely, however, that the addition of the term 'distress' would enhance our comprehension of emotions, unless one wanted to take advantage of the confusion caused by Selye's 'misspelling' of distress.

Residual common effect of 'stressors'

This last assumption provides no help at this stage. Until the residue can be determined, we have no way of finding out its role in our lives. As has been pointed out earlier, Goldstein (1995) has suggested that as more is understood about the specific effects of 'stressors', the less chance there is of the likelihood of a residual component being found.

Distinction between physical and psychological 'stressors'

It seems from our evaluation of both the physical and psychological situations or circumstances that are deemed to be sources of stress, that the existence of stress is very problematic. Attempts to improve on Selye's model have not made 'stress' a more useful concept. In fact, other researchers have not managed to take the concept beyond the status of a generic term encompassing many different and unpleasant circumstances. While this may be advantageous in the descriptive everyday discourse, it has been of little use in scientific discourse where its generality renders it incoherent.

There is, however, still a distinction that needs to be made between physical and psychological agents. The former are usually the result of some interactions between physical elements in the environment and the physical body of living organisms. When that interaction threatens these bodies, they seem to have mechanisms that come into play to counteract the effects of that interaction. At no stage, however, does the organism play a part in consciously provoking and reducing the effect. A possible exception to this may be physical exercise, where the organism can stop the activity, but if the activity is continued, no evaluation or appraisal can diminish the effects.

In certain situations, the physical and the psychological may be difficult to separate. Taking sickness as an example, a distinction needs to be made between 'being sick' and 'feeling' sick. A person can be sick and not feel sick, as often happens in the early stages of cancer. On the other hand, it is also possible to feel sick and not be truly sick, as is the case with feeling dizzy after a ride on a merry-go-around. Sometimes there can be a combination of physical and psychological reactions. We can be sick and feel sick at the same time. The conscious experience of feeling sick may produce physical responses that can become confused with those of being sick. Selye seemed to have overlooked this important distinction when he noted that "the feeling of just being tired, jittery or ill are just subjective sensations of stress" (Selye, 1956).

In conclusion, there are many difficulties associated in trying to assess the role of 'stressors', both physical and psychological. In addition to all the difficulties already discussed, it seems that any generalization from physical to psychological is no more possible than the generalization from one physical 'stressor' to all other physical 'stressors' or from a psychological 'stressor' to all psychological 'stressors'. This, however, has not stopped many researchers from generalizing their findings to all forms of stress.

The use of animals in studies of stress

Animals have made a large contribution to the study of the 'stress' concept and are increasingly doing so. This was to be expected in the light of increasing ethical guidelines in science. Unpleasant events, physical and psychological are a feature of many stress studies. This has resulted in animals being used in many cases. The use of animals in experiments has raised questions about the physical and/or mental harm to these animals some experiments may cause. Many organizations involved in animal welfare have suggested that animal experimentation should be stopped. The crucial question at the core of the debate is whether animals can experience pain and more broadly whether they have feelings at all. It would seem that in experimental science the question has somewhat been implicitly answered in the negative. The use of animals in experiments in which the treatment has been deemed to be too cruel, painful or distressing to be performed on human

169

subjects has been based, one would hope, on the belief that animals are not capable of experiencing pain or distress.[17]

Emotions and animals

Darwin (1871) certainly thought that animals had emotions. "The fact that the lower animals are excited by the same emotions as ourselves is so well established, that it will not be necessary to weary the reader by many details." Dawkins (1998), while agreeing, is more cautious. She feels that we can't really tell with absolute certainty whether animals have feelings, but she argues the same can be said about other people and this has not stopped us from making assumptions about their feelings. Accordingly, she suggests that the same assumptions we make about people could be made about animals. She uses the concept of 'suffering' which she describes as "experiencing one of a wide range of extremely unpleasant subjective (mental) states" as a basis for her argument. Dawkins thinks evidence for suffering can be uncovered through three main sources: physical health, physiological signs and behavior. Physical health can often be observed in the appearance of animals. She concedes that physiological signs are somewhat more tricky to interpret and difficult to relate to possible mental states.

> At the moment this remains a major drawback. Physiological measures, although a valuable indication of what is going on beneath the animal's skin do not tell us everything we want to know about mental states.

The problem with Dawkin's argument

Dawkins' argument that we don't know any more about the feelings of other humans anymore than we know about animals is not without problems. Our faces are much more expressive than most animals, we can share emotions with others, we can discuss and explain how we feel and we can correct misunderstandings about our external display of emotions. We blush when embarrassed and turn white when scared. Animals cannot do all these things. This not to say that animals do not feel, they may very well, but we

---

[17] The alternative seems to be a belief that animals do experience pain or distress.

have no way of assessing that. Even if they did, it is unlikely that their feelings would be comparable to ours. Feelings are closely associated with the cognitive appraisal of events. This appraisal does not appear possible without acquiring the attitudes, beliefs and values of the society in which we live. This acquisition would not seem possible for animals since they do not have the complex form of language that is necessary.

The difficulty in assessing emotions in animals

Many people believe that animals have feelings. The way a dog looks lovingly at its master, the way an angry (or perhaps frightened) cat hisses are used as examples of animals expressing their feelings, but these may be no more than signs of what we assume these things to be. Reactions to pain, possible appraisals of events or 'fretting' are difficult to assess without much speculation. When an animal trembles, it is often assumed that it is scared because we humans tremble when we are scared. But to be scared requires the animal to have a concept of being 'scared'. Whether this is the case can never be directly accessed by humans.

Similarity between humans and animals

Furthermore, for animals to share these emotions and feelings with humans, they would also need to conceive of the world the same way that we do. If animals had emotions and feelings, it is highly improbable that these emotions and feelings would be sufficiently similar to that of humans to make studies of animals' emotions useful to our understanding of human emotions. It can be concluded from this that the use of animals in the study of human stress may not necessarily be useful, especially when that stress is deemed to have been caused by an individual's evaluation of a particular event.

Assumptions about animals

The preceding comments are in agreement with Willner (1993) who rightfully makes the point that "accepting that stress is to be defined subjectively creates serious obstacles to the evaluation of animal models of stress... However,

171

while animals may well have subjective experiences, these are for all practical purposes, outside the scope of scientific enquiry." He adds that the subjective nature of stress addresses the question of construct validity, and that cognitive appraisal, an important aspect of psychological stress, suggested by Lazarus and Folkman (1984), cannot be studied in animal models. Yet, surprisingly, he thinks that the problem is not entirely intractable.

Despite admitting that "an environmental definition of stress is theoretically flawed, it serves well in practice, under extreme conditions", he proposes that these extreme conditions (read extreme 'stressors') would generate stress in virtually all people. In addition, he feels that we can "reasonably assume" that animals also experience severe 'stressors' as 'stressful'. He adds that mildly 'stressful' situations "do elicit effects similar to those of more extreme conditions and... cannot easily be attributed to causes other than stress." On the basis of these assumptions he concludes that animal studies are legitimate and that behavioral and physiological changes found in these studies are markers of the 'stressed' state. Ultimately, Willner seems to be proposing that assumptions, especially reasonable ones, can be a substitute for scientific evidence.

The dilemma

If animals were experiencing extreme and mild conditions as 'stressful', this would confirm the views of animal welfare protesters that experiments with animals were cruel. Furthermore, this seems to create a dilemma for many scientists studying psychological stress in animals. If animals have emotions, then surely the experiments are cruel and should be stopped. In other words, the same ethical principles that are used for humans should apply. However, if animals have no emotion and do not feel anything, the experiments are fine but futile, as they cannot measure psychological stress.

Summing up

This section has highlighted three additional problems associated with the concept of 'stress'. The notion of 'purpose', inherent to teleological theories such as those of homeostasis and stress, cannot be proven. This means that the basic assumption underpinning the theories of homeostasis and stress can never be proven scientifically.

Moreover, the concept of 'stress' cannot legitimately encompass physical as well as psychological 'stressors'. Psychological and physical 'stressors' are distinct phenomena that do not rightly belong under the same label. It has also been argued that generalization from a particular 'stressor', be it psychological or physical, cannot be generalized to all 'stressors' and obviously any findings from studies using a physical 'stressor' cannot be generalized to psychological 'stressors'. Furthermore, it has been shown that when using specific examples, the labeling of a psychological or physical event as a 'stressor' does not appear to enhance our understanding of the effects that event has on people.

Lastly, the use of animals in studies investigating psychological stress seems problematic. It has been shown that we have no way of knowing whether animals have emotions. We may suggest that an animal is frightened because it exhibits behaviors that in human terms are usually associated with fear but we could never know whether that animal or other animals get frightened. If they did, their experience is more than likely to be different to ours. This being the case, generalization from animal studies to humans is not appropriate, especially when the issue of their different physiology is also taken into consideration.

PHYSIOLOGICAL EVIDENCE OF STRESS

In this chapter, research testing the physiological effects of stress is evaluated. The available evidence will be assessed in terms that exclude any preconception of the role of stress. A brief description of the systems allegedly involved in the stress response will be presented to assist, whenever necessary, in understanding particular research findings. This analysis is of particular importance since the value and importance of stress depends to a large extent on its capacity to explain disease. If stress, like its predecessors, fails to fulfil that role, it deserves to be relegated to a mere linguistic and scientifically useless abbreviation. Another possible benefit of this analysis is that while the findings may not successfully implicate stress, they may still be useful in demonstrating the impact different circumstances have on our well-being and health. Should this be the case and should it become evident that stress does not provide a useful explanation for this question, this may also give rise to the realization that the use of the concept of 'stress' has retarded rather than advanced our understanding of what is taking place.

To begin this enquiry, an assessment shall be made of the various factors that have been considered in various studies. Generally, the search for evidence on the effects stress has on the body has involved attempts to correlate what is thought to constitute an example of a 'stressful' situation with an altered function of a particular given body system. When such a correlation has been found, the response has been deemed to be a stress response or at least evidence that this particular function is involved in the stress response. Because of this, it is important to analyze and question the measures or the assumptions that have been used to determine what constitutes a 'stressor' as well as the rationale underlying the choice of body response to be assessed. When this is accomplished, there will still be a need to determine whether the conclusions that have been drawn from the research are justified and whether the findings encountered in the study of one 'stressor' can be generalized to 'stress' and/or whether the altered function can be conclusively linked to a given disease.

A further approach has been used in attempts to connect stress and specific diseases. In some instances stress has been measured in terms of retrospective self-reports of 'stressful' events over given periods of time and these have been correlated with the occurrence of a particular disease. There are many recognized methodological problems encountered in such an approach and these will be discussed later.

There seem to be three main strategies used in the literature to determine events or situations that qualify as 'stressful'. The first is to try to produce experimental scenarios that will introduce a 'stressful' element, the second is to chose subjects already experiencing situations that are deemed to be 'stressful'. The third is to ask people already affected by a disease to recall and report 'stressful' events that could have occurred in a preceding given period. The choice of what constitutes a 'stressor' requires that assumptions be made about the events that have been chosen.

Rationale and problems with the choice of 'stressors'

'Stressors' used in animal studies

In animal studies, numerous 'stressors' have been used such as electric shocks, overcrowding, sleep deprivation, noise, rotation, restraint, immersion in cold water, excessive heat, flickering light for long periods of time, isolation, maternal separation, social defeat (Booth, 1998); avoidance conditioning, social status, disturbances in social order and surgery (Bohus and Koolhaas, 1993). A closer inspection of these 'stressors' shows that some are physical 'stressors' while others would seem to be of a more psychological nature. This is the case with overcrowding, restraint, isolation, maternal separation, social defeat and noise.

The problems of animal psychology and emotions have been discussed earlier but it is still necessary to elaborate a little further on the issue. To label situations as 'stressors', in this case psychological 'stressors', means that some assumptions need to be made since there is no evidence that these situations would have a direct effect on the body. For these situations to possibly have an effect, they would need to be mediated through some sort of psychological or emotional response. For this to be possible, we have to assume that animals are capable of such response. If we ultimately intend to use our findings to assist us in understanding human responses, then we also need to assume that these responses are sufficiently similar to human ones. Even then, a further assumption needs to be made. We must accept that the animals' responses are adverse ones. Our only guide to the nature of their responses is their behavior, but that behavior needs to be interpreted to make sense. All behavior interpretations of human beings or animals are essentially subjective mainly because we can only make sense of the world through our own direct experience. At least with other people we do share many experiences and sometimes find common grounds that we can relate to. Animals and human beings, however, share few experiences. While they may be in the same situation at the same time, this does not mean that the situation has the same meaning for both. Essentially, we cannot think like a mouse or a dog simply because we have never been a mouse or a dog. In fact, we cannot even begin to imagine what it would be like. This does not stop us, however, from interpreting their behaviors and that of other animals and when we do, we do it from our own human perspective.

We think that animals would be unhappy being restrained because we humans would find restraint frustrating. We call their behavior submissive and interpret it as a form of defeat because if we humans behaved that way it would indicate that we have been defeated and humiliated.

Additionally, we would find overcrowding an intrusion on our privacy and therefore an uncomfortable experience. Still, there is a major difference. We know what overcrowding is because we can evaluate that there are too many other people present but it is uncertain whether animals would have that same conscious experience.

With isolation and maternal separation, the same ability to make sense of the situation would seem to be necessary for the circumstances to be deemed to be 'stressful'.

Noise is another type of physical 'stressor' which seems to contain a psychological element. To begin with, there must be some doubt whether noise *per se* causes any physical disturbance. Certain levels of sounds rather than noise can cause physical damage to the hearing system because of the physical effect of sound waves. Sounds can be labeled as music, voice or noise and it is notable that with regard to stress only the effect of noise is investigated. The piercing sound of a high note by a female opera singer could cause potential hearing damage, as would loud rock music. However, music would not be considered by most stress researchers as being something 'stressful'. It seems, then that it is not so much the sound but our interpretation of that sound as noise that could cause 'stress'. When we have control over the noise and stop it, the problem seems to go away. Furthermore, the noise does not have to be physically damaging for it to be deemed 'stressful'. A leaking tap or a buzzing sound at low decibels can still prove to be extremely irritating.

In experiments that use animals, we need to ask whether an animal is capable of making the distinction between a pleasant sound and an unpleasant one and if it could, whether its appreciation of either would be the same as ours.

It is also doubtful that physical 'stressors' could be of use to the study of stress in human beings. Unless the focus of the research is to investigate the biological effects of extreme physical elements, it is not clear what the benefits would be for stress research. Sleep deprivation, electric shock, rotation, immersion in cold water, excessive heat and flickering of light for long periods of time would seem to only occur for human beings in extreme situations that are relatively rarely encountered by most. In fact, if we add to this list, restraint and isolation, these 'stressors' would seem to belong in types of incarceration where physical torture and psychological cruelty were being practiced.

In short, it seems that animal studies involving extreme physical circumstances have little to offer to the study of human stress, especially psychological stress. This will become even more obvious when the physiological effects deemed to occur during 'stressful' episodes are discussed. At this point, however, it has been argued that extreme and physical events, devoid of psychological components, are relatively rare in human everyday life and that the more psychological events are unlikely to be experienced by animals in the same way as human would.

'Stressors' used in human studies

There have been many aspects of life that have been labeled as 'stressors' and whose physiological effects have been investigated. These have included role strain in marriage (Pearlin & Schooler, 1978), anticipation, fear or unpredictability (Frankenhaeuser, 1975; Trap-Jensen *et al*, 1982), alcohol withdrawal (Nut, Glue, Molyneux & Clarke, 1988), urban physical environment (Kaminoff & Proshansky, 1982), sensory deprivation and overload (Goldberger, 1982), noise (Cohen, 1980; Dobson, 1983; Glass & Singer, 1972), work overload (Caplan, 1972), monotony (Quinn, 1975), loss of job, (Cobb & Kasl, 1977), work overload or underload in simulated work situations (Frankenhaeuser, Nordheden, Myrsten, & Post, 1971), defense of a doctoral thesis (Johansson, Collins & Collins, 1983), school children mental testing (Johansson, 1972), preschool children activities in day care centers (Lundberg, Westermark & Rasch, 1993), parenthood of preschool children (Lundberg & Palm, 1989), repetitive work (Lundberg, Granqvist, Hansson, Magnusson & Wallin, 1989), highly mechanized work (Johansson, Aronsson & Lindström, 1978), crowding in urban commuting (Lundberg, 1976), perceived stress (Frankenhaeuser, Sterky, & Järpe, 1962), marriage problems (Ilfeld, 1982), public speaking (Dimsdale & Moss, 1980), and pressured interviews and exams (Sapolsky, 1994).

Others have merely been mentioned as instances capable of producing stress. These have included fluctuations of the stock market, finding a parking place (Miller, Ross, & Cohen, 1985), traffic jams, shortage of money (Dobson, 1983) and society, social organizations, undesired and unscheduled events (Pearlin, 1982).

Most of these situations are either unpleasant or unwelcome or they are assumed to be either unpleasant or unwelcome. At times it has seemed that anything various researchers found unpleasant or unwelcome or anything they felt most people would find so, have been deemed to be 'stressors'. This, however, may be somewhat too simplistic. We must remember that psychological stress has been described by many analysts as being the result of individual subjective evaluation. If this is true, then the various assumptions about what constitutes a 'stressor' cannot be justified.

In fact, making these assumptions renders the studies using unwelcome and unpleasant events as variables, life-events studies. They make the same assumptions made by life-events scales. In some aspects, they are more problematic because at least the scales have a criterion that the event must have a certain degree of disruption in one's life and that the greater that disruption, the greater the score. The use of any unpleasant and unwelcome event as 'stressor' means that anything unpleasant or unwelcome, no matter how trivial, qualifies.

The use of such events as 'stressors' seems to overlook the individual circumstances in which they occur. The reaction to the loss of a job, for instance, may vary greatly with the terms under which it happened, the age of the person, their qualifications, their re-employability, work availability, whether redundancy was paid or not as well as many of the possible effects on their life at that time. These factors will have a bearing on how unpleasant and unwelcome the situation could be to different individuals. There could be circumstances in which the loss of a job could actually be a welcome or pleasant event for some people.

Examinations or disrupted mathematical tasks are often used in human research to measure stress levels in human subjects. Once again, several factors may play a part in affecting the type of response obtained. The basic assumption with examinations is that everyone is nervous, anxious or apprehensive before an exam. This may be so when the exam is of great importance to the student. But it may be much less so if the student is very confident of his capacity to answer most questions on the subject. This may also apply if the student feels competent and views the exam as a mere formality. Additionally, should the student not care for a variety of reasons about the outcome, the student may not feel 'stressed' by the event.

Disrupted mathematical tasks are slightly different. They have been given with the assumption that many people do not like mathematical tasks and furthermore that most people find disruptions and/or the errors that sometimes accompany them frustrating. This is not necessarily true for all people. Some people are very good at mathematics, some people are not easily distracted or don't mind being distracted. Additionally, some people do not really care enough about either mathematics, failure at it or even failure in general to be 'stressed'.

The study of repetitive 'stressful' events is also problematic. It is often suggested in the stress literature that accumulated or prolonged stress can be more severe and is therefore labeled as acute and/or chronic stress, reinforcing the notion of 'stress' as a disease. Taking things like public speaking as an example, we find that the same problem of experience, competence and the importance of the event are present to affect the perception of the event as 'stressful'. It could be suggested that the more someone is exposed to situations in which they have to speak in public, the more it continues to be 'stressful'. However, for some people it seems the more they speak publicly, the less nervous or anxious they become. The lack of experience and perceived fear of being inadequate in performing the task often result in the situation being perceived negatively. With experience, confidence in one's capacity to perform the task increases and fears can disappear to a certain extent for some people. This shows that in some instances repeated exposure to an event can lead to a decrease in the negativity of its perception.

Alternative explanations for 'stressors'

A cursory investigation of the types of events that have been labeled as psychological 'stressors' reveals that most of them have involved at some stage an emotional reaction, if the term 'emotion' is used in its broadest sense. Some of the reactions may in fact be best described as feelings towards the events rather than emotions. Some of these events can result in feelings of anxiety, nervousness, apprehension or fear of failing. They are usually events in which performance is being evaluated (e.g. examinations, public speaking, interviews). Other events in which control is not possible can create a feeling of irritation, frustration and even anger (e.g. noise, road traffic, interruptions to tasks). Other situations may lead to feelings of discouragement, depression and a sense of worthlessness (job loss, end of relationship, unemployment). In fact, most of the adverse situations encountered in one's life are attributed this general feeling of unpleasantness because they result in an emotional reaction or feeling which is usually of a negative nature. Alternatively when 'stressors' are deemed to produce 'eustress', they seem to relate to positive emotions or feelings.

It would be legitimate to ask what difference it would make if emotions and feelings were investigated instead of stress. It seems that there would be many advantages. The first and most obvious would be that the discourse would suddenly become more coherent. We have good and bad emotions (rather than 'eustress' and distress). We also need some emotions (not stress) or else life would not mean much and would probably be boring. Too much emotion (not stress) or strong emotions over too long a period (not chronic stress) and might make it difficult for us to function. Furthermore, we can potentially have the same or different emotions about different things or the same thing. We can also have mixed or ambiguous emotions so that non-specificity is no longer an issue.

The second advantage would be that people, through socialization, seem to learn with varying degrees of success to control their emotions. We do not always display anger when we feel it and we eventually get on with life after traumatic events. The fact that we do not always control these emotions to our complete satisfaction or that of others, only shows that it is not always easy to do so, not that it is not possible.

Another benefit of considering emotions and feelings as an alternative to stress is that, unlike what is happening with stress, people tend to be able to define emotions fairly similarly. There is a reasonably broad agreement among people as to what constitutes anger, frustration, nervousness, anxiety, worry, fear and many other emotions or feelings. We know, for example, that worry involves imagining negative outcomes ahead of time, that frustration usually occurs when we feel that the circumstances of an event appears to be beyond our control or that we are afraid when we are faced with a dangerous situation which we cannot adequately handle. It may therefore be said that emotions and feelings may provide a more defined explanation of a person's state than the poorly defined and little understood concept of 'stress'.

The last and probably the most important advantage of considering emotions and feelings is that they represent an important differentiation in the way we feel about events. The nature of each emotion and feeling says much about the way we interpret the event socially. Feelings and emotions are an important part of life but when their manifestation overwhelms our life to a point where we find it difficult to function, an understanding of their exact nature becomes important. Understanding the specific feeling or emotion behind our unhappiness offers more chance of a solution than a generic, poorly understood, one-fit-all concept like stress. Emotions and feelings reflect the way we look at the world. If some result in extreme unhappiness, understanding this may be the first step towards recovery. Alternatively, the hit-and-miss approach of stress management, with its suggestions of avoidance of 'stressors', relaxation, exercise and a better diet, seem to be treating the symptoms of a misunderstood condition. Adding to these a total change of lifestyle and thinking may prove more of a burden than the original condition for many people.

Self-reports

Recalls of significant events

One type of self-report has involved asking people to recall important or significant events that have occurred in a given period of time, usually from the previous week but also up to six months or even two years ago. This approach has often been used in attempts to link the onset of some disease with stress. There are nevertheless many difficulties associated with this type of attempt to detect stress. The most obvious is that again we have the problem of assessing what constitutes a 'stressful' episode. Typically, many of the events, considered as examples of stress, are related to events in the life-events scale. This does not mean that other events are excluded. In fact, any events that would be reasonably considered unpleasant or upsetting by many people have also been considered 'stressful'.

Other possible sources of problems with self-reports include the lack of accuracy of recall, importance of the event to the individual, as well as specific circumstances surrounding the events. Additionally, people participating in these sorts of experiments may be compliant and eager to please the experimenters (Kienle & Kiene, 1998) and this may cause them to magnify the importance of the event or to discard unhelpful comments. Also, asking people to recall 'stressful' events is suggestive that such events exist and are important. Finally, if one considers and accepts the view proposed by many in the stress literature that stress is a permanent feature of life, to ask someone whether they had experienced 'stressful' events during a given period seems rather superfluous since they would obviously have. Furthermore, if stress were inherent to human life and also caused disease, then everyone would ultimately be permanently ill.

Another important setback for the use of self-reports in attempts to correlate stress and physiological reaction or disease is that correlation does not mean cause and effect. The mere precedence of an event by another event does not mean that one causes the other. So to claim that either a particular response was caused by stress or that stress caused or played a part in the onset of a condition because it preceded it cannot be justified.

Self-reports of feeling 'stressed'

In order to demonstrate the extent of the stress problem, many researchers using surveys, have asked people whether they felt various degrees of stress or how often they experienced it. This approach has also been used in experiments that try to correlate stress with a physiological response or a disease or even to demonstrate the effectiveness of particular stress management techniques.

Self-reports of feeling more or less 'stressed' are plagued with the same problems inherent to all self-reports. Yet they also present additional challenges. The first is the difficulty found in defining stress. With no specific consensus about what stress is, definition is left to the interpretation of the individual. The nature, gravity and importance of the experience are highly individualistic. Furthermore, as was shown in the chapter on popular views, people are reminded every day about how 'stressful' modern living is and how stress levels are rising.

Many doctors promote the view that stress is out there and that it is a cause of many conditions, often invoking stress when they cannot explain their patients' condition. Subsequently, it is not difficult to imagine that some people might feel largely obligated to agree that they were 'stressed' at various times. In instances when people are asked if they feel less 'stressed' as a result of some intervention, compliance, politeness and eagerness to please may again play a part. This is not unique to studies of stress.

Asking people how they feel can also add difficulties. We often ask people how they feel with regard to physiological states and when we do so, it is quite different to asking them about a psychological state. One of the reasons we ask about feelings towards a physical condition is because this is often the only assessment available to us. While a wound or a skin condition can be visual indicators of injury or disease; pain, discomfort and nausea can only be felt. Therefore, their evaluation can be highly subjective. We can rarely assess the extent of tissue or bone damage with only pain as an indicator, nor can we accurately feel our level of temperature during fevers unless we use a thermometer. When we are sick and are asked if we feel better, we cannot always answer with certainty but in an experiment we may feel obliged to report feeling better even we are not. In trying to comply or please, we may unwittingly look harder for the slightest sign of improvement.

People feel 'stressed' because they believe in the first place that feeling 'stressed' is a legitimate condition. Without such a belief, the subjective feeling is not possible. Nevertheless, in everyday language, feelings of being 'stressed' often appear to supplant the use of emotion terms. Instead of feeling 'annoyed', 'worried', 'apprehensive' or 'frustrated', people seem more likely to declare that they are feeling 'stressed' even though it does not necessarily accurately describe to themselves and others what they feel.

The choice of 'stressors': summary

Most, if not all, of the methods that have and are being used to identify stress as an independent variable are less than satisfactory. They are many reasons why this is so but the most basic is that stress has not and probably cannot be defined. An inspection of existing definitions reveals that none of them actually describes stress. There are attempts at telling us what stress does, how it manifests itself or the type of process it is but they do not explain what it looks like or what it feels like (after all it is supposed to be a state). Granted we are told about the 'flight or fight' reaction, but we rarely appear to experience it, in most 'stressful' situations.

The choice of 'stressor', when not arbitrary, is usually dictated by theoretical approaches. Yet many of the theories have defined stress in many different ways. Therefore, the best that can be concluded about this aspect of the research undertaken under the rubric 'stress' is that the results should be confined to the specific independent variable that has been studied. In other words, a study on physiological responses to examinations tells us that the responses may be correlated with the experience of undertaking an examination or maybe even just that particular examination. To say that stress was involved is purely speculative.

The same is true about physiological responses and feeling 'stressed'. All that can be said legitimately is that a feeling of being 'stressed' was correlated with certain physiological responses but we cannot say that stress itself was present as a condition.

Rationale and problems associated with the choice of 'stress responses'

The difficulty in defining stress independently has resulted in attempts to prove its existence by demonstrating its effects on various body systems. Many experiments have been developed to this effect,. Their design has, to a certain extent, reflected the investigator's knowledge about the various body systems that were thought to be implicated in the stress response. Relatively simple studies[18] attempting to investigate the physiological effect of stress have grossly underestimated the complexity of these systems as well as that of their interaction. With this in mind, the following rather succinct description of the various body systems is intended mostly to assist with familiarization with some of the terms used in the physiological discourse and to provide a basic understanding of the function of these systems.

---

[18] These studies may only consider one variable when usually many responses are taking place at once.

According to Goldstein (1995), the body possesses many 'stress effector systems' which act directly or indirectly. They include the sympathetic nervous system (SNS), the adrenomedullary hormonal system (AHS), the hypothalamic-pituitary-adrenocortical system (HPA), the parasympathetic nervous system (PNS), the renin-angiotensin-aldosterone system (RAS) and systems involving vasopressin (AVP) as well as endogenous opioids. All these systems have central as well as peripheral facets. The chemical messengers in use in these systems are released in and act on the brain as well on other organs. Goldstein admits that little is understood about to the usefulness of the simultaneous release in both brain and organs.

The chemical transmission in the sympathetic nervous system (SNS) is provided by the neurotransmitter norepinephrine (also known as noradreneline). The release of norepinephrine, a catecholamine, affects blood flow distribution, cardiac function and glandular activity and comes into effect during mild exercise, high or low environmental temperature and performance of non-distressing locomotor tasks. Goldstein points out that "The SNS consists of so many facets, that no single measurement tool - even direct sympathetic nerve recording - can describe adequately the events mediating sympathoneural regulation of the circulation" (1995).

The adrenomedullary cells in the adrenomedullary hormonal system (AHS) also release the catecholamine epinephrine (also known as adrenaline) in humans directly in the blood stream. Epinephrine not only affects the function of most organs but is also known to increase, amongst other things, heartbeat, rate of breathing and to redirect blood volume toward the heart, brain and skeletal muscle. This is the neurotransmitter thought to be predominant in the 'flight or fight' response.

In the hypothalamic-pituitary-adrenocortical system (HPA), the cortex of the adrenal glands secretes the cortisol hormone into the bloodstream. Cortisol is a glucocorticoid which increases blood levels of glucose and acts as an anti-inflammatory agent. While it also affects most organs, its effects are much slower than that of catecholamines. In relation to stress, however, Goldstein points out that "the bases for the requirement of normal adrenocortical function in order to weather acute stress remain obscure".

Corticotrophin-releasing hormone (CRH) (sometimes labeled a factor and abbreviated as CRF) influences the pituitary secretion of corticotrophin or adrenocorticotropic hormone (ACTH) which, in turn, regulates the release of glucocorticoids. Goldstein mentions that there has been speculation that CRH could be the 'master stress hormone' because of its capacity to simultaneously activate the body's three main 'stress systems': HPA, SNS and AHS.

These four systems, with the addition of the immune system, play the most direct role in the alleged production of stress. The other systems mentioned, as well as some not described here, play either a minor, an indirect, an unknown or no role whatsoever.

Physiological measurement of stress

Findings about the physiological effects of stress have been reported in many articles and have been advanced as providing overwhelming evidence that stress exits and that its effects are well documented. However, this begs the question of how we can possibly know that these effects are caused by stress. If we cannot define something, there must be doubt as to what it actually is or what it does. In reality, the reason the fluctuating levels of particular hormones or neurotransmitters have been used as measures of stress is simply because they had initially been hypothesized by Selye to be indicative of a stress response. Further research trying to confirm his findings has not always succeeded in doing so. Moreover, attempts to liken stress to the 'flight or fight' response have resulted in studies trying to reproduce and validate some of Cannon's findings.

In order to assess the adequacy of findings relating to the physiological effects of stress, two main criteria will be used. The first criterion is that only something deemed to be 'stressful' should produce the effect. If the effect can be produced by something else then it cannot be strictly labeled a 'stress response'. The second criterion is that all 'stressors' should cause that effect. Contradictory findings about various 'stressors' would be evidence that 'stress' is not a legitimate unitary concept. If we are left with a variety of states in response to a variety of social situations and if we already have names for such situations and states, the use of the concept of 'stress' would prove superfluous.

Cardiovascular measures

Many studies, mostly involving animals, have focused on heart rates and blood pressure. The reasons for this are twofold. The first is that these two measures are relatively simple to obtain. The second is that most of these studies have accepted the view that the stress response and those of the 'flight or fight' are one and the same. Cannon (1929) had described the 'flight or fight' response as a natural reaction in animals and humans which was characterized by a mass-discharge and inhibition of the parasympathetic nervous system. Some, like Bohus and Koolhaas (1993), claim this discharge "...has long been considered to be responsible for the 'classical signs' of stress such as the pressor response (increase in blood pressure) and tachycardia (increase in heart rate). It also inhibits the enteric limb of the parasympathetic nervous system, thereby reducing gastrointestinal activity during stress." They acknowledge, however, that the idea of sympathetic mass-discharge has been challenged recently by Jänig and McMaclan (1992) as a result of extensive physiological and neurobiological research on nervous regulation of cardiovascular functions. Goldstein (1995) proposes that Cannon's formulation and Selye's later description of the release of 'adrenalines', a generic term for all the catecholamines from the medulla in his alarm reaction, have proven to be oversimplifications of complex interactions between nerves and hormones. He suggests that there is growing evidence to support the independent regulation of the sympathoneural (SNS) and adrenomedullary system (AHS), thus rejecting their concept of a unitary sympathoadrenal system. However, Lundberg (1995), like many other researchers, still believes

190

that this sympathetic-adrenal medullary system is one of two neuroendocrine systems particularly sensitive to stress. He claims that studies have demonstrated that this system mainly reflects the intensity of stress and arousal whereas the other system, the pituitary-adrenal cortical system, is more sensitive to the affective aspect of the stress situation.

Relatively few human studies have undertaken the measurement of heart rates and blood pressure. A study by Turner, Girdler, Sherwood and Light (1990), however, compared the heart rate and blood pressure of dental and graduate students in four laboratory 'stressful' tasks involving a real-life challenge of presenting their research in front of a small audience. It was found that while the absolute levels of both dimensions in each task correlated significantly with those in the real-world situation, the reactivity scores indicating the amount of increase in levels were not significantly correlated. Another study by Linden (1991) investigated the effect of various protocols used in experiments with 'stressful' arithmetic calculations on cardiovascular responses and found that some were more useful than others.

The small amount of studies of human cardiovascular responses is contrasted by the numerous studies on animals. Many of these studies have suggested that an elevation of blood pressure and heart rate are indicative of stress while other research has concentrated on whether chronic stress can lead to hypertension. Both these types of studies have returned mainly positive findings in rats (Bohus & Koolhaas, 1993). However, these researchers also issue a note of caution, remarking that the common need to handle most animals in experiments itself causes elevated heart rates in most species.

There are, in fact, other factors which can make base rates of cardiovascular responses difficult to assess. These include the use of free moving animals in the studies and the fact that motor activity often accompanies the 'stressor'. Bohus and Koolhaas conclude, nevertheless, that the data they have reviewed clearly show that stress is an additional risk factor for various cardiovascular pathologies in animals and that it is just as clear that it is a comparable risk factor for humans. This is declared without once citing a human study. Interestingly, they add "That stress of various types profoundly affects the function of the cardiovascular system and is in physiological terms, self-explanatory. It is more remarkable that there are different patterns of responses that are not physiologically directly self-explanatory".

These different patterns of responses are explained by proposing that they are dependent on the choice of coping strategies by the animals. This is purely speculative since there is no evidence that animals could make this sort of decision. What is more likely is that the different patterns of responses occurred because different 'stressors' and they must have represented different phenomena, were involved.

Heart rates and blood pressure can increase for reasons that could not be classified as stress. The heart rate can increase purely with increased activity. Any relatively moderate movement will increase it because more blood is needed to perform the task. Some emotional responses, including positive ones, will also increase the heart rate. The rate, however, will return to normal when the task or event is over. This also applies in strenuous exercises. The normal or resting pulse can only be measured after a period of complete inactivity or calm. Fever can also lead to an increased pulse as can the use of certain drugs such as antihistamines, tobacco, tea or coffee.

Furthermore, there are events usually described as 'stressors' that are unlikely to cause a raised heart pulse. Monotony, for example, is unlikely to do so. Unhappy events such as the loss of a job, the loss of a partner or relative, or many events that are likely to sadden people, do not generally seem to produce increased heart rate.

Blood pressure levels will also rise during physical activities. They will also do so with age. The older a person becomes the more likely they are to have raised levels of blood pressure. Again not all 'stressors' increase blood pressure. Only those that contain an element of frustration, anger, anxiety and any other excited states are likely to do so. Rosenman (1996) has also claimed that:

> Although there have been repeated attempts to differentiate SNS and cardiovascular to different emotional states, ambulatory monitoring finds no qualitative differences in blood pressure changes that occur in response to various emotions. For example, the average rise in blood pressure is the same during anger and anxiety, although both are quantitatively higher than occur during happiness.

Even if the animal studies of cardiovascular responses were relevant to humans, their findings would not be convincing. Not only could there have been confounding variables like handling and normal activities, but the difference in response patterns indicates that the results are not solely indicative of a stress response. If various 'stressors' do not always produce the same response and if factors other than 'stressors' can induce the same sort of response as those that are claimed to be a stress response, it can be concluded that increased heart rates or increased levels of blood pressure are not necessarily indicative of the presence or existence of stress.

Neurotransmitter measures: adrenaline, noradreneline and dopamine

Of the three best understood neurotransmitters, adrenaline, has been the most studied. This may be due to the perceived view that Selye believed the 'adrenalines' were the most important part of the stress response, which was not in fact the case. Selye was more preoccupied with inflammation and other hormones than with neurotransmitters. He did, however, acknowledge Cannon's contribution by stating that "The work of Walter B. Cannon and his school at Harvard University has taught us that during acute emergencies the adrenal medulla and certain nerves secrete an excess of adrenaline" (Selye, 1956).

Elevated levels of adrenaline have been found in the study of many 'stressors' such as work overload and underload (Frankenhaeuser et al, 1971), examinations (Johansson, Collins & Collins, 1983), mental testing in children (Johansson, 1972) and commuter passengers confronted with different levels of crowding (Lundberg, 1976). Self-reported stress by individuals has also been found to correlate significantly with high amounts of catecholamine excretion while subjects who where supposed to be experiencing calm and tranquillity exhibited low levels (Dobson, 1983). Lundberg (1995) has also noted that the sympathoadrenal-medullary system is activated in response to positive as well as to negative emotive situations. This confirms previous studies that have indicated that pleasant psychosocial stimuli as well as unpleasant ones produce increased adrenaline excretion (Levi & Kagan, 1980). These authors, in reviewing many studies, reported that in some of them it was found that caffeine, alcohol and exposure to a wide variety of everyday physical events also increased adrenaline levels. Other studies have also shown that adrenaline, as well as noradrenaline, exhibit pronounced circadian variation even under constant conditions of activity and environment.

It has also been found that while acute stress seems to increase the level of catecholamines, in prolonged or repeated stress, the rise of both adrenaline and noradrenaline will peak and decline to basal level before the cessation of stress (Stanford, 1993). These results were obtained in animal studies. There seem to be differences, however between adrenaline and noradrenaline excretion. In repeated episodes of centrifugation stress, only adrenaline and not noradrenaline was found to decline (Frankenhaeuser, 1971). This is the opposite of what happened after repeated immobilization sessions, when noradrenaline concentrations returned to baseline but high adrenaline levels persisted (Kvetnansky & Torda, 1984).

Other studies have shown differences in catecholamine secretions in male and female human subjects. Johansson and Post (1972, as cited in Dobson, 1983), in a comparison of secretion in a 'stressful' situation (an intelligence test under time constraint) and non 'stressful' situation (normal daily activities), discovered that the women's level remained the same during both situations in contrast to men who experienced higher levels in the intelligence test.

Levi (1972) and Frankenhaeuser *et al* (1976) recorded similar results.

Age has also been found to have an effect on levels of noradrenaline. A study by Christensen and Jensen (1994) indicates that responses to exercise, upright posture and oral glucose administration resulted in greater levels of noradrenaline in elderly subjects than it did in younger ones.

As for dopamine, there is conflicting evidence regarding the levels of release when the stress is repeated intermittently over a period of days, leading Stanford (1993) to suggest that the role of dopamine in response and in adaptation to stress is far from understood.

In reference to one of our previously stated criteria, it appears that catecholamine levels can be increased by factors not normally considered 'stressors'. Caffeine and alcohol are not supposed to be 'stressors', nor are they unpleasant stimuli. With everyday psychological stimuli, their 'everyday' tag seems to rule out notions of 'stressfulness'. Furthermore, factors like age and sex are not stress and yet they have an effect on catecholamine levels. The daily fluctuation of these levels also makes them difficult to measure accurately.

With regards to other criterion, Sapolsky (1994) states that "...all stressors do not cause secretion of both epinephrine and norepinephrine, nor of norepinephrine from all branches of the sympathetic system....two identical stressors can cause very different stress signatures depending on the psychological context of the stressors." If we add to this that the release of either adrenaline or noradrenaline has been found to be dependent on the type of emotional responses, the reliability of these catecholamines as markers of stress must be questioned. Glue, Nut and Coupland (1993) did find that noradrenaline is most commonly associated with anger and motor activity, while higher release of adrenaline has been correlated with anticipation, fear or unpredictability.

The subsequent decrease of levels in either adrenaline or noradrenaline, depending on the type of 'stressor', shows

195

that duration and repetition also play a part. Yet if stress was the only condition affecting levels of these neurotransmitters, these levels would be affected in a consistent manner. What seems to be happening is that these two catecholamines are involved in many human activities and especially so in situations when those activities require a greater physical or emotional involvement. Their role in increasing heart rate and blood pressure levels necessary in such situations would seem to support this possibility. Under this scenario, equating stress to an increase in catecholamines would simply imply that all human activities are 'stressful'. Not even Selye ever proposed that this was so.

Measures of hypothalamus-pituitary adrenal secretion

Another important class of hormones, the glucocorticoids, has been implicated in the 'stress' response. These are steroid hormones. It has been hypothesized that in times of stress, the hypothalamus secretes the critical initiating releasing hormone, CRF, [corticotropin releasing factor] into the hypothalamus-pituitary circulatory system which controls the amount of adrenocorticotropic (ACTH) in the blood which in turn controls the activity of the adrenal cortex. The adrenal cortex is responsible for the release of a type of hormone called the corticosteroids and they include the mineralocorticoid, glucocorticoid hormones and sex hormones. The glucocorticoids hormones are mainly cortisol and corticosterone. These hormones are especially important in exposure to heat, cold, injury and infection (Dobson, 1984)[19]. In addition, the pancreas is stimulated to release a hormone called glucagon. All these hormones raise circulating levels of the sugar glucose. Prolactin, another hormone, is also released while both the pituitary and the brains secrete endorphins and enkephalins which help, amongst other things, pain perception. The pituitary also releases vasopressin, an antidiuretic hormone, which is thought to play a role in cardiovascular responses. Other hormones, including reproductive hormones such as

---

[19] This may explain the presence of these hormones in experiments using these variables.

estrogen, progesterone, testosterone, growth hormones and insulin are inhibited during the response (Sapolsky, 1994).

Fluctuation of secretion

Whereas an increase in catecholamines occurs soon after exposure to 'stressors', cortisol peaks about 20-30 minutes after the 'stress episode'. Furthermore, both have diurnal patterns, catecholamines usually peak in the middle of the day, while cortisol does so very early in the morning. However, both their secretion can be influenced by non-stress factors such as alcohol, tobacco and heavy exercise (Lundberg, 1995).

Cortisol and catecholamines are not the only hormones to fluctuate and superimpose on resting levels. It has been known for quite some time that most hormone levels have shown diurnal changes and that these are of a rhythmical nature. Brown, Seggie and Ettigi (1977) have summarized many studies that demonstrated that adrenal steroid secretion fluctuates in the resting state of both man and rat. Prolactin levels have shown 24-hour variation as have growth hormones. Human ACTH and cortisol secretions have seven to nine episodic bursts every 24-hour period. For growth hormones there are up to eight surges. Additionally, age can influence the number of bursts. These authors have warned that:

> Indeed, a pattern of episodic secretion has been found in all anterior pituitary hormones studied to date. The net result of this type of secretion is that the active secretion period for any one hormone may be quite brief and the standard error of average values will thus be very high. In order for maximum information to be obtained from neuroendocrine measures, conditions of sampling must be controlled for time of the day, as well as for a variety of other factors known to alter the levels such as the type of environmental and psychological conditions surrounding the sampling, sex, menstrual phase, age, stage of development of puberty, metabolic factors such as state of nutrition, pharmacological treatment, and perhaps even the season of the year. Adequate control of these factors has rarely been achieved, probably because of the lack of knowledge of these factors.

Finally, they also point out, as does Sapolsky (1994), that there are important differences in responses by species. In human and monkey, for example, situations that have been labeled 'stressful' seem to result in an acute increase in growth hormones which parallels the change in adrenal steroids, whereas in rats there is an acute lowering of blood growth hormones.

Attempts to explain decrease or lack of increase

Cox (1985) suggests that an increase in blood glucose, usually labeled a marker of stress, may not always occur in 'stressful' situations. He quotes several studies on noise as a source of stress which he claims have resulted in both increase and decrease of blood glucose levels. He attempts to explain these contradictions by suggesting that they are due to the varying degrees of stress being experienced. This is similar to what had been proposed by Lazarus and Lanier (1978) who felt that the intensity and quality of the stress response might be more important than the physical characteristics of the 'stressor'. Mason et al (1976) had attempted to explain different adreno-cortical responses in physical 'stressors' such as electric shock by implicating an emotional component in animal studies.

One can conclude, as was the case with catecholamines, that an increased level of most of the hormones can be produced by factors other than stress. Moreover, the same 'stressor' can produce contradictory results. In addition, the variable nature of the resting levels these hormones exhibit, must create some doubt as to the reliability of their measurement. Finally, different cortical responses to the same 'stressor' can be explained in two ways. Either the response is not indicative of stress (since it should be consistently so) or the event cannot be labeled as a 'stressor' because it did not always provoke the response deemed to be representative of a stress state.

Summing up

I have shown that there are serious problems demonstrating the physiological effects of stress. On the one hand, many events or situations that have been hypothesized to represent examples of stress may not necessarily be so. On the other hand, the responses that have been theorized as being those of stress are not always necessarily so. Difficult to measure reliably and influenced by other factors, these responses have not been conclusively proven to be 'stress responses'. The neurology, chemistry and endocrinology of the human body are much more complex than Selye had imagined. Selye (1978) once explained that:

Again and again, in the discussion periods following my lectures before scientific societies, someone would get up and ask why I had to speak of stress, when I actually used Formalin, cold or x-rays. Would it not be more straightforward to say that the adrenals were stimulated by cold when it was cold that my experimental animal was exposed to and the adrenals were enlarged? I tried to point out that it could not be cold itself that was necessary for adrenal stimulation, since heat or any number of other agents produced the same effect.

Sapolsky (1994), however, seemed to disagree:

Central to Selye's conceptualization of the stress-response was the belief that whether you are too hot or too cold... you activate the same pattern of secretion of glucocorticoids, epinephrine, growth hormone, estrogen, and so for forth for each of those stressors. It turns out that the pattern of response is not quite that consistent, however. In general stressors of all kinds particularly massive physical stressors, involve the hormonal changes outlined in this chapter, with the glucocorticoids and sympathetic components being the most reliable. But the speed and the magnitude with which the secretion of some particular hormone changes may vary according to the stressor, especially for more subtle ones. The orchestration, the patterning of hormone release tends to vary from stressor to stressor, and a hot topic in stress research these days is figuring out the hormonal 'signature' of a particular stressor... Despite the dimensions common to various stressors, it is still a very different challenge physiologically to be too hot, too cold, to be extremely anxious or deeply depressed.

His views have been echoed by Goldstein (1995) who pronounced:

Just as no unitary neurocirculatory or neuroendocrine response pattern occurs during different forms of physical stress such as hemorrhagic hypotension and hypoglycemia, no unitary neurocirculatory or neuroendocrine response pattern may occur during different forms of emotional distress.

Considering this admission and his many other criticisms of the 'stress' concept, it is puzzling that Goldstein would still have attempted to develop his own stress theory. As for Sapolsky (1994), he concluded that:

> Despite this, the hormonal changes... which occur pretty reliably in the face of impressively different stressors, still constitute the superstructure of the neural and endocrine stress-response. We are now in a position to see how these responses collectively save our skin during acute emergencies but can make us sick in the long run.

Ultimately, the best that can be said about the findings of the studies that have tried to correlate certain events or situations with certain physiological responses, is that a particular event or situation has been positively correlated with a certain increase in a level of a particular hormone or neurotransmitter. These findings cannot then be generalized to any other event.

The picture that has emerged is that physiological changes have been sometimes observed in various body systems during certain situations that have been theorized to be 'stressful'. The long term and cumulative effects of these changes are poorly understood and the conclusion that they eventually lead to illness remains to be justified. Moreover, the changes in question are not always present. In these instances researchers rationalize that either the nature and intensity of the situation was insufficient to provoke the change or that physiological or psychological individual difference in people accounted for the lack of change. Additionally, these changes can be elicited by factors other than those labeled 'stressful'. These include diurnal changes in individuals. Under these conditions, it is difficult to see what role stress could play or whether the notion of 'stress' serves any useful purpose.

The notion of a threatened homeostasis is itself under threat. Changes in various body systems seem to be an essential part of everyday life resulting in the body being in a constant state of flux. There are some unsafe upper limits to that flux but the long-term effects of particular acute changes or their accumulation need to be better understood before these limits can be established. In the meantime, it seems that people survive reasonably well with this constant state of flux. After all, if there were some teleology behind the design of human beings, it would not have made sense to create beings that are capable of emotional states if these states were ultimately harmful to their survival.

STRESS AND DISEASE

Introduction

The relationship between stress and disease is arguably the most important aspect of the whole stress discourse. As has been mentioned earlier, the link with disease is vital if stress is to be considered as an important subject of scientific evaluation. Had stress been understood to be simply a series of worrying, frustrating, annoying, unwelcome or generally unpleasant short term challenges with little long term consequences, it is highly unlikely that the concept would have enjoyed the recognition and popularity that it has. Consequently, should it emerge that there is no conclusive evidence that stress and disease are linked, the concept would have little to offer. The aim of this chapter is to investigate the available scientific evidence for such a link.

A great deal of recent research has been devoted to studying the effect of various 'stressors' on the immune system. The reason for this is that the immune system has been seen as an obvious generic pathway to disease for 'stressors'. Indeed, it was reasoned that if it could be demonstrated that various 'stressors' affect the immune system in a way that renders it less effective, disease would be more likely to occur. In other words, if the immune system's role is to protect the body against disease, any reduced or suppressed function would mean that that role will be diminished and disease will be able to develop.

The problems associated with the choice of 'stressors' have already been discussed in the previous chapter and obviously still apply to the research on the immune system. The focus of this chapter, therefore, will now be on the immune system itself.

The immune system

The immune system is a complex network of specialized cells and organs whose function is to defend the body against entry by 'foreign' bodies such as bacteria, viruses, fungi and parasites. It displays both enormous diversity and extraordinary specificity. Not only does it seem to be able to 'recognize' many millions of distinctive non-self molecules, it can produce molecules and cells that match up and counteract each one of them. Virtually every body cell carries distinctive molecules that identify it as self. The cells involved in the body's immune defense do not normally attack tissues that carry a self marker. However, when immune cells encounter cells, organisms or fragments carrying molecules that distinguish them as being 'foreign', various elements of the immune system are quickly activated in order to eliminate or neutralize them.

Any substance capable of triggering an immune response is called an antigen. Tissues or cells from another individual, with the exception of an identical twin, also act as antigens. Antigens have intricate and characteristic shapes called epitopes, which protrude from their surface. Most antigens, even the simplest microbes, carry several different kinds of epitopes on their surface; some may carry several hundred. However, some epitopes are more likely than others to stimulate an immune response.

The organs of the immune system are positioned throughout the body. They are generally referred to as lymphoid organs because they are concerned with the growth, development and deployment of lymphocytes, the white cells that are the key elements of the immune system. Lymphoid organs include the bone marrow and the thymus, as well as lymph nodes, spleen, tonsils and adenoids, the appendix and clumps of lymphoid tissue in the small intestine known as Peyer's patches. The blood and lymphatic vessels also carry lymphocytes to and from the other structures.

Cells destined to become immune cells, like all other blood cells, are produced in the bone marrow. The two major classes of lymphocytes, which number around one trillion, are B cells and T cells. B cells complete their maturation in the bone marrow and T cells in the thymus, an organ situated high behind the breastbone. A random process usually referred to as 'cell education', in which any B or T cell binding to any 'self' cell self-destructs, means that only those cells that did not bind to 'self' cells are released into both the lymph and blood circulations. The lymphatic system contains nodes situated in the neck, armpits and abdomen in which production of B and T lymphocytes and other components needed for an immune response takes place when needed.

Each B cell is able to make a specific antibody. For example, a B cell will make an antibody that blocks a virus that causes the common cold, while another produces an antibody relevant to the bacterium responsible for pneumonia. A given antibody matches an antigen much the same as a key matches a lock but the fit can vary quite a bit. Nevertheless, the antibody interlocks with the antigen to some extent and thereby marks it for destruction. Antibodies belong to a family of large molecules known as immunoglobulins. Scientists have identified nine chemically distinct classes of human immunoglobulins (IgG)-four kinds of IgG and two kinds of IgA, plus IgM, IgE and IgD. Each type plays a different role in the immune defense strategy. Of particular interest to research on stress are IgA which concentrates in body fluids - tears, saliva, the secretions of the respiratory and gastrointestinal tracts - guarding the entrances to the body and IgE, which under normal circumstances occurs only in trace amounts and becomes more prominent in allergic reactions.

T cells, on the other hand, work primarily by secreting substances known as cytokines and also contribute to the immune defenses in two major ways. Regulatory T cells are vital to triggering the elaborate immune system. (B cells, for instance, cannot make antibody against most substances without T cell help). Cytotoxic T cells, on the other hand, are killer cells that directly attack body cells that are infected or malignant. They usually carry a marker known as T8. Typically identifiable by the T4 cell marker, helper T cells are essential for activating B cells and other T cells as well as natural killer cells and macrophages.

Natural Killer (NK) cells are yet another type of lethal lymphocyte. Like catotoxic T cells, they contain granules filled with potent chemicals. They are called 'natural' killers because they, unlike cytotoxic T cells, do not need to recognize a specific antigen before going into action. [20]

Finally, another important aspect of the immune system is a group of molecules called cytokines. Cytokines are released by many cells in addition to those normally regarded as belonging to the immune system. Thirteen of them have been renamed as interleukin (1 to 13). Interleukin 1, for instance, causes fever, whereas interleukin 12 activates natural killer cells. Others include interferons, tumor necrosis factors and GMCSF. Cytokines have been sometimes described as being the immune system 'hormones' and can determine the type of immune response that will be encountered (Smith, 1997).

Interaction of the immune system with other systems

The interaction of the immune system with the central nervous system (CNS) and the endocrine system is particularly important to research on stress since it would be otherwise difficult to link external events directly to that system. However, if it can be shown that the physiological reactions of the other systems in turn affect immune responses, an indirect link is created. There has been increased evidence of diverse and extensive interconnections between the immune and neuroendocrine system and this has led Blalock (1989) to deduce that there is considerable potential for mutual influence.

Booth and Ashbridge (1993) have attempted to develop a model of 'teleological coherence' which assumes a shared

---

[20] Adapted from Understanding The Immune System. (National Cancer Institute and the National Institute of Allergy and Infectious Diseases, 1998). [The information was rewritten to avoid any of the military metaphors and the personification of the immune system that are common to most of descriptions of the system].

goal for these systems. Stein and Miller (1993) have suggested that several factors indicate a connection and they include "...the effects of lesions of the hypothalamus on immune responses, the influence of hormones, neurotransmitters and peptides on immune function; and neuroanatomic and neurochemical evidence of direct innervation of lymphoid tissues". But some researchers are more ambivalent about the evidence. Hiramoto *et al* (1997) remark that:

> How the interaction between the brain and immune system takes place has not been clearly defined. Because multiple changes are occurring simultaneously in all organ systems (e.g., cardiovascular, gastrointestinal, reproductive, renal, respiratory, immune, CNS), how many single systems interact with the brain becomes extraordinarily difficult to understand.

Their comment highlights an important consideration. The simultaneity of events cannot guarantee that even an indirect link between stress and immunity exists. Considering what was discussed in the previous chapter, the link between stress and the other systems is at best very doubtful. Even if a direct link could be established between these systems and the immune system, this would not necessarily be proof that stress itself was implicated.

Immune responses in stress studies

Despite the uncertainty in establishing how a link between stress and disease would operate, it is still important to review some of the studies that have attempted to find correlations between stress and some immune functions. Many of the studies have been with animals. Much of the early research on stress in mice concentrated on increased susceptibility to various types of virus such as herpes simplex, poliomyelitis and polyoma. The same type of study, however, reveals an increased host resistance to poliomyelitis in monkeys. More recently, Booth (1998) has claimed that "Indeed it is difficult to find many measurable aspects of the immune system that cannot be altered by some stressor." With regard to human studies, he states:

Where perception of environmental stressors has been assessed using such indicators as daily moods, hassles, anxiety, social support or various coping measures, there has generally been a correlation between high perceived stress and depression of humoral and/or cell-mediated immunological measures. Often the most significant correlation has been with depression of natural killer (NK) cells.

An earlier investigation of nine studies had revealed that natural killer cells and a decreased mitogen, a substance that produces mitosis in T cells, were the two most consistent changes taking place in the immune system. The results from measurement of change in other cells were either inconsistent or indicated that no change took place (Kiecolt-Glaser, Cacioppo, Malarkey, & Glaser, 1992). These authors concluded that it was clear that short-term 'stressors' could produce transient immunological alterations, with some facets of the immune response appearing more susceptible than others.

Nevertheless, there have still been many other claims that stress affects the immune system. Cohen, Tyrell and Smith (1991), for instance, have found that although severe acute 'stressful' life events (less than 1 month long) were not associated with developing colds, severe chronic 'stressors' (1 month or longer) were associated with a substantial increase in the risk of disease. Others have found links of decrease of some immune functions with academic stress among medical students caring for Alzheimer's patients (Keicolt-Glaser & Glaser, 1991) and with conjugal bereavement (Bartop, Lazarus, luckherst & Kiloh, 1977; Schleifer, Keller, Camerino, Thorton, & Stein, 1983). Interestingly the Schleifer *et al* study also revealed the immune aspect under consideration had returned to levels similar to control levels for the majority of subjects soon after the experiment.

Similar findings were encountered by Dhabhar (1995, in May, 1996) who, in an experiment with rats, found that white-cell count had dropped by nearly half after two hours of being confined in Plexiglas tubes but had returned to normal an hour or so after. Additionally, a measurement of levels of lactate dehydrogenase, an indicator of cell damage, indicated that none had occurred. In a further experiment, Dhabhar exposed 'stressed' and non 'stressed' rats to an allergic condition and found that the 'stressed' rats produced a better immune response than the non 'stressed rats' and were found to have more white-cells in their skin. In other words, stress seemed to have enhanced, not suppressed, the immune response.

Some studies have attempted to show that while stress has an adverse effect, its supposed opposite, positive emotion, should have the reverse effect (Berk & Tan, 1996; Valdimarsdottir & Bovbjerg, 1997). Futterman, Kemeny, Shapiro and Fahey (1994) used method actors in an experiment investigating the experience of various moods. Method acting involves actors reliving past personal experiences. The moods included happy, content, satisfied, pleased, loving, friendly, warm, depressed, unhappy, irritated, frustrated, afraid, anxious, tense, calm, relaxed, fatigued, aroused, alert, excited, energetic, bored and unemotional. The authors reported that NK numbers and activity increased after all mood states, but returned to baseline levels after 20 minutes and that more aroused mood states did not have a greater impact on the immune system.

There have been many other instances of contradictory results. It seems that the immune system is much more complex than much of the research implies. It is notable that, as has been the case with other body systems, many other factors can affect elements of immune function. This is why Goodkin and his team, in a 1990 study of HIV affected men, controlled for sleep disturbances, prescription drug use, exercise level, diet, alcohol consumption, caffeine consumption and cigarette smoking (*Science News*, April 6, 1991).

Booth (1996) has pointed out the complexity of the immune system:

> For example, if there are just 10 different factors... involved in generating a particular phenomenon, then the number of possible

interactions among them is greater than 10^{27}. Conceiving of a map of the process as a single logical cascade of interactions is therefore virtually impossible, and yet this is the tacit assumption that informs much of our current effort.

He also reminds us that the 'stressors' used in animal studies do not all produce the same effect and that the acute application of a particular 'stressor' inhibits immune responsiveness, while some chronic exposure seems to sometimes increase immunity (Booth, 1998). As for human research, he suggests that "Thus, there will be conditions under which stressors interfere with immunity, have no effect or even enhance immune responses." He also remarks that most human studies assess blood immune variables but that blood contains less than 10% of the total lymphoid pool and as such is not representative of the whole population of lymphoid cells. Furthermore, he explains that "...the immune system contains a high degree of redundancy and so the fact that an event might alter a particular immune measure need not necessarily indicate any alteration of immune responsiveness within the whole individual."

In another article on emotions and immunity, Booth & Pennebaker (1999, in press), warn that:

Some immune measures, for example, are highly correlated and others are independent. The degree to which a person is resistant to say, a particular cold virus may be completely uncorrelated with their ability to ward off hepatitis. In other words, there is no representative measure of human immune behavior, partly because of the limited access to immune components in humans, but more especially because the notion of a representative measure of the immune system is essentially meaningless. ...the immune system undergoes continual change and immunity is not a unidimensional variable. The experience of a particular stressor associated with a decrease in the number of helper T cells lymphocytes in the blood has too often been interpreted as an example of 'stress suppressing the immune system'. This is a little like claiming that the quality of a symphony orchestra diminishes when the violas play more softly. We have to be careful not to over interpret observed immune changes as evidence of suppression or enhancement.

These comments, however, seem to be contradicted by their views that:

Taken together, a growing body of evidence is indicating that negative emotions can adversely affect immune markers which, directly or indirectly, can contribute to poorer health.

In the same article, they show even less reserve when they propose that "Negative mood (e.g. emotional distress) is known to affect immune function" and "This is abundant evidence that traumatic experiences adversely affect mental and physical health." Booth also implies a connection with disease when he says, "...the impact and direction of the effects of stress on immune behavior and on disease susceptibility depend on such factors as the quality, quantity and duration of the stressor" (Booth, 1998).

The proposition that altered immune response could lead to disease has been advanced by others. Peterson *et al* (1991) while recognizing "...the inherent difficulties in defining and measuring stress" have claimed that "With a few notable exceptions, investigations of viral infections in humans and in animal models support the hypothesis that stress promotes the pathogenesis of such infections." They add, "While many of these studies have substantial limitations, the data nonetheless suggest that stress is a potential cofactor in the pathogenesis of infectious disease."

Hidaka and Amino (1998) have implicated stress with the onset of autoimmune diseases in the title of their study investigating a possible relationship between stress and Graves' disease. Yet they concluded that psychological stress was a risk factor for Graves' disease, although the mechanism by which stress induces autoimmune disease remained unknown.

If stress were truly detrimental to the function of the immune system, one would expect that people infected with the HIV virus would be more severely affected. This, however, does not seem to be the case. In an article in *Science News* (1991), it was reported that psychologist Judith Rabkin of Columbia University in New York City and her coworkers had tested a group of 124 homosexual men who tested positive for HIV, the immunity-weakening virus that can lead to AIDS. Those supposed to be suffering the most depression, emotional distress or 'stressful' life events showed no greater reduction in the number of helper T-cells and no more advanced symptoms of HIV infection than the others.

It seems that there is insufficient evidence to suggest that an alteration of some immune parameters is proof that stress causes a deterioration in immune function. Furthermore, the next step linking stress to disease via altered immune function is not justified given that the immune system can be affected by daily and 'non-stressful' situations. There is also no evidence of a unitary response to stress. Instead, we are left to contemplate a notion of 'stress' with effects that can vary from individual to individual and from 'stressor' to 'stressor'. In addition, the fact that the time, place, duration and severity of the various 'stressors' can result in different findings, confirms that 'stress' cannot be a unitary concept but rather a loosely defined term which has no apparent scientific usefulness other than bringing together a set of adverse conditions which are experienced individually.

Attempts to connect stress with disease have not been limited to the immune system. Various researchers have tried to study the possible effect of stress as either an agent of specific diseases, as a cofactor or as facilitating the onset of such diseases. The reminder of this chapter will analyze evidence regarding these effects.

Disease in general

Selye (1956) had no doubt that most diseases were diseases of adaptation. In fact, by 1977, he continued to believe that stress was associated with every disease with its role ranging from very small to very large. He had some supporters. Humphrey (1992), a fellow of *The American Institute of Stress* who had earlier worked with Selye, claimed to have reviewed the literature by "various medical authorities" and found that diabetes, cirrhosis of the liver, high blood pressure, peptic ulcer, migraine headaches, multiple sclerosis, herpes, lung disease, injury due to accidents, mental breakdown, cancer and coronary heart disease were in some way related to stress.

Rosch (1984), also a member of *The American Institute of Stress*, did not speak about specific conditions but in suggesting that "Good health or resistance to stress depends upon the integration, coordination and communication between complex sophisticated mechanisms designed to maintain the integrity and constancy of this internal environment", he makes good health synonymous to stress resistance; the corollary of this being that an inability to resist stress will result in poor health. By 1996, he would be more explicit. While talking about the "automatic, archaic 'flight and fight' responses" he would postulate that, "Repeatedly invoked, it is not difficult to understand how they could contribute to such 'diseases of Civilization' as hypertension, diabetes, heart attack, stroke, peptic ulcer, muscle spasm, etc...." (1996) and added:

> ...the important role of stress, is being increasingly confirmed in patients with hypertension, coronary heart disease, peptic ulcer, allergic conditions, psoriasis, low back pain and a variety of mental and emotional disorders...it may be appropriate to insert cancer near the top of this list of 'Diseases of Civilization'.

Sometimes the link between stress and disease seems fairly complex and subject to many suppositions. Leon and Shkolnikov (1998), for example, have attempted to blame stress for increased mortality in Russia. While they do not claim a direct link, they first suggest that economic hardship caused by the collapse of Soviet Union may be partly to blame. This, they reason, has resulted in severe stress in urban areas which in turn might have led to increased alcohol consumption by men and women, with the 30 to 49 age group being the most affected. They compare the current decline in life expectancy with an earlier period of increase which they attribute to Gorbachev's 1985 anti-alcohol campaign. However, in drawing their conclusion, these writers seem to have discounted the possibility that the increased mortality rate may have been due to the discontinuation of the anti-alcohol campaign.

Levi (1996) has also tried to link stress and death and has argued that a number of studies in different countries have shown a relationship between environmental 'stressors' and morbidity and mortality. Despite recognizing that "Although correlation is not causation", he felt that the evidence was strong enough to justify measures to prevent or reduce stress".

Sapolsky (1994) does not appear to agree. He notes that "Everything bad in human health now is not caused by stress, nor is it in our power to cure ourselves of all our worst medical nightmares merely by reducing stress and thinking healthy thoughts full of courage and spirit and love. Would it were so. And shame on those who would sell this view". Surprisingly though, earlier in his book he had pronounced that "Put in the parlance with which we have grown familiar, stress can make us sick and a critical shift in medicine has been the recognition that many of the damaging diseases of slow accumulation can either be caused or made worse by stress".

The preceding examples indicate that proponents of the theory of stress 'as an agent of disease' do not offer compelling evidence of such agency. Generally, the effects are inferred but not conclusively proven. With regard to mortality rates, these can hardly be a yardstick by which to measure the incidence and/or the effects of stress on morbidity and mortality in a particular country. This is probably best exemplified by what has happened in the U.S and Canada. In 1920, life expectancy was 59 years in Canada, 73 years later it had increased to 77 (*Statistics Canada*, 1998). Gist (1998) reports that in the U.S.A. it was only 54 in 1920, and that by 1995 it had risen to nearly 76 [21]. He also points out that in the 17th century, life expectancy was only 30 to 35. The figures for many other

---

[21] These figures are indicative of life expectancy at birth and would have been substantially affected by a decrease in infant mortality. Nevertheless, the increased life expectancy is still significant.

Western countries are very similar. If 'modern life' and/or stress were the main factors for an increased mortality, then it would seem that 'modern life' or stress must be non-existent in these countries or else plays an insignificant role in reducing life spans.

Some researchers have tried to link stress with particular diseases. Many diseases have been investigated but most of the attention has been directed toward those diseases perceived to be the main sources of mortality in people. Studies probing the links between stress and heart diseases as well as links with cancer dominate the field. Because of this, most of the remainder of this analysis will deal with these conditions. The role of stress in peptic ulcers will also be discussed.

Cancer

Selye (1986), despite his admission that we knew "very little about the possible relationship between stress and cancer", speculated that stress and cancer were related essentially in three ways. He proposed that cancer could produce considerable stress in patients, stress could cause or aggravate cancer and stress could inhibit or even prevent cancer. He claimed that several researchers had found that the most common precursors of cancer were the loss of a significant figure (parent, child, spouse, etc.) through death or separation, frustration of significant life situations and goals and a tendency towards despair, hopelessness and grief when encountering stress, frustration and/or loss. "Although none of them has been definitely proven, all these findings suggest that distress is a predisposing element in carcinogenesis". The absence of scientific proof did not seem to worry Rosch (1984) either, when he stated that:

> Anecdotal but irrefutable reports of cancer cures from shrines, faith healing, various non-traditional approaches such as laetrile, krebiozen, acupuncture, macrobiotic diets, etc., also suggest that the benefits derived may be due to resultant emotional or psychological attitudes rather than therapies judged to be medically worthless.

In other words, emotional or psychological attitudes could cure cancer. If there was any doubt that the reverse also applied, this was clarified by Rosch when he stated that:

While it may not be possible to scientifically define stress, it is quite clear that its hallmark is being out of control. It is becoming increasingly apparent that progressive loss of control is a characteristic of civilization and cancer rates may correlate with such stressful and disruptive effects on the 'internal environment' and homeostasis.

A few years later, Rosch (1996) appeared to have changed his mind, lamenting that:

Unfortunately, some pop psychologists and self-help zealots have gone overboard, by implying that certain types of cancer are usually stress related. Nothing could be crueler than adding to the stress and guilt of cancer patients by insinuating that their illness, or failure to improve with treatment is due to some deficiency in their character.

His sentiments were shared by Sapolsky (1994) who commented:

It is bad enough to have cancer without being led by some perversion of psychoneuroimmunology into thinking that it is your fault that you have it and that it is within your power to cure it.

It must be noted that Sapolsky believed that stress could influence some aspects of tumor growth in the laboratory setting but that these influences were not particularly strong.

Rosch's change of views (1996) seemed to have been complete when he went as far as suggesting that:

Even if we could confirm that stress-induced neuroendocrine, immune system, or other pathways that induce malignant changes, this is not proof that stress can cause cancer. It is essential to emphasize that association never proves causation, this simply signifies some statistical association, rather than proving a causative, or even contributory role.

Despite the two previous comments, he still remained attached to the view that stress must somehow still play some part in cancer:

216

Psychosocial stresses such as poverty, social isolation, and low societal status appear to be risk markers for malignancy... Various constellations of personality traits seem to be connected with increased cancer tendencies and possibly predispose to behaviors and lifestyles that are risk factors...

He stated further:

Although we cannot define stress, all of our research confirms that the sense of being out of control is always distressful. That also happens to be an accurate definition of the cancer cell.... A domineering and dogmatic determination, firm and forceful faith, and aggressive attitude, all reflect the development of a strong sense of control. These are common themes in reports of patients who triumphed over seemingly fatal malignancies.

In other words, triumph over cancer was still possible with the right attitude. If this were so, it is difficult to see how those without the 'right stuff' could escape from the feeling of guilt which Rosch was so eager to spare them.

Some researchers have investigated the mechanism by which stress might be implicated in cancer. Brown, Seggie and Ettigi (1986) have proposed that stress may influence cancer via the immune system. Cox (1984) has attempted to develop a model for stress and cancer in which stress may effect the initiation of the cancer process and thus play an etiological role. In this model, "stress may also effect the promotion of malignant transformation through the suppression of immune surveillance and play some role in the development of cancers".

However, he has conceded that the effects of stress may be small compared to those of biological events. This seems to confirm the conclusion reached by Temoshok and Heller (1984) who thought that while numerous authors had provided theory, clinical observations and research data pertinent to the relationship of psychosocial factors to cancer initiation and/or progression, no psychological construct had emerged for cancer.

A different approach has been to study the effect of stress on the progression of cancer. Anderson (cited in

217

Henderson, *Cancer Weekly plus*, 1998), in a study of women with breast cancer, found that:

This stress [of diagnosis and breast cancer surgery] can affect the immune system, possibly reducing the ability of individuals with cancer to resist disease progression and metastatic spread [the spread of cancer cells throughout the body] (1998).

Incidentally, stress in the experiment was measured by using a standardized stress test which required women to respond to such items as "I had dreams about being a cancer patient" and "I was aware that I still had a lot of feelings about cancer, but I didn't deal with them." "It actually measures traumatic stress," Andersen was quoted as saying in a telephone interview. "It's above and beyond someone feeling tense or anxious or nervous." Her conclusions were not endorsed by some of her colleagues. In the same article, Cohen and Rabin, two prominent researchers in psychoimmunology, both reported that the findings were interesting. They noted, however, that many studies had shown stress could suppress the immune system, but that these effects were short-lived and that no one had yet shown stress could make cancer worse.

Their views seem to be shared by the *U.S National Cancer institute* and the *National Institute of Health*. In an Internet Web page titled *Cancer facts*, (CancerNet, 1996) it is emphasized that the complex relationship between physical and psychological health is not well understood. Whilst acknowledging that stress may cause changes in the immune system, it is pointed out that the immune system can be affected by a number of other factors and that so far it has not been shown that stress-induced changes in the immune system directly cause cancer. The findings by some studies that have indicated an increased incidence of early death, including cancer death, among people who have experienced the recent loss of a spouse or other loved one, are dismissed as unjustified. The reason given is that most cancers have been developing for many years and are diagnosed only after they have been growing in the body for a long time (i.e. from 2 to 30 years). This fact, it is suggested, mitigates against an association between the death of a loved one and the triggering of cancer.

Cardiovascular diseases

There have been many anecdotal reports of the effects of modern life and stress on health. Tache (1977), a close collaborator of Selye, had sated that:

> Cardiovascular diseases-such as myocardial infarction and hypertension, two of the paramount killers in our age are known to be associated with stress, which ranks with smoking, overweight, and lack of physical exercise as a prime factor. The role of stress in these diseases is described by some as being that of a permissive factor and by others as that of a triggering agent.

Selye (1977) thought that even good stress "...is by definition agreeable, but if sudden and very intense, it can kill instantly, presumably as a result of cardiac fibrillation". Steppe (1993) has proposed that a limited amount of longitudinal data has suggested that people with larger than average cardiovascular reactions to mental stress were more likely to develop hypertension, particularly in the presence of other risk factors such as a high body weight and disturbances of sodium metabolism. However, in the absence of control for these two risks, some doubt must remain about these findings.

Sapolsky (1994) categorically stated that "Chronic stress causes atherosclerosis". He quoted studies with mice and primates to support his claim but none with humans. He explained:

> ...if chronic stress has made a mess of your blood vessels each individual new stressor is even more damaging, for a very insidious reason. It has to do with myocardial ischemia- a condition that arises when the arteries feeding your heart have become sufficiently clogged that the heart is partially deprived of blood flow and thus oxygen and glucose.

This, he stated, would result in angina pectoris and that "...all sorts of psychological stressors could trigger them, public speaking, pressured interviews, exams". He also claimed that the consensus among cardiologists was that sudden cardiac death was simply an extreme version of

219

acute stress causing ventricular fibrillation and severe ischemia in the heart. This meant that even joyful experiences could kill you in the same way as grief, so that a murderous rage and a thrilling orgasm might have the same effect on your coronary arteries.

He also suggested that another consequence of stress may be diabetes:

> Suppose that you're in your fifties, overweight, and just on the edge of adult-onset diabetes. Along comes a period of chronic stress; even more glucose and fatty acids in the bloodstream, plus those glucocorticoids repeatedly urging cells to listen to insulin even less. Enough of this and you pass the threshold for becoming overtly diabetic, set up for more atherosclerosic trouble.

In contrast to Sapolsky, Hinkle (1987) after reviewing the evidence available, concluded that, "So far as I am aware, the data that would allow one to obtain a quantitative answer to this hypothesis about the relation of 'stress' to illness in modern society do not exist". He explained that ischemic heart disease was much more prevalent in modern societies than it was in the past, partly because people now lived longer. Furthermore, it was a disease of well-nourished people who had a high caloric and saturated fat diet; the sort of diet prevalent in modern life. These factors, combined with a lower level of exercise, would have enhanced the probability of its occurrence. Turning his attention to both myocardial infarctions and sudden arrhythmic deaths, he pointed to a study that showed that most of them happened in the morning hours and have often seemed to happen after heated arguments, exciting events or strenuous exercise. He added:

> However, when one looks more closely at the data relating to all of these events, one sees, for example, that the vast majority of the sudden deaths that occur to people after activities such as running for a bus, or pull-starting a lawn mower, and that those who die under these circumstances have engaged in these and similar activities many times before without dying. In addition, one sees that many of the people who die suddenly, die during or after activities such as urinating or defecating, which cannot easily be considered as 'stresses' of modern life.

220

He concluded that in most cases when stress has been blamed for heart conditions, elevated blood lipids, smoking and hypertension have also been present.

Cox (1985) has also expressed some doubt. While claiming that the weight of available evidence underlines the importance of the experience of stress in coronary heart disease, he cautioned that, "...because most of the studies have been retrospective, it is not always possible to say that the reported high experience of stress was a cause or an effect of the disease". Byrne and Byrne (1990, cited in Goldstein, 1995), looking at the effects of 'stressful' life events, have found that the literature is inconsistent about whether life change inventory scores predict any specific cardiovascular morbid events.

Farber (1982) felt that factors other than stress have been neglected, particularly the fact that coronary disease tends to run in families. She quotes several studies, including hers, which have estimated blood pressure, including hypertension, to be due to heredity. She claims that despite this evidence, epidemiological studies of heart disease have preferred to focus on 'stressors' such as diet, inactivity, type A and B personalities, high cholesterol, high blood pressure, smoking, drinking.

Goldstein (1995) has made a clear distinction between people with healthy or diseased hearts. After admitting that "Whether chronic emotional stress accelerates the development of hypertension, coronary disease or any cardiovascular disorder in otherwise healthy people is unknown", he suggested that in an individual with underlying coronary heart disease, it can precipitate myocardial ischemia or sudden death. Finally all Dobson (1983) could offer to justify his claim that there was a close correspondence between stress and cardiovascular disease, was a suggestion that "...this is hardly surprising since the heart has always been regarded as the seat of emotions".

Again, there is no direct evidence of stress, in the guise of 'modern life' or of its more specific 'stressors', being the cause of heart disease. There is much anecdotal evidence, much speculation and assumptions but little proof. There is some evidence that people with an already diseased heart can suffer a heart attack. However, to suggest that in this situation, stress or any other factors, triggered the heart attack is like proposing that one drop of water (the last one) caused water in a glass to overflow, when it was the collective presence of many other drops that had made the occurrence of such event possible in the first place.

As for stress being the cause of heart disease and heart attack, consensus among cardiologists was not evident in a recent article dealing with heart attacks occurring at a relatively young age. Professor Terry Campbell, a cardiologist at St. Vincent's hospital in Sydney was reported by Nicholas (*The Sydney Morning Herald*, 1999), as saying that heart disease started when men were in their teens and early 20s, particularly if they had a family history of the illness, drank alcohol, exercised little or ate badly. Heart disease in young women, on the other hand, was extremely rare because their hormones protected them against the disease. He commented further that the notion that stress was linked to heart disease was a myth not borne out by medical evidence.

Peptic ulcers

Stomach ulceration had for a long time been the subject of much research by those interested in stress. Prompted by Selye's finding of ulcers in his experiments with rats, many experimenters have investigated the role of psychological stress in peptic ulcers but there has been some disagreement amongst them as to whether stress can cause ulcers. Dobson (1983), for instance, felt that there was no evidence to suggest that there was a direct connection between stress and ulcer formation.

Sapolsky (1994) was not sure what percentage of ulcers was caused by stress. The subject, he contended, remains highly controversial, but this did not stop him suggesting that "....stress is not at the top of list of causes, but near the top, with the capacity to worsen the effects of some of the more common causes such as genetics or diet. Surprisingly enough, it's also not yet clear how stress causes ulcers". Finally, Thompson (1988) thought that the overall pattern of findings of both laboratory and clinical studies strongly suggested that emotional states might play a part in the onset and recurrence of peptic ulcers. However, like Sapolsky, he acknowledged that identifying how this happened had proven to be extremely difficult.

The debate has now changed markedly and this is due mainly to the discovery by two scientists, Marshall and Warren, of the bacterium *Helicobacter pylori*. Marshall (1995) describes how their work, which started in 1981, culminated with the discovery that this particular bacterium may be responsible for the majority of peptic ulcers. At first it was believed that the bacterium was involved in only half of the cases of ulcers. This was because of the limitation of the original antibiotic treatments. Improvement to the treatment in the form of a cocktail of antibiotics has meant that Marshall can now claim a cure for almost 100% of peptic ulcers.

Researchers have discovered that *H. pylori* is present in nearly 100% of patients who have duodenal ulcers and 80% of those with gastric ulcers (Ateshkadi, Lam, & Johnson, 1993). Soon after, participants in a conference sponsored by the *National Institutes of Health* [NIH] concluded that *Helicobacter pylori* causes most cases of peptic ulcer disease (NIH Consensus Conference, 1994). At the same time, the U.S Food and Drug Administration approved five *H. pylori* treatment regimens.

Despite the discovery and the official recognition of the role of the bacterium, the message has been slow to reach all sections of the population. In 1994 and 1996, national surveys of primary-care physicians and gastroenterologists about knowledge of the association between *H. pylori* infection and peptic ulcers indicated that approximately 90% of these physicians identified *H. pylori* infection as the primary cause of peptic ulcers. However, the physicians reported treating approximately 50% of patients with first-time ulcer symptoms with anti-secretory agents without first testing for *H. pylori* whereas gastroenterologists reported treating approximately only 30% of these patients with these agents (Novelli, 1997).

In 1995, a study by the *American Digestive Health Foundation and Opinion Research Corporation* (1995) found that most members of the public (72%) were unaware of the association between *H. pylori* and ulcers. In 1997, another survey by the U.S. Department of Health and Human Services revealed that approximately 60% of respondents still believed that ulcers were caused by stress, while another 17% thought that the consumption of spicy foods caused peptic ulcers. The results of these surveys were instrumental in the creation of an awareness and education program.

It had seemed that the discovery of the bacterium would mean the end of research trying to prove the role of stress in producing ulcers. Spiro (1998) commented that for a long time "...the ruling notion had held that peptic ulcer represented a wound-stripe of civilization, the burden (or pride) of the ambitious, the strenuous and the hard-working—all those poor urbanized folk 'under pressure'. Now ulcer patients no longer need to reprove themselves for their pain". Not so, claims Levenstein (1998). Having in previous papers demonstrated the effect of stress on peptic ulcers, she feels that:

> The discovery that Helicobacter pylori is a cause of peptic ulcer has tempted many to conclude that psychological factors are unimportant. But this is dichotomized thinking. There is solid evidence that psychological stress triggers many ulcers and impairs response to treatment, while helicobacter is inadequate as a mono-causal explanation as most infected people do not develop ulcers.

She argues that:

By the time H. pylori had been discovered, many pieces of the ulcer puzzle, from cigarette smoking to type O blood, had already been found and fitted together, although we did not know exactly where they belonged in the larger picture.

One of the reasons she gives for urging the continuation of research on peptic ulcers is that stress was still fashionable in other areas of medical research:

Ironically, while the gastroenterological community seems to view those who have continued to support a psychosomatic etiology for Ulcer disease as stubbornly clinging to obsolete views, psychosocial factors have the glitter of novelty for researchers in other specialties, who are happily exploring whether you can die of fright or get the sniffles from stress.

While she acknowledges that "No direct data are available as yet for stress but there is no reason to expect that infection with *H. pylori* is related to any particular psychological state. In most cases, however, stress probably functions as a cofactor with *H pylori.*" But she concedes that "Again, little empirical evidence exists on the relation between stress and *H pylori*". This does not stop her however from speculating about many possibilities.

Levenstein's reaction is not totally surprising. In fact, it probably is symptomatic of most of the research that has attempted to link stress with many conditions. It must be remembered that research on peptic ulcers had started to expand in the mid 1950's. By all accounts, it can hardly be said to have been successful. After nearly 50 years, there are still more unanswered questions than there are answers. The only things that have been found are a multitude of correlations. Often, writers eager to find some signs that stress may play a role have elevated these correlations to the status of evidence. Yet no empirical evidence for a direct connection with stress is available and when such a connection is advanced, it cannot be explained. Moreover, interventions based on resulting theoretical assumptions seldom show any more than a perceived, self-reported, minor improvement in people, but never a cure.

In contrast, the discovery of *H. pylori* has resulted in the eradication of ulcers in most of the cases when the correct treatment has been applied. Here, the theory has been proved useful and practical and even Levenstein cannot argue against this, yet in order to find a role for stress, she seeks to exploit the fact that the bacterium is not always active in carriers. With no clear basis to explain that role, she is prepared to settle for an obscure cofactorial role for stress, a common occurrence in many areas of stress and disease research. However, one must wonder what benefit could result even if Levenstein were right. Even if stress were a contributing factor in the activation of *H. pylori*, this would not impact on the treatment and eventual cure. While it might be useful in terms of prevention, such prevention would require a lifetime of stress avoidance, something very difficult to achieve if stress is inevitable. On this occasion, it appears that the cure (an antibiotic treatment) might be easier than prevention.

Summing up

There is no evidence to support the view that stress causes disease. To invoke the much weaker position that stress is a cofactor or a contributing factor may be an attempt to hide the lack of evidence by confounding stress with other factors. This is reminiscent of many 'miracle' dieting products that guarantee that the product offered will help you lose weight as long as you follow a carefully controlled diet and exercise regularly. Those who do so will never know how much weight they would have lost without the product.

It should also be noted that while some studies have controlled for things such as smoking and drinking alcohol, others have included these as 'stressors'. Other alleged effects of stress such as high cholesterol, high blood pressure and diet have also been deemed to be 'stressors'. Considering the generosity with which the role of 'stressor' has been conferred, the sheer number of factors supposed to be causing stress might surely have offered ample opportunities to find a link, if such a link ever existed. Instead, the only thing stress researchers can show for their efforts over many years is a plethora of correlations. This should not be surprising. After all, most human activities involve some sort of physical changes and if enough of them are labeled 'stressful' some correlation is bound to be found.

AN ALTERNATIVE EXPLANATION

This chapter is important in several respects. It is not sufficient to just demonstrate that stress is not a useful scientific concept. It is also necessary to answer the simple question that results from this finding: if it is not stress, then what do people experience when they say they are 'stressed'? Before I begin with this task, some clarifications are needed. They are needed because the concept of 'stress' has created a great deal of confusion about many important issues. These issues therefore need to be addressed before progressing further.

The impact of life on health

Once the concept of stress is taken out of the picture, it may leave some people with the impression that the issue relating to the effect of life on health is not completely resolved. This, however, reflects two possible understandings. One is that life itself can directly be responsible for affecting our health. The other is that it is the way we respond to life events that can have such an impact.

The cause

The first possibility can only be envisaged if we accept that life, as such, is capable of such an effect. The particular concept of 'life' in this example is indicative of an abstraction. Since abstractions cannot be causal agents, an abstract 'life' cannot impact on our health. Additionally, even if we were to accept that life could have an impact on our health, we would also have to agree that the mere fact of being alive would be sufficient for such an impact to occur.

This leaves us with the second possibility. What we usually call 'life' is mostly made up of events, situations and incidents. Our responses to them can be pleasant, unpleasant or indifferent. The events, situations or incidents themselves are neutral. That is, they do not come into being with 'built-in' pleasantness, unpleasantness or indifference. We only react to various moments in our life because they have varying degrees of importance to us. That importance is mostly determined by their social significance. The more socially important an event is, the more likely it is to be reacted to in a similar fashion by many people. This is what may sometimes give the impression that there is some sort of inevitability in the emergence of a particular reaction. For example, the death of someone close is often going to be a very sad event for many people but this is not always the case. Many circumstances can affect our reaction to this particular event[22]. Despite this, many seem to accept that it is not only normal or desirable to have a specific reaction, it is also an integral part of the event. This acceptance has led to claims that some events are 'stressful' or 'traumatic' when in fact they only appear to be so only because we confer them such 'qualities'. We only do so, however, when these events have a personal impact on us. Considering someone dying again, unless that person is known to us or liked by us, we are unlikely to react.

The effect

Now that we know that our reactions to events rather than the events themselves are what we need to understand, we should turn our attention to the impact these reactions have on people. On which basis, can it be asserted that our reactions to events impact on our health. Surely, it cannot be on the evidence available. The preceding chapters have shown that there is no conclusive evidence that stress has any detrimental effect on our health. Most of what has been deemed to be stress has involved mostly negative reactions to specific events. Therefore, these events as given examples of stress, cannot be linked to poorer health.

This is not to say that our reactions to events do not have an effect on our well-being. Indeed, reactions to various events often result in varying degrees of physical reactions. This seems to occur regardless of the quality of these reactions.

---

[22] Many of these circumstances were discussed in the section on the live events approach in the chapter on *Other theories*

Positive, as well as negative reactions seem to elicit physical effects. Crying and laughing both involve physical changes. It is worth noting that crying can sometimes produce a soothing experience, whereas laughing, especially in its hysterical form, can sometimes become physically unbearable. This serves to show that while most of the time there is a similarity to the quality of both the response and its physical equivalent, this is not always the case. In other words, a pleasant response cannot always be guaranteed to be accompanied by a pleasant state of being, nor an unpleasant response by an unpleasant state.

To say that reactions, be they feelings or emotions, have an effect on our well-being does not automatically mean that they affect our health. I previously discussed how easily we can be mistaken to think that the way we feel is also the way we are. In doing so I pointed out how in everyday language we commonly ask sick people how they feel. This often results in the notions of 'sickness' and 'feeling' being easily confused. The same can be said about 'well-being' and 'sickness' and other concepts like 'illness' and 'disease'. Not only are these words often interchanged in everyday conversations, feeling unwell is usually interpreted as being ill or sick. Under these circumstances, it becomes quite difficult for people to truly understand the nature of their feelings. Many of us have experienced feeling a bit strange and then worrying about it and feeling even worse. When this happens it also becomes difficult to pin point what we are actually feeling. Our confusion about what it is we are feeling makes it possible to believe the view that negative reactions will ultimately end up making us sick and even kill us.

Our impression of well-being, however, has more to do with our level of comfort than our health. A violent bout of screaming can be quite exhausting and make us feel very uncomfortable. Likewise, feeling sad or unhappy can make us feel sometimes that life is not really worth living. Incidentally, in times of sickness the same unhappy feeling can be experienced. Once again, the similarity adds to our confusion. Most of that confusion revolves around the

229

notion of 'feel'. We use the words 'feel' and 'feeling' in many different circumstances and in relation to various phenomena so that it is hardly surprising that confusion would result.

The various use of the term 'feel'

Physical 'feel'

The verb 'feel' and the noun 'feeling' are used in many different situations. We can indeed feel in a physical sense. We can, for instance, feel (touch) a piece of wood and a piece of metal and be aware that they are different in terms of their surface, their temperature or even their respective weight. We can also feel that someone is touching us, providing our senses are not impaired in any way. A crack on the wall can be detected by feel (touch). We can feel (experience) the wind and humidity, the heat and the cold as well as pins and needles or numbness. We also feel (experience) pain, tiredness, hunger and thirst or cramps in our stomach or elsewhere. In the latter example, it must be said that what we feel is not really hunger but hunger pangs. Likewise, we do not truly feel thirsty but we experience a dryness in our mouth which we recognize as a sign of being thirsty.

Psychological 'feel'

When we feel happy, unhappy, disappointed, sad or ecstatic are these the same feelings as those we have when we feel rejected, ignored, isolated or even a sense of relief? It seems that in the first group what we are describing are our moods, i.e. what we think we are experiencing. The second group, on the other hand, seems to refer to our judgment, impression or awareness about particular situations. In these cases, 'feel' is used as a substitute for 'think'. Similarly, we can feel the importance of the moment, that it is time to go or that things will be fine eventually. In these cases, 'feel' becomes synonymous with 'realize'. Finally, we can also feel good, bad or indifferent about something.

The superimposing of physical and psychological 'feel'

On certain occasions, because of our lack of attention regarding the demarcation between the two broad meanings of 'feel', we are not aware of the distinction between them. This is probably best evidenced by situations during which a physical sensation is followed soon after by an anxious response. Say we feel some pain in our chest. We may become more aware of our heart and start to worry about a potential problem with our heart.

There are, however, times when physical and psychological 'feelings' are more difficult to separate. When you are cold or tired for instance, you have some psychological feelings about the fact that you are cold or tired. You may, for instance, be unhappy about experiencing these states. Similarly, if you were hungry, you would first experience hunger pangs but they may soon be accompanied by the feeling that you need some food rather urgently. The longer you have to wait the worse it gets, yet, you may have noticed that if you are busy with other preoccupations, the hunger pangs eventually disappear.

There are indeed countless occasions when physical and psychological feelings can be easily intertwined. This is mostly due to our lack of awareness between abstract and physical experiences. Ever since our introduction to the world, abstractions and physical objects have never been properly differentiated. This has resulted in a perception that feelings are always physical. To most people, all the experiences that can be labeled 'feelings' seem to have blended into one. For most people, it seems that just as the presence of a name always gives the impression that it must have a physical existence, the presence of a feeling seems to have the same effect. In both situations, the abstract nature of what is being described makes it possible. With feelings, the confusion is greater simply because when we feel psychologically, this may lead to physical reactions in the form of releases of additional hormones and neurotransmitters

Consequences of our reactions

I have demonstrated that life itself cannot have any impact on our health but that our reactions to events in our life can have an effect on our well-being. Furthermore, I have argued that well-being and health are different and separate phenomena. What does this mean for the way we deal with these reactions?

Accepting that various reactions to events do not have a detrimental effect on our health does not mean that it is no longer necessary to be concerned about their effects. Physical health is only one facet, albeit an important one, of human existence. Another important aspect is psychological well-being. Because what we call 'life' is the total sum of our experiences, the way we feel psychologically about such a life or rather about the events that are part of it, is vital in evaluating the quality of our life. A life evaluated as being unpleasant would not be coveted by most people. Most of us aspire to some degree of psychological comfort in our life. This comfort is very important. Without it, performance of everyday tasks, or indeed of any tasks, is more difficult. It is only when we are comfortable that can we function easily. People rarely perform adequately when feeling embarrassed, self-conscious, nervous or worried.

Once we accept that discomfort rather than ill heath should be our main preoccupation, we can begin to investigate the source of such discomfort.

The importance of feelings and emotions

So far I have spoken mostly about reactions rather than feelings and emotions. This is because feelings and emotions are also abstractions. There have been many attempts to define and distinguish both but it is not so easy to differentiate between them. Are emotions also feelings? After all, we feel emotions don't we? Yet, it is difficult to know whether we experience them physically or psychologically. There have also been theories questioning whether the physical aspect comes before the psychological

232

one or whether the reverse occurs. There have also been discussions debating whether individual emotions are feelings or states. In fact, much of the research on emotions has been concerned with trying to understand the nature of emotions and as well as their display. Less attention, however, has been devoted to the role and sources of emotions in our social life.

The problem for researchers involved in the study of emotions and feelings is that there is as much difficulty determining what emotions and feelings are as there is demonstrating what stress is. While it may be easier to get agreement among people as to what emotions and feelings are, since they are more specific than stress, many difficulties still exist when trying to explain them clearly.

Individual 'feelings' and 'emotions' are really just labels for reactions to events or things in our lives. To be jealous is understood by most people to mean that people so labeled are envious of someone or are concerned about their partner's loyalty. To be angry is often recognized by some accepted signs. These may include facial or bodily reactions, screaming, swear words and tone of voice. These observable signs lead us to conclude that anger is a physical phenomenon not than the abstraction that it is. Indeed, we can never see anger itself or any other emotions. All we can do is assume their existence.

I do not deny that emotion and feeling labels are quite useful as explanations of behavior in everyday life. However, in our present discussion these labels are not useful. Furthermore, not using them makes it possible to avoid all the possible pitfalls a discussion of feelings and emotions could bring. For the purpose of this discussion, labeling these reactions does not improve the analysis. If anything, it is more likely to confuse the picture by detracting from the more important issue. What is important in this context, is not what specific emotion is involved but rather what effect experiencing any reaction could have on our level of comfort.

The role of reactions in our life

There seems little doubt that reactions play an important part in our life. Because these reactions are closely related to the way we interpret events, they make life more interesting. We interpret events in relation to their importance to us. If few things are of interest, we get a reaction we label as 'boredom'. The reverse, of course, brings great excitement. Despite this up and down effect, reactions are very much part of human social life. Without them, life would seem very dull. It could be argued that we do not really need negative reactions and that life would be much more pleasant without them. Although we don't need misery, we do at least need some sort of contrast between reactions. In order to recognize that some reactions are pleasant, we need some less pleasant ones to compare them to. Even a life of constant bliss could end up being labeled as 'boring'. If we always got what we wanted immediately, we would eventually cease to appreciate most of what we had.

It appears that we need some variety in our life to make it more exciting. This does not mean that we need unpleasantness. Unpleasant reactions, are the ones we will investigate because they are the cause of our discomfort.

Another interesting aspect of reactions, when labeled 'feelings' or 'emotions', is our attitudes towards them. In many cultures, the attitude is ambivalent. In these cultures, feelings and emotions are often contrasted with logical and rational thinking. It is often believed that the two are not compatible. Objective thinking is often thought only possible when devoid of feelings or emotions. To be described as being 'too emotional' usually indicates a judgment of inadequate or inappropriate behavior. Indeed in most cultures, the propriety of emotional display is fairly regulated. It is more acceptable, for example, for women to openly display emotions, yet this often results in women being burdened with the 'too emotional' tag.

The fact that we can accuse people of 'over-reacting' shows that there are certain assumed relationships between events and reactions. The appropriate relationship, however, is often a matter of personal and self-interested judgment.

There are also definite social situations in which the display of emotions and feelings is deemed necessary while being frowned upon in others. For example, it would not only be acceptable for both parents of a dead child to display very strong emotions and feelings, it would be highly expected. Alternatively, screaming or crying in the presence of a customer would be considered so inappropriate that it could lead to the dismissal of an employee..

Nevertheless, reactions are here to stay. For better or for worse, we need our feelings or emotions. The question, therefore, becomes how do we deal with them so that our comfort is not too compromised. The answer to this question lies with the way these reactions come into being.

The source of reactions

The frequent labeling of events as 'traumatic', 'distressing', 'tragedies' or 'unpleasant' has meant that little attention has been paid to the origin of our reactions. To many people, reactions are an inevitable consequence of certain events occurring. For that reason, the event is seen as the cause of our reaction. The seemingly direct link between event and reaction is not as direct as may first appear. If the reaction depends, as it does, on the way we appreciate a particular event, such a reaction is more directly linked to our appreciation than it is to the event itself.

Interestingly, our appreciation sometimes differs when compared to that of other people. It is common knowledge that various events provoke a different response from various people. In some cases, no response occurs. If there are variations in appreciation then this is what needs to be investigated. Understanding not only how but why reactions occur or fail to occur becomes necessary.

Factors that affect appreciation

Our appreciation of various events is largely influenced by the extent to which they are important to us. As I suggested earlier, in some situations we are expected to react and in others we are not. In between, there are many situations to which we can more or less react according to our personal choice. There is, however, a common denominator to all our reactions. Whether we react as we should or whether we do it as we please, we only react when we have expectations about a given situation. When we have no expectation, we don't really care and therefore don't react.

Expectations are guided mostly by the way we have been socialized. Once we have accepted some state of affairs as true or valid, we expect it to occur as we have been led to believe. Those who believe in justice are likely to be upset when their expectation is not fulfilled (injustice). The greater the belief in 'justice', the greater the upset. Additionally, the extent to which the injustice affects an individual personally also has a bearing on the intensity of the reaction.

This example may be useful to better understand what is meant by 'socialization' in this instance. We are told about justice and all the related issues that are connected with it. The concept is closely tied up to the concepts of 'fairness', 'right' and 'appropriateness'. When justice occurs the bad get punished and the good get rewarded. As children we are often told that bad people get punished and that good people always win the day. The same view is heavily promoted in movies, television series and books. The good guy always wins, even despite the odds. The constant reminders through various media means that many people believe in justice. Consequently, some people feel that they have a strong sense of justice, when in fact what they really have are strong expectations about justice.

In would be fair to say that the stronger people's expectations are, the stronger their reactions will be. This can apply to expectations about other facets of life. If you strongly expect, for example, that Christmas should be spent with your family, being alone at that time would engender a very negative reaction.

You may have noticed that the word 'should' was used in the previous sentence. The term is often used in connection with expectations. This is because by definition, expectations convey notions of 'certainty' and 'obligation'. A certainty that not only whatever you expect will happen, but also that it should or must happen. The 'should' or 'must' part of an expectation is what creates the most basic negative reaction which we label 'disappointment'. Once we have expectations, we want them or need them to be fulfilled.

Fulfilment of expectations

Expectations do not necessarily have to be fulfilled to bring on a positive response. In effect, an expectation that things will go wrong can bring a positive reaction if it is not fulfilled. There seems to be a mathematical pattern with expectations and fulfillment.

A positive expectation (+) positively fulfilled (+) brings on a positive (+) reaction. Something we want to happen, happens and we are pleased.

A negative expectation (-) positively fulfilled (+) brings on a negative (-) reaction. Something we don't want to see happen, happens and we are displeased.

A negative expectation (-) negatively fulfilled (-) brings on a positive (+) reaction. Something we don't want to happen, does not happen and we are pleased.

A positive expectation (+) negatively fulfilled (-) brings on a negative (-) reaction. Something we want to see happen, does not happen and we are displeased.

Reactions to events

When we consider reactions in relation to our psychological well-being, two factors seem to be of importance: namely intensity and duration. As the duration of a negative reaction to an event increases, there is a greater likelihood that it will start to impact adversely on the life of the person experiencing it. The impact can also be greater if the event is of great importance to the person (e g: loss of someone close) and results in an a very intense reaction..

It seems from this that intensity and duration together with high levels of expectations are the main three factors that could be manipulated in situations where individuals feel so overwhelmed that they can no longer function adequately.

Inadequate functioning is the key to whether some form of intervention is needed. Most of us experience negative reactions just as much as we do positive ones. This is part of social human life. Various reactions to events, not 'stress', makes life interesting. Generally, most of the time, people are able to cope with most situations in the long run or even adapt to what have been dramatic events for them.

In some cases, however, problems do occur. When nothing is important and we don't care about anything around us, we also react negatively. The ups and downs of life are often reactions to events people have little control over. At times individuals experience more downs than ups over a certain period, sometimes to the point when they can no longer react positively to things as they once did. In such situations, labeling their states as either 'depression' or 'stress' and blaming their conditions on some sort of vague unproven biological imbalance or weakness in personality, will not be of great assistance, neither will the prescription of sedatives or anti-depressant medication.

What may be more useful is to help people understand what is taking place and why it is taking place. Rather than treating symptoms, the legitimate causes can be investigated so that the correct solution can then be applied. This approach is more likely to eliminate the problem rather than just contain it. This may not be of great benefit to the many people making a living out of the 'stress' or 'depression' industry, but it would undoubtedly be very welcome by the many people left to 'helplessly' cope.

The situations described above are not diseases or conditions. They are states of mind. So-called 'psychosomatic diseases' are not diseases, they are about how we feel, not about how we are. If states can be caused by our imagination, then surely not using our imagination will result in these states not occurring. The important thing to remember here is that the way we react is responsible for us feeling unwell. Furthermore, our imagination can be used to make us feel good or bad.

The role of imagination in "mental conditions"

We seldom realize the extent to which we use our imagination in making ourselves unhappy or even happy. We have the ability to imagine unpleasant past events and re-live them repeatedly. We can also imagine various possibilities what could occur in the future. With the former, usually labeled as 'trauma', we can also re-live the feelings and sensations that had been previously experienced. With the latter, we can feel as if the event was already taking place. Imagining and reacting in the future is usually described as 'daydreaming' for pleasurable experiences and 'worry', 'apprehension', 'anxiety' and 'fear' when it involves undesirable experiences.

Trauma

In most cases of trauma, the event or situation that caused the trauma has finished, sometimes a long time ago. By re-living and experiencing the feelings, the individual continues the experience and its effects. It seems rather puzzling why people would want to keep re-igniting the unpleasantness but it is not difficult to understand if we consider the way we deal with these events. Often we treat the event as the cause of the problem. Rape, war, natural disasters and child abuse are often cited as major causes of trauma. When people have been involved in such situations, it is not only assumed that they must have been traumatized, we expect it. This is evidenced by a tendency to send counselors to the scene of man-made or natural disasters. In many instances, people are counseled whether they asked to be or not. These events receive a great deal of media attention and assist in the perception that they are 'traumatic' events which, as their name indicates must, traumatize people.

This tendency to attribute events with 'traumatic', 'stressful', 'saddening' or 'shocking' qualities, which they

239

cannot possess, reinforces the view that events not people's reactions to them are responsible for various psychological states. Because of this and the tendency of therapists and the media to legitimize and encourage the expression of 'traumatized' behavior, most people do not seem to be aware that they, in fact, traumatize themselves by re-living and hence re-experiencing all the reactions of the original events.

Whenever this is pointed out to people, it seems to be a genuine revelation. This is not to say that forgetting events we found extremely unpleasant will always be easy but accepting that the event is no longer taking place and that we are solely responsible for its imaginary continuity would seem to be an important starting point for recovery.

Psychological injury

Sometimes 'conditions' like trauma, stress and anxiety have also been labeled psychological injuries. The concept of 'psychological injury' is misleading in the sense that it gives the impression that actual injury has occurred in the mind when what we are mostly dealing with are unpleasant memories. What renders these memories unpleasant is that they relate to events that fulfil some of our probably most unwanted expectations. These events are re-visited and experienced repeatedly, as if in a state of disbelief that these events could have ever taken place.

The metaphorical use of the term 'injury' also implies that something physical is taking place in the mind. This is not entirely surprising considering that often writers studying emotions will often personify them by talking of the neurobiology, psychobiology or even biology of emotions. What these writers fail to understand is that biological factors are a part of us and not a part of our emotions

Worry, apprehension, anxiety and fear

These labels are usually used when dealing with future undesirable events. The events are imagined together with their possible unwanted consequences. When this happens, the reactions are similar to those that would normally be experienced should the situation actually occur as imagined. This may happen repeatedly over a period of time. In many cases, the unwanted event never eventuates, so that the 'imagined' reactions have created unnecessary unpleasantness. Often these repeated imagined reactions can be strong enough to affect comfortable functioning. Worry, apprehension, anxiety and fear express different nuances of the same phenomenon: the contemplation of the occurrence of undesired events accompanied by reactions similar to those that would take place should they actually occur.

Pressure, tension and self-consciousness

Imagination also makes it possible to feel pressure or feel the tension 'in the air' when none is present. In fact, even in situations when most people would agree that there is pressure or tension, it is only a metaphorical explanation of what is really taking place. What is usually taking place is that the outcome of a potential event is of great significance for the individual or individuals involved. Until the outcome becomes known, the people involved with the event are tense and apprehensive. The tension is not 'in the air' or in the situation but in people's muscles, with their imagination doing the rest. Furthermore, tension is usually 'felt' when there is a fear that expectations will not be fulfilled.

Imagination also plays a part if we were to fall in public. Most people would be embarrassed simply because they would think that everyone witnessing the incident would think they were clumsy or silly. (people falling on their face are a great source of fun in comedy). They would probably be convinced that everyone not only has noticed their fall but also that those witnessing the incident would care. Yet we know, from our own experience as a witness of this sort of incident, that when we see people falling we are more likely to be concerned about their welfare. So in this instance, accepting that falling in public is 'embarrassing', creates an unjustified and unnecessary unpleasant reaction.

Similarly, imagination plays a part in the placebo effect. Taking a sugar pill in experiments sometimes has been known to make someone feel better merely because they think this will cure them. It must be noted that this will only work if the condition was itself one that was brought about by imagination to begin with. Conditions that have been labeled psychosomatic are not so much instances of the mind causing disease but of our imagination first making possible the impression that we are sick[23]. and later making us feel that we are better. In other instances, what we call the placebo effect is just a case of feeling better rather than being better.

The placebo effect is not a case of mind over matter as some people would suggest but rather a case of mind over mind. If it was a case of mind over matter then just putting a non-active cream on a wound would make it heal quicker when the patient believed it would. Most examples of placebo effects involve two types of experiments: One when the patient's belief has affected the way they feel; the other when the patient's belief has resulted in a subtle change of behavior which may have contributed to an improvement in their behavior.

Putting it together

I have argued that what we experience when we are uncomfortable can be explained by understanding the factors involved in our reactions to events. I have suggested the following sequences:

Socialization results in expectations. Expectations are either fulfilled or not. Whenever positive expectations are not fulfilled or negative ones are fulfilled, we have a negative reaction. Imagination often plays a part in the whole process by making the psychological appear physical. It also makes it possible to continue reacting after an event is finished or to react by anticipating what could occur, even though it may never happen.

---

[23] This was discussed in the *Historical Perspective* chapter.

All that is needed now, is to discuss what can be done to impact on the various factors involved in our potential discomfort.

The danger of prescription

One thing must be understood before discussing any solution to deal with adverse reactions,. I am not going to suggest that you have to, or should, do anything. Neither should you think that should or have to anything. The reason for this is quite simple. To propose that you should do anything, should you accept it as correct, can only create an expectation. The expectation here might be that you should be able to all the things that are suggested. Should you for some reason not be able to do them, this would bring a negative reaction.

This has already happened to most people. Anything, we feel bad or guilty about is related to something we could not do while believing that we should. If this happens too many times it can lead to sentiments of failure, inadequacy or of being overwhelmed by events. This is exactly what the concept of 'stress' is trying to explain. This is the very problem that is being addressed here.

I am suggesting that many of the problems the concept of 'stress' was trying to deal with were problems of prescription. If this is so, the last thing any of us need is more prescription. This is why I want to make it absolutely clear that the advice or solution to the problem at hand is to be followed, only if and when the need and desire to solve it arises. In other words, I am not saying that you should do what I am saying but you can try. The choice is yours. If in your particular situation, the cure should turn out to be worse that the condition, you are better off leaving it as it is. You will feel more comfortable because it will be your decision. Being in control of situations is a very important part of being comfortable.

For example, say you had a problem at work and you need to confront the boss. However, if you realized that the prospect of doing so was more uncomfortable than living with the problem, you would probably be much better off not confronting the boss. Realizing and accepting what you can or want to do, on the balance of things, sometimes makes the situation less overwhelming and easier to accept.

How to deal with discomfort

We often feel uncomfortable. Sometimes, the discomfort is mild and/or of a short duration. When this happens, it does not really present a problem. At other times, however, discomfort can be so strong or over too long a period that it becomes a problem. In these situations, it begins to affect your everyday functioning. This is when you may feel a need to redress the situation. These are the basic options that are available to you:

1-Lower the level of expectations

2-Try to decrease the intensity of the reaction

3-Try to reduce the duration of the reaction

It is important to realize that all this can only be done gradually over a relatively long period of time. No one can instantly forget many years of habitual living and reacting. It is never that easy but it does not mean that it is hard work. It will also be much easier to do if and when a strong desire to change is present.

Lowering the level of expectations

If high positive expectations results in strong negative reactions when not fulfilled, it makes a great deal of sense to try to reduce their levels. This is not suggesting that this should be done immediately since this would be very difficult. Instead, expectations can be lowered gradually over time. Many people do that over a life time. As children, most of us had very high expectations. Most children, you may have noticed, largely think in black and white terms. For many children, things are either good or bad or right or wrong. There is little in between. By the time the child becomes a teenager and then an adult, many of the expectations have been greatly toned down.

244

A good example of this is our attitude about being told the truth.. Most young children tend to believe what they are told. Adults, on the other hand, tend to be more cautious when deciding whether to believe what they are being told. The reactions of adults are often explained by suggesting that they are more cynical than children. Whether people's caution in accepting explanations reflect cynicism or realism is not the main issue. The more important consideration here is that most of us lower our expectations when we have reasons to believe that they are either too high or unrealistic.

Repeated disappointments are common when expectations have not been fulfilled. Eventually, it becomes evident that there is little likelihood that they will ever be fulfilled. Having a high expectation that people should always tell the truth will often result in great disappointment.

The problem with having to wait for repeated non-fulfilment of our expectations is that sometimes we still react strongly while we are waiting to get the message. Furthermore, there are some expectations we do not really want to lower. These barriers, however, are not insurmountable.

Remembering that the purpose of lowering our expectations is not to stop reacting altogether but rather to lessen the impact of the reactions so that they no longer stop us from functioning habitually. With that in mind, all that needs to be considered are mostly the reactions that have such an impact. Once the causes (the expectations) of these reactions are found, it becomes obvious which ones need to be lowered. Often, it will be evident that these expectations have seldom been fulfilled in the past and have often resulted in unpleasant reactions. Such a realization will make it easier to lower them.

Intensity of the reaction

There may be, for a multitude of reasons, a difficulty in lowering expectations. We do not usually, for instance, expect someone close and dear to die suddenly. No matter

245

how much we could try, it is not an expectation that could be easy to tone down. In this sort of situation, the intensity of the reaction will be great. In some cases, it may not just be the loss of a dear one, it may also be all the implications that accompany such a loss. Someone losing a partner, would indeed, react to many of the aspects of that loss.

It is notable, however, how people still manage to control their reactions to the loss of someone close. It is evident that the greater the attachment, the more intense the reaction is. Controlling the reaction can be somewhat tricky. Controlling too much can result in denial or in delaying the outcome.

Reactions are better expressed to their fullest. Restraining reactions can sometimes lead to greater problems than those resulting from the full expression of the original reaction. If something did upset you repeatedly, for example and you didn't say anything, eventually, not having said how you felt may add other reactions such as frustration, annoyance and feeling that you should have said something. Often in these situations, saying something becomes increasingly difficult and creates even more frustration.

In most circumstances, reacting strongly will be better than reacting in a restrained manner. It is after all difficult to react strongly forever. How long for instance, can one scream or cry? Surely there must be a limit. In fact, you often hear of people saying that they have run out of tears.

The duration of the reaction

The duration aspect of reactions is probably the most significant after that of lowering expectations. Lowering expectations sufficiently will eliminate the problem altogether but when this is not possible, the shortening of the duration is likely to be the next most beneficial.

There are many reasons why people react to an event for a long time. In the previous example of someone losing someone close and dear, the loss may be perceived to be so great that it takes a very long time to get over it. This is when long term problems can occur.

If it is agreed that unpleasant reactions can affect our normal functioning, the longer such reactions last, the longer our discomfort will last. This is why it is important to shorten the duration of our reactions. So what factors that will help here?

Expressing reactions to their fullest has already been discussed in the previous section. That in itself should help reduce the duration. Also of help is to remember what whilst reactions can last a long time, the events that brought them about are often quickly over. In other words, our reactions more often than not outlive the events which made them possible. In many, but not in all cases, it is only our imagination that continues our reactions by reliving the event constantly and reacting as if it was still happening. Realizing that this is what is taking place can help reduce the intensity.

On other occasions, we may look at the reasons for our reactions. If they do not make sense, this can help. For example, it could be something someone did to us. In such cases, continuing our discomfort means that someone is getting to us in two ways. The first is by what they did to us and the second is that by continuing our reaction we indirectly let them get to us for even longer. In a way, we are helping them prolong the effects of what they did to us.

Ultimately, the key to reducing the duration of a reaction is to accept what took place. To do this means also accepting the consequences of what took place. While it may not be easy, it is in no way impossible. People are remarkably resilient. Most of the time, they realize that sooner or later, they will have to get on with their life. This is especially true when other people are involved.

We often hear of people getting over their grief, for instance, because they felt they had to be strong for other people who were also affected by the situation. It seems that in these situations, the strong desire to function comfortably is forced upon them. It is also possible that

247

while they are busy helping others cope, they do not have time to reminisce. They do not have time to relive and re-experience. If people cope when others are involved, one would think that it would be reasonable to expect people to do for themselves what they can do for others. Yet many do not seem to realize that they can have some control over their reactions.

It is notable, that many people have an 'all or nothing' attitude towards emotions and feelings but this is not necessary. There is no weakness in having emotions and feelings, nor is there any reward for controlling them. There is no need to control our feelings. What we need is to make sure that we do not contribute to our misery by acting as if our feelings were inevitable. After all, when reactions are disrobed of their social decoration, their mechanism can be understood and acted upon. Once we understand and accept that we alone are making these reactions possible, it is easier for us to stop them from making our life more difficult than it need be.

Summing up

I have outlined the process which makes the reactions we label 'emotions' or 'feelings' possible. I have argued that we need these reactions to make our life interesting. I have also argued that it is only when these reactions make our life difficult to the point where we can no longer function comfortably that we should do something to redress the situation.

There are three basic elements that can be manipulated to that end. I have explained that we already do some of the things that can help._Once we realize that some of our reactions are the source of our problems, we can become aware of another important fact: Wittingly or wittingly, *WE* react. Indeed *NOTHING* makes us react. There is no inevitability about reacting. This is best evidenced by the fact that not everyone reacts similarly to the same event. If *WE* react, *WE* therefore make ourselves unhappy but the good news is that *WE* can also stop it if *WE* really want to.

It may not be easy but it can be done. It may take a while to get better at it but it can be done.

Undoubtedly, talks of pseudo-diseases like depression and stress have convinced many people that they are powerless to act. Once they have been told that they are suffering a medical condition, they have no reason to find ways of counteracting these diseases. These conditions seem very attractive at first. They offer us something else to blame for the guilt felt at not being able to fulfil many of the highly idealistic social expectations. To be told it is not our fault, has lured many people into a false sense of short term security. The many pills that are being swallowed to provide this sense of security are the most convincing evidence yet that they are not the solution to the problem.

A young girl I was helping, told me that once she asked her psychiatrist how long would she have to take the antidepressant medication she had just been prescribed. She was told, "it is hard to say. It depends". Asking what it depended on, she was puzzled by the reply: "It depends on how long it will take you to get better". Surely if these pills were the answer, there would be no need to keep taking them and hence using them as a perpetual crush. It seems that we are only condemned to a lifetime of pills and their accompanying side-effects when the cause of our problems have not been found. Dealing with the symptoms seems to be an acknowledgment of such failure.

CONCLUSION

The word 'stress' originally meant hardship and difficulties. Engineers borrowed the term to determine a pressure or a force, while biologists adopted the hardship version. However Hans Selye changed all that. In developing a theory of stress, he created a totally new meaning for stress and also offered a new possible explanation for a somatic view of illness. This theory filled the vacuum left by the demise of vapors, nerves, neurasthenia, psychasthenia and nervous tension. It gave psychosomatic medicine a much needed boost after the decline of psychoanalysis. From its modest origin under the name of 'G.A.S' in 1936, it would be twenty years before it became popularized as 'stress' and another 20 years before the media and ultimately the public would adopt the concept. This adoption would be so complete that many people today can no longer imagine a world without stress. In fact, there are now suggestions that stress has always been part of life and that even cavemen suffered their own version of stress. These are contrasted by declarations that stress is the epidemic of modern times. This book has shed some light on this debate and shown that there has been indeed a preoccupation with trying to understand the relationship between the performance of human social life and health. The concept of 'stress', as an explanation for the consequences of such a relationship, is relatively recent and was preceded by many other concepts which ultimately failed to provide a satisfactory explanation. Stress, it would appear, is doomed to the same fate.

An analysis of some of the stress theories has shown that a great deal of confusion, regarding the nature of stress, still persists. Selye's original formulation was soon followed by other researchers who attempted to remedy some of the obvious problems and contradictions of his theory. Yet instead of clarifying Selye's views, they introduced more contradictions which Selye himself was quick to embrace in his obvious pride at seeing the growing popularity of the concept. In some of his writings he would provide the latest overall tally of publications about stress (Selye, foreword in Albrecht, 1979; Selye, 1986). More than 44 years after the publication of *The Stress of Life,* little progress has been made in understanding what stress is or does. Indeed many of the original issues involved in the stress debate have still not been resolved and are unlikely to be so. Many medical, neurological, endocrinological, immunological and psychoneuroimmunological studies have become increasingly sophisticated. Understanding their findings has become increasingly beyond the reach of lay people. They hide, however, some basic problems. The most important is that stress is not a legitimate scientific concept. It is flawed in many ways. It was doomed from the beginning because stress was always an invention, a creation. It was born out of the failure of Hans Selye to discover a new sex hormone. When he could not find a new scientific fact, he invented one. Based on the idea that sick people seem to suffer a common syndrome of 'being sick', he proposed his theory of General Adaptation Syndrome. It was many years later that the term 'stress' was somehow added to this syndrome where it fitted rather uncomfortably[24]. Even Cannon, whom Selye admired, could not agree with his theory. It is therefore ironical that many years later Cannon would be credited with the co-invention of the 'stress' concept or as being one of its pioneers. Cannon's inclusion in the stress debate has meant that the stress response has often been likened to the 'flight or fight' response. Yet, it has been shown that many so-called 'stressful' episodes do not involve a 'flight or fight' response.

The concept of 'appraisal' introduced by Lazarus (1966) should have meant the end of the notions of 'stressor' or of 'stressful life since that concept and these two notions are mutually exclusive. Yet these terms have continued to co-exist and have often been used together in explanations of stress. It has also been shown that the theory underpinning

---

[24] In his early work, he had described stress as a cause of the GAS, later it would become unclear what the relationship between them was.

the view that we need some stress but not too much was fatally flawed because it confused an awakened state with an excited one. Furthermore, the analysis of attempts by Wheaton and Goldstein, to create new models of stress, has emphasized that no matter how sophisticated these theories have become they cannot ultimately render stress coherent.. Goldstein after promising a more appropriate explanation of stress could, by his own admission, only offer speculation.

Finally, Albrecht's elucidation of stress was presented because it was representative of depictions of stress which serve to frighten people into a cure for the treatment of a 'devastating epidemic invading the world'. That Selye would support such an endeavor says much about him. Nevertheless, an analysis of the various theories and stress-related concepts has shown that despite many years of research in the field, the concept of 'stress' is, if anything, less coherent or useful. Kasl (1996) gave some pertinent reasons as to why the concept has ceased to be useful:

> It would seem that the concept of stress has served us well in the past in directing us to additional situations and experiences and psychosocial characteristics of individuals… However, these aspects of usefulness of the concept may be seen as reflecting the earlier stages of research with a broad concept, when the integrative function of a concept and the hypotheses it generates are particularly important. But as a particular research domain matures, we expect the concept to help us fine tune the theory and to guide us towards sharper differentiation from other concepts and towards more precise measurements. However, it does not appear that in this sense the concept of 'stress' has continued to be useful with the greater maturity of the stress and health research domain.

Three other aspects of the present analysis have also proven to be problematic for the concept of 'stress'. The first has been that 'stress' is not only an abstract concept, it is also a broad concept. The vagueness of such concepts makes the search for a universally agreed definition impossible. Secondly, there is the teleological nature of the 'stress' concept and of the related concepts of homeostasis and adaptation. The purpose that these theories have proposed has not been proven, nor have they been adequately explained. Moreover, the existence of a purpose can never be scientifically demonstrated. The same in fact can be said about the third aspect: the use of animals in experiments trying to investigate responses to psychological stress. These studies have assumed one of two things: either that physical stress is no different to psychological stress or that animals have emotions and/or cognition similar to that of people.

It has been argued that various physical events were often quite different from each other and that the same was true for psychological events. Furthermore, it was demonstrated that physical and psychological events are experienced differently. It was also argued that we can never know whether animals have emotions, and that if they did, these might differ from ours. The same conclusion was reached for cognition. For these reasons, it is concluded that animal experiments are of little value in understanding the effects of psychological stress on people and this does not even take into account inter-species physiological differences.

Even if the lack of usefulness of animal studies is overlooked, there are still more difficulties to be encountered when trying to evaluate the alleged effects of stress. It has been demonstrated that the choice of variables is always problematic. In the absence of a definition that can be agreed upon, determining what constitutes stress would always prove to be a challenge. However, some stress scientists have tried to overcome the problem by deciding that anything unpleasant or adverse could qualify as a 'stressor'. Others have implicitly accepted that certain changes are signs of stress and therefore anything that causes those changes must be stress. The problem with the former is that unpleasantness and adversity can range from minimal to extreme. As for the latter, many 'non-stressful' events or conditions can produce physiological changes. Ultimately, the result is the same, with both of them mislabeling an event as 'stress'. All that can be shown is some correlation. In crude terms, all that has been found is that an event labeled as 'stress' has occurred before an biological change that has been theorized to be a sign of experiencing stress. In situations when findings have not fulfilled expectations or have been found to contradict other studies, this has been rationalized as a sign of variability among 'stressors'. However, the potential usefulness of the concept of 'stress' depends largely on its unitary role. Any evidence of variability can only cast doubt on such a role.

Rationalization has also taken place when responses have not been consistent. When responses fail to recur, adaptation is evoked. When subjects in experiments do not react, they are described as having good coping mechanisms or simply as being 'hardy'. Rationalization also takes place even when people do not turn up to stress seminars. Their absence is explained by suggesting they are afraid of admitting the condition when in fact there is ample evidence from surveys that people will readily declare that they are 'stressed'. In the final analysis, the evidence that has emerged from studies of physiological effects has not proved the existence of stress. On occasions when correlations have been found, limited understanding of various body systems and their interaction have prevented useful explanations.

Studies of the physiological effects of stress have also failed to provide legitimacy for claims of a link between stress and disease. The various avenues that have been tried have proven to be unfruitful. Some scientists had hoped, and a number still do, that investigating immune responses could prove a connection. Often thinking of the immune system in quasi-military terms, researchers have hypothesized that if the body's defenses were lowered, then diseases would be allowed through. This has been shown to be simplistic. There are many elements that form what is described as the immune system. A decrease in quantity of any of these elements, often labeled as immunosuppression, does not necessarily mean that the whole system is compromised. Furthermore, studies show that various 'stressors' have different impacts or even no impact at all on people. This again is a problem for the unitary potential of the 'stress' concept, but even if the responses were

255

uniform, it still would not guarantee that these responses constitute evidence that stress can cause illness. In the immune system, levels of various cells and elements fluctuate, just as hormones and neurotransmitters do in other systems. This is part of the process of being alive. It seems therefore, that increases or decreases of many physiological variables are not sufficient to explain the occurrence of disease. There have been other retrospective studies attempting to link disease and stress. The results from these studies have yielded more correlations but direct evidence of concrete links has not been forthcoming so that the much needed proof that stress was bad for health has not been provided.

This book has shown that the concept of 'stress' is not flawed in just one aspect. In all the areas that have been investigated the concept has been found wanting as a legitimate object of scientific study. Historically, it does not offer more than its predecessors did. In one aspect, it is less useful than hysteria, vapors, nerves or neurasthenia. These conditions were theorized to be of physical origin and internally based. To paraphrase Martensen (1994), their diagnosis provided people with a scientifically and socially legitimate explanation of their inability to perform their expected roles. Stress, on the other hand, was first hypothesized to be externally based but the introduction of the concept of appraisal and coping has meant that people were again seen as responsible for their actions. This has possibly made the concept more detrimental than useful in the sense that it has given people who are struggling to deal with some aspect of life the added burden of feeling inadequate in dealing with stress as well as the aspect in question.

Stress also fails another test as a unitary term. The introduction of the concept was supposed to help do away with many other terms. However, some explanatory value is lost when stress is used instead of various specific emotions or physical events like hot or cold. Its biggest failure, however, is the lack of evidence of a connection with disease. If stress cannot be shown to be harmful to health, then its importance as a scientific object of study is lessened dramatically. If stress did exist, but were harmless, there would be no need to change our behavior or our lifestyle. Alternatively, if stress did not exist, it could not possibly affect our health. If this were the case, then the continuation of a belief in the legitimacy of stress can only retard our understanding of the relationship we have with events in our lives.

This understanding was provided in the last chapter where the impact of life on people was discussed. The alternative view that was developed showed that only our reactions to events can have an impact on our well-being. This may at first seem very similar to the transactional view of stress. There are, however, some major differences. Unencumbered by the concept of stress, the view I propose does not dwell on the role of the perceiver of the situation. Instead, the reason for our reactions are investigated and consequently shown to be our expectations. Once this is done, the solution becomes clearer. Furthermore, doing away with the inevitability of stress makes it possible to deal with the problem rather than the symptoms.

The problem is no longer whether our reactions to events can cause disease or even death since most of what has been labeled psychological stress has implicated adverse reactions. It can be therefore safely concluded that a link between adverse reactions and disease would be just as elusive. Instead, there seems little doubt that many reactions are capable of creating psychological or even physical discomfort. The effect this has on our well-being cannot be ignored. The alternative explanation I offer accounts for this. After all, most of what we call social life is made of abstractions but because we have imagination we can feel whatever we believe strongly enough including the best and the worst. Sometimes unwittingly, we let our feelings make our life more uncomfortable that it needs to be.

To live up to sometimes impossible to achieve ideals is difficult enough. We hardly need to told that coming to terms with that difficulty may end up making sick or killing us.

BIBLIOGRAPHY

Abrahams, A. (1917). Soldier's Heart. *Lancet.* 1, 442-4

Ackernecht, E. H. (1982).The History of Psychosomatic Medicine. *Psychological Medicine.* 2, 17-24.

Acte, K., Tuulio-Henriksson, A., & Henriksson, M. (1994). Psychosomatic Medicine past and present. *Psychatria Fennica.* 15 (2), 41-51.

Adamson, T., Johnson, G., Roher, T., & Lam, H. (1997). *Metaphors We Ought Not to Live By Rush Limbaugh in the Age of Cognitive Science.* University of Oregon Philosophy Department [On Line]. Available: http://darkwing.uoregon.edu/~roher/rush.htm.

Adessa, M. (1989). Gut Emotions. Stress and Irritable Bowel Syndrome. *Psychology Today.* March. 23 (2), 72-72.

Albrecht, K. (1979). *Stress and the Manager: Making it Work for You.* New York: Simon & Schuster.

Alexander, F. (1939). Psychoanalytic Study of a Case of Essential Hypertension. *Psychosomatic Medicine.* 1,139-152.

_____ (1950). *Psychosomatic Medicine, its Principles and Applications.* New York: Norton.

Alford, S. S. (1881). Defective Nerve-Power as a Primary Cause of Disease. *British Medical Journal.* 1, 591-593.

Allbut, T. C. (1870). The Effects of Over-Work and Strain on the Heart and Great Blood-Vessels. *St. George's Hospital Reports.* v, 28.

_____ (1872). The Effect of Overwork and Strain on the Heart and Great Blood Vessels. *Restrospect of Practical Medicine and Surgery.* 64, 72-78.

_____ (1878). On Brain Forcing. *Brain.* 1(1),60-78.

_____ (1895). Nervous Diseases and Modern Life. *Contemporary Review.* 67, 210-231.

_____ (1909). Over-Stress of the Heart. In *System of Medicine.* 2nd Volume: Disease of the Heart and Blood Vessels. London: MacMillan.

_____ (1910). On Neurasthenia. In *System of Medicine.* 2nd Volume: Diseases of the Brain and Mental Diseases. London: MacMillan.

American Digestive Health Foundation and Opinion Research Corporation. (1995). *Familiarity With H. pylori Among Adults with Digestive Disorders and Their Views Toward Diagnostic And Treatment Options.* Bethesda, Maryland.

American Psychiatric Association (1987). *Diagnostic and Statistical Manual of Mental Disorders.* 3rd Ed, revised. American Psychiatric Association: Washington, DC

Anderson, H. B. (1905). Strain as a Factor in Cardio-aortic lesions. *British Medical Journal.* ii, 840-845.

259

Anon (1996). *Workload Accepted As Cause of Stress In UK Landmark Case* [On Line]. Available: http://www.werple.net.au/~militant/nov96/uk_stres. htm.

Arbetter, S. (1992, Oct 2). Handling Stress: The Balancing Act. *Current Health.*. 19 (2), 7.

Armon-Jones, C. (1986). The Thesis of Constructionism. In Harre, R. (Ed). *The Social Construction of Emotions* (pp. 32-56). New York: Basil Blackwell.

Arnold, M. B. (1960). *Emotion and Personality*. New York. Columbia University Press.

Ateshkadi, A., Lam, N., & Johnson, C. (1993). *Helicobacter pylori* in Peptic Ulcer Disease. *Clinical. Pharmacy.* 12 (1), 34.

Bach Flower Remedies. (1996, November 11). *Celebrity Stress Beaters.* Two Ten Press News Release [On Line]. Available: http://releases. twoten.press.net/releases/date/1996/11/11/HEALTHFlower_Remedies.html.

Bagby, E. (1927). A Compulsion And Its Motivation. *Journal of Abnormal and Social Psychology.* 22, 8-11.

Bairey- Merz, N. (1997, Feb 17). Heart Disease: The Stress Connection. *Newsweek.*

Banking Insurance and Finance Union [BIFU]. (1996, June 30). *Union Launches "Stress Register"*. Two Ten Press News Release [On Line]. Available:http://releases.twoten.press.net/releases/date/1996/06/30/ UNION-Stress_Clydesdale.Html.

Bargen, J. A. (1950). Psychosomatic Relationships in the Digestive System. *Gastroenterology.* 15 (4), 581-591.

Bartop, R. W., Lazarus, L., Luckherst, E., & Kiloh, L. H. (1977). Depressed Lymphocyte Function after Bereavement. *Lancet.* 1, 834-386.

Baum, A. (1990). Stress, intrusive imagery, and chronic distress. *Health Psychology.* 9, 653-675.

Beam, S. F. (1938). The irritable colon and its complications. *Radiological-Review-and-Mississippi-Valley-Medical-Journal.* 60, 14.

Beard, G. (1869). Neurasthenia, or Nervous Exhaustion. *BMSJ.* Vol. 80:217-22.

Bell, J. C. (Ed). (1918). War and Credulity. Journal of Educational Psychology. May; 9.5, 298-300.

Bennett, A. E. (1945). War Nerves. *Diseases of the Nervous System.* 6, 43-48.

Bernard, C. (1859). *An Introduction to the Study of Experimental Medicine.* New York: Dover Publications. Translated, 1957.

Berk, L., & Tan, S. (1996). *The Laughter-Immune Connection* [On Line]. Available: http://touchstartpro.com/ laughbb3.html.

Bernik, V. (1997). *Stress: The Silent Killer* [On Line]. Available: http://www.epub.org.br /cm/n03/doencas/stress_i.htm.

Bilkent University Counseling Center. (1996). *Coping With Stress* [On Line]. Available: http://www.bilkent.edu.tr/~Bilnews/doc12/stress. html.

260

Billig, M. (1988). Social Representation, Objectification and Anchoring: a Rhetorical Analysis. *Social Behavior.* 3 (2), 1-16.

Bishop, J. (1846). On the Causes, Pathology, and Treatment of Deformities in the Human Body. *Lancet.* i, 122-125.

Blalock, J. E. (1989). A Molecular Basis for Bidirectional Communication Between the Immune System and Neuroendocrine Systems. *Physiological Reviews.* 69, 1-32.

Bohus, B., & Koolhaas, J. M. (1993). Stress and the Cardiovascular System: Central and Peripheral Physiological mechanisms. In Stanford, S. C., & Salmon, P. (Eds). *Stress: From Synapse to Syndrome* (pp. 76-106). London: Academic Press, Harcourt Brace & Company, Publishers.

Booth, R. J. (1996). Contrary to Lloyd, the Animating Idea of Psychoneuroimmunology Has Not Lost Its Heuristic Value. *Advances: The Journal of Mind-Body Health.* 12,1-16

_____ (1998). Stress and the Immune System. In Roitt, I. M., & Delves, P. J.(Eds) *The Encyclopaedia of Immunology* (pp. 2220-2228). (2nd Ed). London: Academic Press.

Booth, R. J., & Ashbridge. K. R. (1993). A Fresh Look at the Relationship Between the Psyche and Immune System: Teleological Coherence and Harmony of purpose. *Advances: the Journal of Body- Mind Health.* 9 (2), 4-21.

Booth, R. J., & Pennebaker. J. W. (1999). Emotions and Immunity. In Lewis, M., & Haviland-Jones. J. (Eds). *Handbook of Emotions.* 2nd (Ed). Academic Press: New York (in press).

Bores, L. D. (1996). *The Babylonians* [On Line]. Available: http://www.getnet.com/ `labores/babylonia.html.

Boschen, H. (1997). *The Juice Guy 1997* [On Line]. Available: http://www.csn.net/ healthinfo/disease.html.

Bourgignon, A. (1989). Les outils intellectuels de la psychiatrie. *Psychiatrie Francaise.* 20 (4), 9-14.

Bower, B. (1991, April 6). Questions of Mind over Immunity: Scientists Rethink the Link Between Psychology and Immune Function. *Science News.* 139 (14), 216-218.

Bowman, G. (1998*). Some Commonly Asked Questions About Stress* [On Line]. Available: http://www.hsc. edu/stu/counseling/stress.html.

Boyd, R. S. (1997, October 29). Stress Can Lead To Long-Term Physical Problems, Researchers Say. *Free Press.*

Braud, W. G. (1994). The Role of Mind in the Physical World: A Psychologist's View. *European Journal of Parapsychology.* 10, 66-77.

Breznitz, S., & Goldberger, L. (Eds). (1982). *Handbook of Stress: Theoretical and Clinical Aspects.* New York: The Free Press. A division of Macmillan, Inc.

_____ (Eds). (1993). *Handbook of Stress: Theoretical and Clinical Aspects.* New York: The Free Press. A division of Macmillan, Inc.

Briquet, P. (1859). *Traité clinique de thérapeutique de l'hysterie.* Paris: J.B Baillière.

261

Brown, G. M., Seggie, J., & Ettigi, P. (1986). Stress, Hormones Responses, and Cancer. In Day, S. B. (Ed). *Cancer, Stress, and Death* (pp. 21-31). New York: Plenum medical Book Company. Inc.

Brown, J. F. (1929). The Methods Of Kurt Lewin In The Psychology Of Action And Affection. *Psychological Review*. 36, 200-221.

Brown, T. M. (1993). Mental Diseases. In Bynum, W. M., & Porter. R. (Eds). *Companion Encyclopedia of the History of Medicine* (pp. 438-463). Volume 1. London: Routledge.

Bruer, J., & Freud, S. (1895). *Studies in Hysteria*. English translation.(1955). Harmondsworth: Penguin. 1974.

Buchanan, A. (1870). On The Force of The Human heart. *Lancet*. 2, 665-666.

Burtchfield, S. R. (1979). The Stress Response: A New Perspective. *Psychosomatic Medicine*. 4 (8), 661-673.

Burton, R. (1621). *The anatomy of Melancholy*. Oxford : Printed by John Lichfield and James Short for Henry Cripps.

Business Day Online (1996). *Transcendental Meditation 'Helps Beat Stress'* [On Line]. Available: http://www.bday.co.za/96/1003/special/ ma4.htm.

Bynum, W. F. (1993). Nosology. In Bynum, W. M., & Porter. R. (Eds). *Companion Encyclopedia of the History of Medicine* (pp. 335-358). Volume 1. London: Routledge.

Cadogan, W. (1772) A Dissertation on the Gout and all Chronic Diseases. Philadelphia: William and Thomas Bradford.

Cameron, R., & Meichenbaum, D. (1982). The Nature of Effective Coping and the Treatment of Stress Related Problems: A Cognitive-Behavioral Perspective. In Breznitz, S., & Goldberger, L. (1982). Eds). *Handbook of Stress: Theoretical and Clinical Aspects* (pp. 695-709). New York: The Free Press. A division of Macmillan, Inc.

CancerNet. National Cancer Institute. (1998). *Cancer facts* [On Line]. Available: http://NISC8A.upenn.edu /pdq_html/6/engl/600317.html.

Cannon, W. B. (1911). The Stimulation of Adrenal Glands by Emotional excitement. *Journal of the American Medical Association*. 56, 742.

_____ (1927). The James-Lang Theory of Emotions: A Critical Examination and an Alternative Theory. *American Journal of Psychology*. 39, 106-24.

_____ (1929). Organization for physiological homeostasis. *Physiological Review*. 9, 399-431.

_____ (1935). Stresses And Strains Of Homeostasis. *American Journal of Medical Sciences*. 189, 1-14.

_____ (1939). *The Wisdom of the Body*. New York: W W Norton.

Caplan, R. D. (1972). Organizational Stress and Individual strain: A Social Psychological Study of Risk Factors in Coronary Heart Disease Among Administrators, Engineers and, Scientists. *Dissertation Abstracts International*. 32 (11B), 6706B.

Chesney, M. A., & Rosenman, R. H. (Eds). (1985). *Anger and Hostility in Cardiovascular and Behavioral Disorders*. Washington, DC: Hemisphere.

Cheyne, G. (1733). *The English Malady*. Reprint, 1976. New York: Scholars Facsimiles & Reprints

Christensen, N. J., & Jensen. E. W. (1994). Affect of Psychosocial Stress and Age on Plasma Norepinephrine levels: A Review. *Psychosomatic Medicine*. 56, 77-83.

Clark, F. (1883). Some Remarks on Nervous Exhaustion and on Vasomotor Action. *Journal of Anatomy and Physiology*. 18, 239-256.

_____ (1986). Some Observations Concerning What Is Called Neurasthenia. *Lancet.*. 1, (1), 1-2.

Cobb, S., & Kasl, S. V. (1977). *Termination: The Consequences of Job Loss*. Cincinnati: National Institute for Occupational Safety and Health.

Cofer, C. N., & Appley, M. H. (1964). *Motivation. Theory and Research*. New York: John Wiley & Sons, Inc.

Cohen, S. (1980). After effects of Stress on Human Performance and Social Behavior: A Review and Theory. *Psychological Bulletin*. 88, 82-108.

Cohen, S., Tyrell, A. J., & Smith, A. P. (1991). Psychological Stress and Susceptibility to the Common Cold. *New England Journal of Medicine*. 325, 606-612.

Condon, J. C. (1966). *Semantics and Communication*. New York: MacMillan.

Cook, M., Young, A., Taylor, D., & Bedford, A. P. (1996). Personality Correlates of Psychological Distress. *Personality and Individual Differences*. 2 (3), 313-319.

Coriat, I. H. (1909-1910). Certain Pulse Reactions as a Measure of The Emotions. Journal of Abnormal Psychology. Oct-Nov; 4, 261-279.

_____ (1915). Stammering as a Psychoneurosis. *Journal of Abnormal Psychology*. 9, 417-430.

Cory, H. A. (1944). Present Wartime Personnel Problems Relating To Office Workers. *Texas Personnel Review*. 3, 27-30.

Cottington, E. M., Matthews, K. A., Talbot E., & Kuller, L. H. (1980). Environmental Events Preceding Sudden Death in Women. *Psychosomatic Medicine*. 42 (6), 567-574.

Cox, T. (1984). Stress: a Psychophysiological Approach to Cancer. In Cooper, C. L. (Ed). *Psychosocial Stress and Cancer* (pp. 149-172). Chichester: John Wiley & Sons.

_____ (1985). *Stress*. Hampshire: MacMillan Publishers Ltd.

Cox, T., Mackay, C. J., Cox, S., Watts, C., & Brockley, T. (1978*). Stress and Well-Being in School Teachers: Psychophysiological Response to Occupational Stress*. Paper Presented to the Ergonomics Society Conference, Nottingham University, Nottingham, England.

Cremieux, A. (1930). Position Actuelle Du Probleme Des Nevroses. / The Present Position Of The Problem Of Neuroses. *Actualites Medico Chirurgicales*. 75-123.

Curtis, J. M. (1982). Emotional Elements of Mental Illness: Psychological Concomitants of Stress. *Psychological Reports*. 50, 1207-1213.

DaCosta, J. M. (1871). On Irritable Heart: A Clinical Study of a Form of Functional Cardiac Disorder and its Consequences. *The American Journal of the Medical Sciences.* January.

Dana, C. L. (1906-1908). The Limitations Of The Term Hysteria With A Consideration Of The Nature Of Hysteria And Certain Allied Psychoses. *Journal of Abnormal Psychology.* Feb; 1, 269-278.

Daquin, J. (1787). Topographie Medicale de la Ville de Chambery. Chambery: Gorrin.

Darwin, C. (1871) *The descent of man* [On line]. Available: http://infidels.org/library/historical/charles_darwin/descent_of_man/chapter_03.html.

Davidson, J. (1998,). Slowing The Hectic Pace Of Stress. *Public Management.* April. p.14-18.

Dawkins, M. S. (1998). The Scientific Basis for Assessing Suffering in Animals [On Line]. Available: http://arrs.envirolink.org/essays/ assess.html

Dawes, R. M. (1994). House of Cards. Psychology and Psychotherapy built on Myth. New York: The Free Press.

Dawson, W. R. (1929). *Magician and Leech.* London: Methuen.

Dean, T. N. (1928). The Value Of Curative Work In Workmen's Compensation Cases. *Occupational Therapy and Rehabilitation.* 7,11-20.

De Brabander, B., Hellemans, J., Boone, C., & Gerits, P. (1996) Locus of Control, Sensation Seeking, and Stress. *Psychological Reports.* 79, 1307-1312.

De Geus, E. J. C., Van Doornen, L. J. P., De Visser, D. C., & Orlebeke, J. F. (1990). Existing and Training Induced Differences in Aerobic Fitness: Their Relationship to Physiological Response Patterns During Different Types of Stress. *Psychophysiology.* 27 (4), 457-478.

Demand, N. (1997). *Medicine In Ancient Mesopotamia* [On Line]. Available: http://www.indiana.edu/~ancmed/meso. HTM.

Derogatis, L. R., & Coons, H.L. (1993). Self-report Measures of Stress. In Breznitz, S., & Goldberger, L. (Eds*). Handbook of Stress: Theoretical and Clinical Aspects* (pp. 200-233). New York: The Free Press. A division of Macmillan, Inc.

Dimsdale, J. E., & Moss, J. (1980). Plasma Catecholamines in Stress and Exercise. *Journal of the American Medicine Association.* 243, 340-342.

Ditto, B. (1993). Familial influences on heart rate, blood pressure, and self - report anxiety responses to stress: Results from 100 twin pairs. *Psychophysiology.* 20, 635-645.

Dobson, C. B. (1983). *Stress: The Hidden Adversary.* Ridgewood New Jersey: George A. Bogden & Son, Inc.

Duckworth, D. H. (1985). Is the 'organizational stress' construct a red herring? A reply to Glowinkowski and Cooper. *Bulletin of the British Psychological Society.* 38, 401-404.

Dunbar, H. F. (1935*). Emotions and bodily changes: A survey of literature on psychosomatic relationship: 1910-1933.* New York: Columbia University Press.

Dupau, J. A. (1819). *De L'erethisme Nerveux Ou Analyze Des Affections Nerveuses.* Montpellier: Martel.

Eder, M. D. (1916). The Psycho-pathology of War Neuroses. *Lancet.* 2: 264-268.

Ellis, C., & Thompson, D. (1983, June, 6). Stress: Can We Cope? *Time.*

Eliot, R. S. (Ed). (1988). *Stress and the heart. Mechanisms, Measurements, and Management.* Mount Kisco, NY: Futura Publishing Co.

Endröczi, E. (1991). *Stress and Adaptation.* Budapest: Akademiai kiado.

Engel, S. M. (1995). *What Is the Fallacy of Hypostatization?* [On Line]. Available: http://www.shss.montclair.edu/inquiry/summ95/ engel.html.

Farber, S. L. (1982). Genetic Diversity and Differing Reaction to Stress. In Breznitz, S., & Goldberger, L. (Eds). *Handbook of Stress: Theoretical and Clinical Aspects* (pp. 123-133). New York: The Free Press. A division of Macmillan, Inc.

Farquarson, R. (1870). The Influence of Athletic Sports on Health. *Lancet.* 2, 513-515, 545-546.

Farr, C. B., Leuders, C. W., & Bond, E. D. (1925). Studies of gastric secretions and motility in mental patients. *American Journal of Psychiatry.* 5, 93-101.

Favoretto, G. (1988). Research into work stress in Italy: a review. *Work and Stress.* 2 (20), 113-121.

Flögel, Dr. (1845). Etiology of Diseases of the Heart. *Lancet.* 2, 596.

Fontaine, O., & Salah, D. (1991). Stress D' Origine medicale et "Education" du Patient (Latrogenic Stress and Patient Education). *Science et Comportement.* 21 (4), 259-272.

Forbes Magazine. (1995, March 13). *Second Opinion. Stressed For Success.*

Forbes Magazine. (1996, Nov 18). *Stress Can Cause - Um, I Forgot. (Research Shows That Long-Term Stress May Shrink Part Of The Brain That Keeps People Intelligent).* p.105.

Fox, C. D. (1910-1911). Psychogenetic Convulsions. *Journal of Abnormal Psychology.* Apr-May; 5, 1-19.

Frank, L. K. (1928). The Management Of Tensions. *American Journal of Sociology.* 33, 705-736.

Frankenhaeuser, M. (1975). Experimental Approach to the Study of Catecholamines and Emotion. In Levi, L. (Ed), *Emotions: Their Parameters and Measurement* (pp. 209-234). Raven Press: New York.

Frankenhaeuser, M., Nordheden, B., Myrsten, A. L., & Post, B. (1971). Psychophysiological Reactions to Understimulation and Overstimulation. *Acta Psychologica.* 35, 298-308.

Frankenhaeuser, M., Sterky, & K., Järpe, G. (1962). Psychophysiological relations in habituation to gravitational stress. *Perceptual and Motor Skills.* 15, 63-72.

Frankenhaeuser, M., Von Wright, M. R., Collins, A., Von Wright, J., Sedvall, G., & Swahn, C. G. (1976). Sex Differences in Psychoneuroendocrine Reactions to Examination Stress. *Report No 489.* Department of Psychology. University of Stockholm.

French, N, K. (1991). Elementary Teachers Perceptions Of Stressful Events And Stress Related Teaching Practices. *Perceptual and Motor Skills.* 72, 203-210.

Freud, S. (1916). *Introductory Lectures on Psychoanalysis.* New York : Norton, 1966.

Futterman, A. D., Kemeny, M.E., Shapiro, D., & Fahey, J.L. (1994). Immunological and Physiological Changes Associated with Induced Positive and Negative Mood. *Psychosomatic Medicine.* 56:499-511.

Galenica, B. V. (1996). *Galen* [On line]. Available: http://www.euromed.nl /alenuse.html.

Gamow, K., & Gamow, D. (1998). *Research on Stress and Meditation* [On line]. Available: http://www. jps.net/dkgamow/clarsrch.htm.

Gist, M. (1998). *They All Died So Young* [On line]. Available: http://ourworld.compuserve.com/ homepages/ Mark _Gist/age.htm.

Glass, D. C., & Singer, J.E. (1972). *Urban Stress: Experiments on Noise and Social Stressors.* New York: Academic.

Glue, P., Nut, D., & Coupland, N. (1993). Stress and Psychiatric Disorder: Reconciling Social and Biological Approaches. In Stanford, S. C., & Salmon, P. (Eds). *Stress: From Synapse to Syndrome* (pp. 53-75). London: Academic Press, Harcourt Brace & Company, Publishers.

Goldberger, L. (1982). Sensory Deprivation and Overload. In Breznitz, S., & Goldberger, L. (Eds). *Handbook of Stress: Theoretical and Clinical Aspects* (pp. 410-418). New York: The Free Press. A division of Macmillan, Inc.

Goldstein, D. S. (1995). *Stress, Catecholamines, and Cardiovascular Disease.* New York: Oxford University Press.

Gonzalez-Galvan, J. M. (1949). Moderno Concepto psicosomatico de la digestopatias. / The modern psychosomatic concept of the digestive disorders. *Clinica y Laboratoria.* 48, 53-63.

Goodman, S. (1994). Infertility: Could Stress Be To Blame? *Health.* Nov-Dec. 8 (7), 42-44.

Gordon, C. (1990, March 12). Bulging veins as status symbols. *Maclean's.* p.13.

Gould, R. L. (1997). *Understanding Stress* [On Line]. Available: http://www.insight.com/ creators.htm.

Gray, K. (1998). *Stress fills high school life* [On line]. Available: http://www.netins.net/ showcase/ahschool/ needle/needle.htm.

Grayling Co. (1997, November 19). *Owning A Pet Is Just As Good As Social Support.* Two Ten Press News Release[On Line].Available: http://releases.twoten.press.net/ releases/date/1997/11/19/ SOCIAL-Pets.html.

Greenaway, N. (1997, December, 17). Quebecers And Women Are Canada's Most Stressed People. *The Ottawa Citizen.*

Greg, W. R. (1853). *England as it is. Essays on Political and Social Science.* Volume 1. London: Longman, Brown, Green & Longmans.

Grinkler, R. R., & Spiegel, J. P. (1945). *Men Under Stress.* Philadelphia: Blakiston; New York: McGraw-Hill.

266

Guggensheim, F. (1997). *Somatoform Disorders* [On line]. Available :http://www.uams.edu/department_of_psychiatry/syllabus/somatoform/ somatoform.htm.

Gutierrez-Noriega, C. (1940). Teoria De La Descarga De Energia Nerviosa Y De Su Accion Neurofilactica En La Terapeutica Onvulsivantes. / Theory Of Discharge Of Nervous Energy And Its Neurophilactic Action In Therapy By Convulsants. *Revista de Neuro Psiquiatria.* Lima. 3, 163-189.

Haan, N. (1982). Assessment of Coping, Defense, and Stress. In Breznitz, S., & Goldberger, L. (Eds). *Handbook of Stress: Theoretical and Clinical Aspects* (pp. 354-269). New York: The Free Press. A division of Macmillan, Inc.

Hall, S. B. (1927). The blood pressure in psychoneurosis. *Lancet.* 213, 540-543.

Harms, H. E., & Soniat, T. L. L. (1952). The meaning of fatigue. *Medical Clinics of North America.* Mar, 311-317.

Harre, R. (1986). An Outline of the Social Constructionist Viewpoint. In Harre, R. (Ed). *The Social Construction of Emotions* (pp. 2-14). New York: Basil Blackwell.

Harrison, C. J. (1990).Teaching Abstract Concepts in Psychology. *Journal of Instructional Psychology.* 17 (2), 68-70.

Haughton, S. (1868). The Relation of Food to Work Done by the Body. *Lancet.* 2, 209-211.

Health Response Ability Systems, Inc. (1995). *Reduce Stress: Take Responsibility and Control!* [On line]. Available: http://home.navisoft. com/solemom/stress.htm.

Hebb, D. O. (1955). Drives and the Conceptual Nervous System. *Psychological Review.* 62, 243.

Heinroth, J. C. A. (1818). *Textbook of Disturbances of Mental Life.* Translated by Schmorak, T. (1975). 2 Vols. Baltimore, MD: John Hopkins University Press.

Heller, T. (1930). Hoerstummheit. / Mutism with comprehension. *Archiv fuer die Gesamte Psychologie.* 77, 265-272.

Henderson, C. W. (1998, January, 19). Study Finds Stress Can Affect Cancer (Breast Cancer). *Cancer Weekly Plus.* p. 13.

Herbert, T. B., & Cohen, S. (1993). Stress and Immunity in Humans: A Meta-Analytic Review. *Psychosomatic Medicine.* 55, 364-379.

Hicks, R. A., Conti, P. A., & Nellis, T. (1992). Arousability and Stress-Related Physical Symptoms: A Validation Study of Coren's Arousal Predisposition Scale. *Perceptual Motor Skills.* 74, 659-662.

Hidaka, Y., & Amino, N. (1998). Stress, Endocrine, and Immune System; Stress Induces   the Onset of Auto-immune Diseases. *Rinsho Byori.* 46 (6), 581-586.

Hinkle, E. Jr. (1987). Stress and Disease: The Concept after 50 Years. *Social Science and Medicine.* 25(6), 561-566.

Hiramoto, R. N., Rogers, C. F., Demissie, S., Hsueh, C. M., Hiramoto, N.S., Lorden, J.   F., & Ghanta, V. K. (1997). Psychoneuroendocrine Immunology: Site of Recognition, Learning and Memory in the Immune

System and the Brain. *International Journal of Neuroscience.* Dec; 92 (3-4), 259-85.

Holmes, T. H. (1979). Development and application of a quantitative measure of life change magnitude. In Barrett, J. E., Rose. R. M., & Klerman, G. L. (Eds). *Stress and Mental Disorder* (pp. 37-53). New York: Raven.

Holmes, T. H., & Rahe, R. H. (1967). The Social Readjustment Scale. *Journal of Psychosomatic Research.* 11, 213-218.

Holroyd, K.A., & Lazarus, R. S. (1982). Stress, Coping, and Somatic Adaptation. In Breznitz, S., & Goldberger, L. (Eds). *Handbook of Stress: Theoretical and Clinical Aspects* (pp. 21-35). New York: The Free Press. A division of Macmillan, Inc.

Horin, A. (1997, August 16). You can't blame stress for a cancer diagnosis. *The Sydney Morning Herald.*.

Houtman, I. L. D., & Bakker, F. C. (1991a). Individual Differences in Reactivity to Coping with the Stress of Lecturing. *Journal of Psychosomatic Research.* 35,(1),11-24.

_____. (1991b). Stress and Coping in Lecturing, and the Stability of Responses Across Practices. *Journal of Psychosomatic Research.* 35 (2/3), 323-333.

Humphrey, J. H. (1992). *Stress among Women in Modern Society.* Springfield, Illinois: Charles C Thomas Publisher.

Humphries, D. (1998, January 26.). Stress Claims Hurting Employers. *The Sydney Morning Herald.*

Humphries, D., & Delvecchio, J. (1998, January 26). Stressed Workers Cost Companies $60 Million. *The Sydney Morning Herald.*

Ilfeld, F. W. (1982). Marital Stressors, Coping Styles, and Symptoms of Depression. In Breznitz, S., & Goldberger, L. (Eds). *Handbook of Stress: Theoretical and Clinical Aspects* (pp. 483-495). New York: The Free Press. A division of Macmillan, Inc.

Impoco. J. (1991, March 18). Dying to work. (karoshi: overwork leading to serious illness or death in Japan). *U.S. News & World Report.* p. 24.

Jacobsen, G. (1999, April 5). Stressed-out workers costly, bosses told. *The Sydney Morning Herald.*

Jacobson, E. (1934). *You must relax; A Practical Method of Reducing the Strains of Modern Living.* New York, London: Whittlesey House: McGraw-Hill Book Company Inc.

James, S. (1994). *Medical Consultants Network, Inc (MCN) Home Page* [On line}. Available: http://www.mcn.com/ioi/1994/stress.htm Stress.

Janet, P. (1903). *Les Obsessions et la Psychasthenie.* Paris: Felix Alcan.

Jänig, W. & McMaclan, E. M. (1992). Characteristics of Function-specific Pathways in the Sympathetic Nervous System. *Trends in Neuroscience.* 15, 475-481.

Johansson, G. (1972). Sex Differences in the Catecholamine Output of Children. *Acta Physilogica Scandinavia.* 86, 569-572.

Johansson, G., Aronsson, G., & Lindström, B. O. (1978). Social psychological and neuro- endocrine stress reactions in highly Mechanized work. *Ergonomics.* 21,583-599.

Johansson, G., Collins, A., & Collins, V. P. (1983). Male and Female Psychoneuro- endocrine Response to Examination Stress: A Case Report. *Motivation and Emotion*. 7, 1-9.

Johnson, M. (1991). Selye's Stress and the Body in the Mind. *Advance*. 7 (2), 38-44.

Johnston, E. O., Kamilaris, K. C., Chrousos, G. P., & Gold, P.W. (1992). Mechanisms of Stress: A dynamic Overview of Hormonal and Behavioral Homeostasis. *Neuroscience and Biobehavioral Reviews*. 16, 115-130.

Jones, E. (1907-1908). Mechanism of a Severe Briquet Attack as Contrasted With That of Psychasthenic Fits. *Journal of Abnormal Psychology*. Dec-Jan; 2, 218-227.

Kaminoff, R. D. & Proshansky, H. M. (1982). Stress as a Consequence of the Urban   Physical environment. In Breznitz, S., & Goldberger, L. (Eds). *Handbook of Stress: Theoretical and Clinical Aspects* (pp. 380-409). New York: The Free Press. A division of Macmillan, Inc.

Kaplan, H. B. (Ed). (1996). *Psychosocial Stress: Perspectives on Structure, Theory, Life Course, and Methods*. San Diego: Academic Press.

Kasl, S. V. (1996). Theory of Stress and Health. In Cooper, C. L. Ed.). *Stress, Medicine and Health* (pp. 13-26). Boca Raton: CRC Press.

Kasl, S. V., & Cobb, S. (1982). Variability of Stress Effects among Men Experiencing Job Loss. In Breznitz, S., & Goldberger, L. (Eds). *Handbook of Stress: Theoretical and Clinical Aspects* (pp. 445-465). New York: The Free Press. A division of Macmillan, Inc.

Katkin, E. S., Dermit, S., & Wine, S. F. (1993). Psychophysiological Assessment of Stress. In Breznitz, S., & Goldberger, L. (Eds). *Handbook of Stress: Theoretical and Clinical Aspects* (pp. 142-157). New York: The Free Press. A division of Macmillan, Inc.

Keicolt-Glaser, J. K., & Glaser, R. (1991). Stress and the Immune Function in Humans. In Ader, R., Felten, D.L., & Cohen, N. (Eds). *Psychoneuroimmunology* (2nd Ed) (pp. 849-867). San Diego: Academic Press.

Kerr, W. A. (1942). Psychological effects of music as reported by 162 defense trainees. *Psychological Record*. Vol. 5, 205-212.

_____ (1942). Factor Analysis Of 229 Electrical Workers' Beliefs In The Effects Of   Music. *Psychological Record*. 5, 213-221.

Kesteven, W. H. (1884). *Work and Worry, From a Medical Point of View*. London: Diprose & Bateman, Lincoln's Inn Fields.

Kiechel III, W. (1986, June 23). Now Some Good News About Stress. *Fortune Magazine*. p.157-158.

Kienle, G., & Keine, H. (1997). The Placebo Effect: Fact or Fiction? *Journal of Clinical Epidemiology*. 50 (1), 1311-1218.

Kiecolt-Glaser, J. K., Cacioppo, J. T., Malarkey, W. B., & Glaser, R. (1992). Acute Psychological Stressors and Short-Term Immune Changes: What, Why, For Whom, and to What Extent? *Psychosomatic Medicine*. 54, 680-685.

Kimball, C. P. (1982).Stress and Psychosomatic Illness. *Journal of Psychosomatic Research*. 26 (1), 63-67.

Kirby, J. (1997). Eat to Beat Stress. *American Health For Women.* Dec, 16 (10), 81.

Koch, F. (1929). Einstellung zur Krankheit und ihre Beziehung zur sozialen Lage. / Absences due to illness and their relation to the social milieu. *Allgemeine Aerzliche Zeitschrift fuer Psychotherapie und Psychische Hygiene.* 2, 217-231.

Kopp, M., & Skrabski, A. (1989). What does the legacy of Hans Selye and Franz Alexander mean today? (The psychophysiological approach in medical practice. *International Journal of Psychophysiology.* 8, 99-105.

Kövecses, Z. (1991) Happiness: A Definitional Effort. *Metaphor and Symbolic Activity.* 6 (1), 29-41.

Kropiunigg, U. (1993). Basics in Psychoneuroimmunology. *Annals of Medicine.* 25, 473-479.

Kuglemann, R. (1992). *Stress: The Nature and History of Engineer Grief.* Westport, Connecticut: Praeger Publishers.

Kvetnansky, R., & Torda, T. (1984). Heart Adrenergic System Activity in Rats during Adaptation to Repeated Stress. In Beamish, R.E, Panagia, V., & Dhalla, N. S. (Eds). *Pathogenesis Of Stress-Induced Heart Disease* (pp. 3-19). Boston: Maritinus Nijhoff.

Lafontaine, A. (1991) L'epidemiologie du 'stress' and les problemes qu'il pose sur the plan medical et social. Le cas particulier des reactions psychiques aigues a un psychotraumatisme. *Bulletin de l'Academie Nationale de Medecine.* 79 (3), 449-462.

Lakoff, G. (1992). *The Contemporary Theory of Metaphor* [On line] Available: Http://rowlf.cc.wwu.edu:80/market/semiotic/Ikof_met.html.

Lamb, D. H. (1979). On the Distinction Between Physical and Psychological Stressors: A Review of the Evidence. *Motivation and Emotion.* 3 (1), 51-61.

Laux, L., & Vossel, G. (1982). Paradigms in Stress Research: Laboratory Versus Field   and Traits Versus Processes. In Breznitz, S., & Goldberger, L. (Eds). *Handbook of Stress: Theoretical and Clinical Aspects* (pp. 203-211). New York: The Free Press. A division of Macmillan, Inc.

Lazarus, R. S. (1966). *Psychological Stress and the Coping Process.* New York: McGraw-Hill.

_____ (1991). *Emotion and Adaptation.* New York: Oxford University Press.

_____ (1993). Why We Should Think of Stress as a Subset of Emotion. In Breznitz, S., & Goldberger, L. (Eds). *Handbook of Stress: Theoretical and Clinical Aspects* (pp. 21-39). New York: The Free Press. A division of Macmillan, Inc.

Lazarus, R. S., & Cohen, J. B. (1977). Environmental Stress. In Altman, I., & Wohlwill, J. F. (Eds). *Human Behavior and Environment* (pp. 90-127). Vol. 2. New York: Plenum.

Lazarus, R. S., & Folkman, S. (1984). *Stress, Appraisal, and Coping.* New York: Springer Publishing Company.

270

Lazarus, R. S., & Launier, R. (1978). Stress-related Transactions between Person and Environment. In Pervin, L. A, & Lewis, M. (Eds). *Perspectives in Interactional Psychology* (pp. 287-327). New York: Plenum.

Leon, D. A., & Shkolnikov, V. M. (1998). Social Stress and the Russian Mortality Crisis. *The Journal of the American Medical Association*. 279 (10), 790792.

Les Dernières Nouvelles D'Alsace. (1996, November, 22). *De Lourdes Contraintes Horaires.*

Le Soir, (1997, November 8). *Le Stress Consume Tous Les Travailleurs.*

Le Soir, (1997, November 22). Pour Vivre Vieux, Soyons Sociables. Et Mangeons Tôt !

Le Vay, D. (1952). Hans Selye And A Unitary Conception Of Disease. *British Journal for the Philosophy of Science*. 3, 157-168.

Levenstein, S. (1998). Stress and Peptic Ulcer: Life Beyond Helicobacter. *British Medical Journal*. 7130, 538-542.

Levi, L. (1972). Stress and Distress in Response to Psycho-social Stimuli. *Acta Medica Scandinavia* (supplement), 528.

_____ (1996). Spice of Life or Kiss of Death. In Cooper, C. L. (Ed). *Handbook of Stress, Medicine and Health* (pp. 1-12). Boca Raton : CRC Press.

Levi, L., & Kagan, A. (1980). Psychosocially-Induced Stress and Disease - Problems, Research Strategies, and Results. In Selye, H. (Ed). *Selye's Guide to Stress Research* (pp. 118-130). Volume I. New York: Van Nostrand Reinhold Company.

Levine, S., & Ursin, H. (1991). What is stress? In Brown, M. R., Koob, G. G., & Rivier, C. (Eds) *Stress. Neurobiology and Neuroendocrinology* (pp. 3-21). New York: Marcel Dekker.

Lewis, R. (1949). The psychological approach to the preschool stutterer. *Canadian Medical Association Journal*. 60, 497- 500.

Linden, W. (1991). What do Arithmetic Stress Tests Measure? Protocol Variations and Cardiovascular Responses. *Psychophysiology*. 28 (1), 91-102.

Lindsley, D. B. (1952). Psychological phenomena and the electroencephalogram. *Electroencephalogram Clinical Neurophyiology*. 4, 443

Lipowski, Z. J. (1986a). Psychosomatic medicine: Past and Present. Part I. *Canadian Journal of Psychiatry*. 31(1), 1-7.

_____ (1986b). Psychosomatic medicine: Past and Present. Part II. *Canadian Journal of Psychiatry*. 31 (1), 8-13.

_____ (1986c). Psychosomatic Medicine: Past and Present. Part III. *Canadian Journal of Psychiatry*. 31, 1:14-21.

Lough, J. E., Solomons, L.M., & Stein, G. (1896). Studies from the psychological laboratory of Harvard University: The Relations Of The Intensity To Duration Of Stimulation In Our Sensations Of Light; Normal Motor Automatism. *Psychological Review*. Sep; 3 (5), 484-512.

Lundberg, U. (1976). Urban Commuting. Crowdedness and catecholamine excretion. *Journal of Human Stress*. 2 (3), 26-32.

_____ (1995). Methods and Application of Stress Research. *Technology and Health Care.* 3, 3-9.

Lundberg, U., Granqvist, M., Hansson, T., Magnusson, M., & Wallin, l. (1989). Psychological and Physiological Stress Responses During Repetitive Work at an Assembly Line. *Work and Stress.* 3 (2), 143-153.

Lundberg, U., & Palm, K. (1989). Workload and Catecholamines Excretion in Parents of Preschool Children. *Work and Stress.* 3 (3), 25-260.

Lundberg, U., Westermark, O., & Rasch, B. (1993). Cardiovascular and Neurendocrine Activity in Preschool Children: Comparison Between Day-Care and Home Levels. *Scandinavian Journal of Psychology.* 34 (8), 774-779.

Lynn, G.T (1998). *Distress and Eustress* [On line]. Available: http://ourworld.compuserve.com/homepages/GeorgeLynn/rage.htm.

Mackenzie, J. (1916). Soldier's Heart. *Lancet.* I, 117-131.

Mandler, G. (1984). *Mind and Body: Psychology of Emotion and Stress.* New York: W Norton & Company.

Manning, M. R., Williams, R. F., & Wolfe, D. M. (1988). Hardiness and the Relationship between Stressors and Outcomes. *Work & Stress.* 2, 205-216.

Manufacturing, Science & Finance Union [MSF]. (1997, October, 9). *MSF Takes Stress Prevention Message On The Road.* Two Ten Press News Release [On Line]. Available: http://releases.twoten.press.net/releases/date/1997/10/09/UNIONStress_Seminars.html.

Manufacturing, Science & Finance Union [MSF]. (1997, October, 6). *London Tops Workplace Stress League.* Two Ten Press News Release [On Line]. Available: http://releases.twoten.press.net/releases/date/ 1997/10/06/ HEALTH-Msf_Stress_London.html.

Marquis, D. P., Sinnett, E. R., & Winter, W. D. (1952). A psychological study of peptic ulcer patients. *Journal of Clinical Psychology.* 8, 266-272.

Marshall, B. J. (1995). *Helicobacter pylori*: the etiologic agent for peptic ulcer. *The Journal of the American Medical Association.* 274 (3), 1064-1067.

Martensen, R. L. (1994). Was Neurasthenia a 'Legitimate Morbid Entity?' *The Journal of the American Medical Association.* 271 (16), 243.

Mason, J. W. (1971). A Re-evaluation of the Concept of 'Non-specificity' in Stress Theory. *Journal of Psychiatric Research.* 8, 323-333.

_____ (1975). A Historical View of the Stress Field. *Journal of Human Stress.* 1 (1), 6-12.

Mason, J. W., Maher, J. T., Harley, L. H., Mogey, E., Perlow, M. J., & Jones, L. G. (1976). Selectivity of Corticosteroid and Catecholamine Responses to Various Natural Stimuli. In Serban, G. (Ed). *Psychopathology of Human Adaptation* (pp. 147-172). New York and London: Plenum press.

May, M. (1996). Skin-Deep. *Science Observer.* May-June 1996.

Mayeaux, E. J. (1989). *A History of Western Medicine and Surgery* [On line}. Available: http://lib-sh.lsumc.edu/fammed/grounds/history.html.

McCowan, P. K., & Quastel, J. H. (1931). Bloodsugar Studies In Abnormal Mental States. *Lancet.* 221, 731-736.

272

McEwen, B. S., & Mendelson, S. (1993). Effects of Stress on the Neurochemistry and Morphology of the Brain: Counterregulation versus Damage. In Breznitz, S., & Goldberger, L. (Eds). *Handbook of Stress: Theoretical and Clinical Aspects* (pp. 100-126). New York: The Free Press. A division of Macmillan.

McGrath, J. E. (1970). *Social and psychological factors in stress.* New York: Holt.

McKeown, P. (1989). Esophageal Pain: Another Price Of Success. (Stress Related Diseases). *Nation's Business.* 77 (11), 89.

Medical News. (1873). *Heart Disease From Over-Exertion..* p. 98-99.

Menninger, W. (1946). Modern Concepts of War Neuroses. *Bulletin of Menninger Clinic.* 10.

Merelman, D. (1997, June 2). On My Mind. What's Worrying Top Executives. *Forbes Magazine.*

Meyer, J. (1998). *Home page* [On line}. Available: http://www. counselingreferrals.com/ people/csis.html.

Miller, L. H., Ross, R. & Cohen, S. I. (1985). *Stress.* Sydney: Bay Books.

Milstein, M. & Farkas, J. (1998). The Over-Stated Case of Educator Stress. *Journal of Educational Administration.* 26 (2), 232-49.

Milsun, J. H. (1985). A Model of the Eustress System for Health/Illness. *Behavioral Science.* 30, 179-186.

Mindell, E. (1997). *Earl Mindell's Secret Remedies* [On line]. Available: http://www.iherb.com/iherb/stress.html# overview.

Moersch, F. P. (1924). Psychic Manifestations in Migraine. *American Journal of Psychiatry.* 3, 698-716.

_____ (1943). The Psychoneuroses of War. *War Medicine.* Chicago. 4, 490-496.

Moracco, J. C., D'Arienzo, R. V., & Danford, D. (1983), Comparison of Perceived Occupational Stress Between Teachers Who Are Contented and Discontented in their Career Choices. *Vocational Guidance Quarterly.* 32 (1), 44-51.

Morgan, E. (1998). *Stress Management* [On line}. Available: http://www.islandnet.com/ ~emorgan/articles/ immherbs.html.

Morrish, J. (1996, August 10). Frantic Semantics *Electronic Telegraph.*

Moruzzi, G., & Magoun, H. W. (1949). Brain Stem Reticular Formation and Activation of the EEG. *Electro-encephalic Clinical Neurophysiology.* 1, 455-73.

Muirhead, I. B. (1916). Shock and the Soldier. *Lancet.* 1, 1021.

Mulhall, A. (1996). Cultural Discourse and the Myth of Stress in Nursing and Medicine. *International Journal of Nursing Studies.* 33 (5), 455-468.

Munson, M. (1995, March) Watch the washout: can stress affect your medications? *Prevention,* p.36-37.

Nando Times. (1998, March 26). *Multiple Sclerosis Appears To Be Exacerbated By Stress* [On Line]. Available: http://www.nandotimes.net.

Nando Times. (1998, April 4). *Stress Hormone Linked To High-Fat Snacking In Women* [On Line]. Available: http://www.nandotimes.com/.

273

National Cancer Institute and the National Institute of Allergy and Infectious Diseases. (1998). *Understanding The Immune System.* National Institutes of Health, National Cancer Institute, U.S. Department of Health and Human Services Public Health Service [On Line]. Available: http://www.mfmdesign.com/NCI_WEBSITE/PATIENTS/INFO_TEACHER / bookshelf/NIH_immune/index.html.

Nation's Business. (1988). *Calm People Get Ulcers, Too.* Feb. 76 (2), 77.

Neel, R. G. (1955). Nervous Stress in the Industrial Situation. *Personnel Psychology.* 8, 405-415.

New York Times. (1976, February 14). *Stress Quiz.*

Newman, P. (1998). *Stressed? - blame your brain.* BBC news [On line}. Available: http://news.bbc.co.uk/hi/english/sci/tech/newsid_111000/111227.stm.

Newsweek. (1988, Apr 25). Stress on the Job. p.40-45.

Newton, T. J. (1989). Occupational Stress and Coping with Stress: A Critique. *Human Relations.* 42 (5), 441-461.

Nicholas, G. (1999, January, 12). *Denton delivers heart-felt advice.* The Sydney Morning Herald.

NIH Consensus Conference. (1994). *Helicobacter pylori* in peptic ulcer disease: NIH Consensus Development Panel on *Helicobacter pylori* in Peptic Ulcer Diseases. *JAMA.* 272 (1), 65.

Novelli, P. (1997, October 24*).* Knowledge about causes of peptic ulcer disease -United States, March-April 1997. *Morbidity and Mortality Weekly Report.* 46 (42), 985-987.

Norman, R. M. G., & Malla, A. K. (1993). Stressful Life Events and Schizophrenia. II. Conceptual and Methodological issues. *British Journal Psychiatry.* 162, 166-174.

Nurofen. (1997, May 21). *Life's A Pain - And Women Are The Cause Says Survey.* Two Ten Press News release [On Line]. Available: http://releases.twoten.press.net/releases/date/1997/05/21/SURVEY-Stress_Men.html.

Nut, D. J., Glue, P., Molyneux, S., & Clarke, E. (1988). Alpha 2-Adrenoreceptor activity in Alcohol Withdrawal: A Pilot Study of the Effects of I.V. Clonidine in alcoholics and Normals. *Alcohol Clinical Experimental Research.* 12,14-18.

O'Brien, D. B. (1981). Coping With Occupational Stress. *Journal of Physical Education, Recreation & Dance.* 52 (9), 44-48.

Oedegaard, E. O. (1932). A Case Of Oculogyric Fits In Encephalitis Accompanied By Obsessions And Disturbance Of Ideation. *Acta Psychiatrica et Neurologica KjoBenhavn.* 7, 855-865.

Office for National Statistics. (1997, May 8). *Health In England: What People Know, What People Think, What People Do.* Two Ten Press News Releases [On Line]. Available: http://releases.twoten.press.net/releases/date/1997/05/08/ SURVEY-Health.html.

Ohio State University. (1998). *Men, Women Disagree On What Causes Stress* [On line}. Available: http://www.ag.ohio-state.edu/~ohioline/ lifetime/lt1-3l.html.

Organics. (1997, November 7). *Hair That's So Stressed Out It's Falling Out - The Answer To Working Women's Latest Worry.* Two Ten Press News Release [On Line]. Available: http://www.twoten.press.net/stories/97/11/07/headlines/HEALTH_Hair_Women.html.

Osler, W. (1910). On Angina Pectoris. *Lancet.* 2, 697-702.

Osnato, M. (1925). Industrial neuroses. *American Journal of Psychiatry.* 5, 117-131.

Otto, J. (1990). The Effects of Physical Exercise on Psychophysiological Reactions under Stress. *Cognition and Emotion.* 4 (4), 341-357.

Ouellet-Kobasa, S. C. (1979). Stressful Life Events, Personality, and Health: An Inquiry into Hardiness. *Journal of Personality and Social Psychology.* 37, 1-11.

_____ (1993). Inquiries into Hardiness. In Breznitz, S., & Goldberger, L. (Eds). *Handbook of Stress: Theoretical and Clinical Aspects* (pp. 77-100). New York: The Free Press. A division of Macmillan, Inc.

Palmer, H. (1941). Military Psychiatric Casualties: Experience with 12,000 cases. *Lancet.* 2, 454-457.

Palsane, M. N., Bhavsar, S. N., Goswani, R. P., & Evans, G. W. (1986). The Concept of Stress in the Indian Tradition. *Journal of Indian Psychology.* 5 (5), 1-12.

Panksepp, J. (1989). The Neurobiology of Emotions: Of Animal brains and Human Feelings. In Wagner, H., & Manstead, A. (Eds). *Handbook of Social Psychophysiology* (pp. 5-26). Chichester: John Wiley & Sons Ltd.

Parsons, C. D., & Wakeley, P. (1991). Idioms of Distress: Somatic Responses to Distress in Everyday Life. *Culture, Medicine and Psychiatry.* 15, 111-132.

Pearlin, L. I. (1982). The Social Context of Stress. In Breznitz, S., & Goldberger, L. (Eds). *Handbook of Stress: Theoretical and Clinical Aspects* (pp. 367-379). New York: The Free Press. A division of Macmillan, Inc.

Pearlin, L. I., & Schooler, C. (1978). The Structure of Coping. *Journal of Health and Social Behavior.* 19, 2-21.

Pedrabissi, L., Rolland, J. P., & Santinello, M. (1993). Stress And Burnout Among Teachers In Italy And France. *The Journal of Psychology.* 127 (5), 529-536.

Perkins, D. V. (1982). The Assessment of Stress Using Life Events Scales. In Breznitz, S., & Goldberger, L. (Eds). *Handbook of Stress: Theoretical and Clinical Aspects* (pp. 320-331). New York: The Free Press. A division of Macmillan, Inc.

Pesareva, L. V. (1948). Nervniyie diettee v domie./ Nervous children in the home. *Semia I Shkola.* Jan; 32-33.

Peterson, P. K., Chao, C. C., Molitor, T., Murtaugh, M., Strgar, F., & Sharp, B. M. (1991). Stress and Pathogenesis of Infectious Disease. *Review of Infectious Disease.* 13 (4), 710-20.

Pichot, P. (1994) Neurasthenia, yesterday and today. *Encephale.* Nov, 20 Spec. 3:, 45-549.

Pine, D. (1988). She's Got The Blinding Blues: Link Found Between Stress And Blindness. *Health.* Jan. Vol. 20, (1), 20.

275

Plutchik, R. (1994). *The psychology and Biology of Emotion.* New York: Harper Collins   College Publishers.

Pollock, C. (1988). On the Social Stress: Production of a Modern Mythology. *Social Science Medicine.* 26, 381-392.

Pomme, P. (1763). *Traite des Affections Vaporeuses des Deux Sexes.* Lyon.

Pope, A. U. (1941). The Importance of Morale. *Journal of Educational Sociology.* 15, 195-205.

Porter, R. (1996). *The Cambridge Illustrated History of Medicine.* Cambridge: Cambridge University Press.

Posen, Dr. (1994). *Stress Management* [On line}. Available: http://www.mentalhealth.com/mag1/p51-str.html.

Prince, N. (1905). Some of the present problems of abnormal psychology. *Psychological Review.* Mar-May; 12 (2-3), 118-143.

Psychology Today. (1996). *Stress...It's Worse Than You Think.* January/February.

Purcell, J. (1702). *A Treatise of Vapors, or Hysterick fits.* London.

Quinn, R. P. (1975). *What Makes Jobs Monotonous and Boring?* Paper presented to the annual meeting of the American Psychological Association, 1975. Chicago.

Rees, L. (1981a). Medical Aspects of Unemployment. *British Medical Journal.* 283, 1630.

_____ (1981b). The Development of Psychosomatic medicine During the Past 25 Years. *Journal of Psychosomatic Research.* 27, (2), 157-164.

Rees, R. (1997, May 18). This Is The Age Of The Strain. *Sunday Times.*

Reuttner, T. (1997). Communication Can Overcome Stress, Says Lipkin. *Business Day* [On line}. Available: http://www.bday.co.za/97/1106/special/x22.htm.

Rhein, J. H. W. (1919). Neuropsychiatric problems at the front during combat. *Journal   of Abnormal Psychology.* Apr-Jun; 14 (1-2), 9-14.

Riadore, J. E. (1835). *Introductory Lectures to a Course On Nervous Irritation, Spinal Affections.* London: Churchill.

Richardson, B. W. (1869). On Physical Disease from Mental Strain. *Journal of Mental Science.* 15, 350-362.

Riddering, P. (1998). *Stress. Is it necessary?* [On line}. Available: http://www.healthandfitness. co.nz/articles/stress.htm.

Rivers, W. H. R. (1918). War Neurosis and Military Training. *Mental Hygiene.* 2 (4), 513-533.

Robbins, S. P. (1993). *Organizational Behavior.* 6th Ed. Englewood Cliffs, N.J: Prentice-Hall, Inc.

Robson, R. (1886). The Wear and Tear of London Life. *Fortnightly Review.* 39, 200-208.

Rombouts, J. M. (1934). Affektdynamik und Psychotherapie. / Emotional Dynamics And Psychotherapy. *Zentralblatt fuer Psychotherapie.* 7, 340-347.

Rosch, P. J. (1984). Stress and Cancer. In Cooper, C. L. (Ed). *Psychosocial Stress and Cancer* (pp. 3-19). Chicester: John Wiley & Sons.

_____ (1996). Stress and Cancer: Disorders of Communication, Control, and Civilization. In: Cooper, C. L. (Ed). *Handbook of Stress, Medicine and Health* (pp. 27-60). Boca Raton: CRC Press.

Rose Medical Center. (1993). *How To Fight & Conquer Stress* [On line}. Available: http://www.coolware.com/health /medical_ reporter/stress.html.

Rosenberg, C. E. (1992). *Explaining epidemics and others studies in the history of medicine.* Cambridge: Cambridge University Press.

Rosenman, R. H. (1996). Personality, Behavior Patterns, and Heart Disease. In Cooper, C. L. (Ed). *Stress, Medicine and Health* (pp. 217-232). Boca Raton: CRC Press.

Roy, C. S., & Adami, J. G. (1888). Remarks of Failure of the Heart from Overstrain. *British Medical Journal.* ii, 1321-1326.

Russell, B. (1921). *The Analysis of Mind.* London: George Allen & Unwin: New York: The Macmillan Company.

Sandberg, N. (1998). *Stress - What's It All About?* [On line}. Available: http://www.relax-uk.com/stressedout/.

Sapolsky, R. M. (1994). *Why Zebra Don't Get Ulcers: A Guide to Stress, Stress-related Diseases, and Coping.* New York: W.H. Freeman and Company.

Saunders, C. (1997). *Men & Stress.* Sydney: Harper Collins Publishers.

Scadding, J. G. (1990). The semantic problems of psychiatry. *Psychological Medicine.* 20, 243-248.

Schleifer, S. J., Keller, S. E., Camerino, M., Thorton, J.C., & Stein, M. (1983). Suppression of Lymphocyte Stimulation Following Bereavement. *Journal of the American Medical Association.* 250, 374-377.

Schulz, P. (1994). Biological Uniqueness and the Definition of Normality. Part 1. The Concept of 'Intrinsic' Homeostasis. *Medical Hypotheses.* 42, 57-62.

Selye, H. (1936). A Syndrome Produced by Diverse Nocuous Agents. *Nature.* 138, 32.

_____ (1954). On the nature of disease. *Texas Reports on Biology and Medicine.* 2, 390-422.

_____ (1956). *The Stress of life.* New York: McGraw-Hill.

_____ (1975). Implications of Stress Concept. *New York State Journal of Medicine.* 75 (12), 2139-2145.

_____ (1976). Forty Years of Stress Research: Principal remaining Problems and Misconceptions. *Canadian Medical Association Journal.* 15 (1), 53-56.

_____ (1978). *The Stress of Life.* New York: McGraw-Hill.

_____ (1979). Foreword. In Albrecht, K. *Stress and the Manager: Making it Work for You* (pp. v-vii). New York: Simon & Schuster.

_____ (Ed). (1980). *Selye's Guide to Stress Research.* Volume 1. New York: Van Nostrand Reinhold Company.

_____ (1982). History and Present Status of the Stress Concept. In Breznitz, S., &Goldberger, L. (Eds). *Handbook of Stress: Theoretical and*

Clinical Aspects (pp. 7-20). New York: The Free Press. A division of Macmillan, Inc.

_____ (1986). Stress, Cancer, and the Mind. In Day, S. B. (Ed). *Cancer, Stress, and Death* (pp. 11-19). New York: Plenum Medical Book Company.

Selye, H., & Fortier, C. (1950). Adaptive reaction to stress. *Psychosomatic Medicine.* 12, 149-157.

Seppa, N. (1997). *Growing Toll Of Job Stress Hikes Compensation Claims* [On Line]. Available: http://www.apa.org/monitor/oct96/work.html.

Shaskan, D. A. (1946). The development of group psychotherapy in a military setting. *Research Publications of the Association for Research in Nervous and Mental Disease.* 25, 311-315.

Shawver, L. (1977). Research Variables in Psychology and the Logic of Their Creation. *Psychiatry.* 40, 1-16.

Shimizu, Y., Makino, S., & Takata, T. (1997). Employee Stress Status During the Past Decade (1982-1992) Based on a Nation-Wide Survey Conducted by the Ministry of labor in Japan. *Industrial Health.* 35, 441-450.

Shorter, E. (1992*). From Paralysis to Fatigue: A History of Psychosomatic Illness in the Modern Era.* New York: The Free Press.

Shorter, E. (1997). *A History of Psychiatry: From the Era of the Asylum to the Age of Prozac.* New York: John Wiley & Sons, Inc.

Simon, N. (1984). The Myth About Ulcers. *Working Woman.* June. 9, 134-136.

Smith, N. (1997). *Lecture Notes in Immunoregulation.* University of Technology, Sydney.

Solomon, M. (1917). Need for a stricter definition of terms in psychopathology. *Journal of Abnormal Psychology.* Aug; 12 (3), 195-199.

Somerville, H. (1923). The War Anxiety Neurotic of the Present Day: His "Dizzy Bouts" and Hallucinations. *British Journal of Medical Psychology.* 3, 309-319.

_____ (1923). The War Anxiety Neurotic of the Present Day: A Clinical Sketch. *Journal of Mental Science.* 69, 170-180.

Sparks, D. (1983). Practical Solutions for Teacher Stress. *Theory into Practice.* 22 (1), 33-42.

Speirs, R. l. (1992). Stress and the Immune System. *Dental Update.* 19 (9), 388-391, 393-394.

Spiney, L. (1997, March 17). Economy Losing Billions As Stress Taking Toll On Staff. *Electronic Telegraph.*.

Spiro, H. M. (1998). Peptic ulcer: Moynihan's or Marshall's disease? *Lancet.* 352 (9),128:645.

Stanford, S. C. (1993). Monoamines in response and adaptation to stress. In Stanford, S. C., & Salmon, P. (Eds). *Stress: From Synapse to Syndrome* (pp. 282-331). London: Academic Press, Harcourt Brace & Company, Publishers.

Statistics Canada. (1998). *Catalogue No. 82-221-XDE* [On Line]. Available: http://johns.largnet. uwo.ca shine/health/ lifeexp.htm.

278

Stein, M., & Miller, A. (1993). Stress, the Immune System, and Health and Illness. In Breznitz, S., & Goldberger, L. (Eds). *Handbook of Stress: Theoretical and Clinical Aspects* (pp. 127-141). New York: The Free Press. A division of Macmillan, Inc.

Steinberg, A., & Ritzmann, R. F. (1990). A Living Systems Approach to Understanding the Concept of Stress. *Behavioral Sciences.* 35, 138-146.

Steptoe, A. (1993). Stress and The Cardiovascular System: A Psychosocial Perspective. In Stanford, S. C., & Salmon, P. (Eds). *Stress: From Synapse to Syndrome* (pp. 120-141). London: Academic Press, Harcourt Brace & Company, Publishers.

Stone, M. H. (1997). *Healing the Mind: A History of Psychiatry from Antiquity to the Present.* New York: W. W. Norton & Co.

Stratakis, C. A., & Chrousos, G. P. (1995). Neuro-endocrinology and Pathophysiology of the Stress System. *Annals of the Academy of Science.* 771, 1-18.

Stress Free Net. (1998). *The Stress Epidemic* [On Line]. Available: http://www.stressfree.com.

Strongman, K. T. (1987). *The Psychology of Emotion.* 3rd Ed. Chichester: John Wiley & Sons.

Sullivan, M. D. (1990). Reconsidering The Wisdom Of The Body: An Epistemological Critique Of Claude Bernard's Concept Of The Internal Environment. *Journal of Medical Philosophy.* 15, 493-514.

Sunday Times (1997, May 18). *Stress At Work: How Your Job Rates.*

Tache, J. (1986). Stress as a Cause of Disease Day, S. B. (Ed*). Cancer, Stress, and Death* (pp. 1-10). New York: Plenum Medical Book Company.

Tache, J., & Selye, H. (1985). On Stress and Coping Mechanisms. Special Issue. Stress and Anxiety. *Issues in Mental Health nursing.* 7 (1-4), 3-24.

Temoshok, L., & Heller, B. W. (1984). On Comparing Apples, Oranges and Fruit Salad: a Methodological Review Of Medical Outcome Studies in Psychosocial Oncology. In Cooper, C. L. (Ed). *Psychosocial Stress and Cancer* (pp. 231-260). Chicester: John Wiley & Sons.

The American Institute of Stress. (1998). *Home page* [On Line]. Available: http://www.stress.org.

The Canadian Mental Health. (1997). *Canadians Name Mental Health As Top Priority.* Sponsored by the Canadian Mental Health Association. Canada NewsWire [On Line]. Available: http://www.newswire.ca/releases /May1997/01/c0008.html

The Mental Health Foundation. (1997). *Information Sheet: Stress and Anxiety* [On Line]. Available: http://www.mentalhealth.org.uk/factanx.htm.

The Spectator. (1894). Nerves and Nervousness. *Eclectic Magazine.* 60, 278-281.

Theodora. (1998). *Stress - There's More To It Than You Think* [On Line]. Available: http://www.oro.net ~theodora/book.htm.

Thompson, J. G. (1988). *The Psychobiology of Emotions.* Plenum Press: New York.

Thompson, N., Murphy, M., & Stradling, S. (1994). *Dealing with stress.* Hampshire: MacMillan Press Ltd.

279

Time. (1983, Aug 1). *Increasing Signs of Stress.* (Japan). p 67.

Tissot, S. A. (1769). *An Essay on Diseases Incident to Literary and Sedentary Persons.* 2nd ed. London: J. Nourse, and E. & C. Dilly.

Toates, F. (1995). *Stress. Conceptual and Biological Aspects.* Chichester: John Wiley & Son.

Trap-Jensen, J., Carlsen, J. E., Hartling, O. J, Svendsen, T. L, TangØ, M., & Christiansen, N. J. (1982). Beta-Adrenoreceptor Blockage and Psychic Stress in Man. A Comparison of the Acute Effects of Labetolol, Metoprolol, Pindolol, and Propanolol on Plasma Levels of Adrenaline and Noradrenaline. *British Journal of Clinical Pharmacology.* 13 (391), S-5S.

Treadwell, J. B. (1872). Observation upon Overwork and Strain of the Heart. Boston *Medical and Surgical Journal.* 10, 157-160.

Triesen, D. & Williams, M. J. (1985). Organizational Stress among Teachers. *Canadian Journal of Education.* 10 (1), 13-34.

Trinca, H. (1997, October 20). Stress On The Job Worries Workers. *The Sydney Morning Herald.*

Trotter, T. (1807). *A view of the Nervous Temperament.* London: Longman, Hurst, Rees, & Orme.

Trade Union Congress [TUC]. (1996). *Survey of Safety Reps. Stressed To Breaking Point. How Managers Are Pushing People To The Brink! (Initial Findings)* [On Line]. Available: http://www.stress.org.uk:80/tuc.htm.

Turner, J. R., Girdler, S. S., Sherwood, A., & Light, K. C. (1990). Cardiovascular Responses to Behavioral Stressors: Laboratory-field Generalization and Inter-task Consistency. *Journal of Psychosomatic Research.* 34 (5), 581-589.

Tyler, M. (1998). *Stress Can Kill!* [On Line]. Available: http://www.netlink.co.uk/ users/phillips/clients/breakaway/ stress.html.

University of Illinois University at Urbana-Champaign Counseling Center. (1996). Str*ess Management* [On Line]. Available: http://domino.odos.uiuc.edu/ Counseling_Center/stress.htm.

University of Indiana. (undated) *Ancient Medicine* [On Line]. Available: http://www.indiana. edu/~ancmed/.

University of Texas Counseling Services. (1998). *Looking at Stress* [On Line]. Available: http://www.utexas.edu/student/cmhc/1998.

Ursin, H., & Olff, M. (1993). The Stress Response. In Stanford, S. C., & Salmon, P. (Eds) *Stress: From Synapse to Syndrome* (pp. 4-22). London: Academic Press. Harcourt Brace & Company, Publishers.

Valdimarsdottir, H. B., & Bovbjerg, D. H. (1997). Positive and Negative Mood. Association with Natural Killer Cell Activity. *Psychology and Health.* 12 (3), 319-327.

Van Urk, H., Duin, N., & Sutcliffe, J. (Eds). (1992). *A History of Medicine: From Prehistory to the Year 2020.* London: Simon Schuster.

Vincent, J-D. (1990). *The Biology of Emotions.* Oxford: Basil Blackwell.

Vinokur, A., & Selzer, M. L. (1975). Desirable Versus Undesirable Life Events: Their Relationship to Stress and Mental Distress. *Journal of Personality and Social Psychology.* 32 (2), 329-337.

Wagner, H. (1989). The Peripheral Physiological Differentiation of Emotion. In Wagner, H., & Manstead, A. (Eds). *Handbook of Social Psychophysiology* (pp. 77-98). Chichester: John Wiley & Sons Ltd.

Wallis, C. (1983, June, 6.). Stress. Can We Cope? *Time.*

Warner, R. (1976). The Relationship Between Language and Disease Concepts. *International Journal of Psychiatry in Medicine.* 7 (1), 57-68.

Weir Mitchell, S. (1887). *Wear and Tear: Or Hints for the Overworked.* 5th Ed. Philadelphia: J.B Lippincott Company.

Westra, H. A., & Kuiper, N. A. (1992). Type A, Irrational Cognitions, and Situational Factors Relating to Stress. *Journal of Research in Personality.* 26,1-20.

Wheaton, B. (1996). The Domains and Boundaries of Stress Concepts. In Kaplan, H. B.(Ed) *Psychosocial Stress: Perspectives on Structure, Theory, Life-Course, and Methods* (pp. 29-70). San Diego: Academic Press.

White, G. M. (1982). The Role of Cultural Explanations in 'Somatization' and 'Psychologization'. *Social Science & Medicine.* 16, 1519-1530.

White, W. A. (1932). The Study of the Mind. *Science.* 76, 90-92.

Wilks, S. (1875). On Overwork. *Lancet.* 1, 886-887.

Williams, G. (1982, October 6). Stress: one thing that is booming. *The Sydney Morning Herald.*

Williams, T. A. (1919). Tremor following explosions. Journal of Abnormal Psychology. Feb; 14(6), 393-405.

Willner, P. (1993). Animal Models of Stress: An Overview. In Stanford, S. C., & Salmon, P.(Eds). *Stress: From Synapse to Syndrome* (pp. 145-165). London: Academic Press, Harcourt Brace & Company.

Wittkower, E. D., & Spillane, J. P. (1944). *The Neuroses of War.* New York: MacMillan.

Wood, P. (1941). DaCosta's Syndrome. *British Medical Journal.* 1, 767-772.

Woolley, L. E. (1929). Studies in obsessive ruminative tension states. I. Relation to paraergastic reactions. *American Journal of Psychiatry.* 9, 1113-1158.

Wozniak, R. H. (1992). *Mind and Body: René Descartes to William James* [On Line]. Available: http://serendip. brynmawr.edu.

Zheng, Y. P., & Lin, K. M. (1994). A Nationwide Study of Stressful Life Events in   Mainland China. *Psychosomatic Medicine.* 56, 296-305.

INDEX

284

homeostasis, XI, XII, 2, 19, 38, 70, 71, 84, 104, 122, 142, 143, 151, 154, 155, 157, 159, 173, 200, 216, 253, 262

hormones, 6, 17, 25, 28, 86, 93, 104, 111, 113, 115, 162, 189, 190, 193, 196, 197, 198, 206, 207, 222, 231, 256

hypertension, 24, 191, 213, 219, 221

hypochondria, 51, 72, 78, 86

hypocondriasis, 49, 62

hypostatization, 92, 94

hypothalamic-pituitary-adrenocortical system, 188

hypothalamus-pituitary adrenal secretion, 196

hysteria, 43, 47, 49, 50, 51, 55, 64, 65, 66, 69, 70, 72, 74, 77, 78, 86, 88, 256

hysterical conversion, 52, 68, 73, 86

I

imagination, X, XI, 46, 78, 92, 99, 118, 133, 238, 239, 241, 242, 247, 257

immune response, 204, 205, 206, 207, 208, 209, 210, 211, 255

immune system, 24, 94, 161, 189, 203, 204, 205, 206, 207, 208, 209, 210, 211, 212, 216, 217, 218, 255

immunoglobulins, 205

information processing, 134

interleukin, 206

irritable bowl syndrome, 24

irritable heart, 58, 66

J

Janet, 65, 268

K

killer cells, 205, 206, 208

L

Lazarus, 82, 83, 84, 107, 127, 128, 130, 134, 142, 165, 172, 198, 208, 252, 260, 268, 270, 271

Levi, 84, 134, 135, 136, 165, 194, 195, 214, 265, 271

life events, XII, 21, 91, 101, 108, 111, 123, 124, 125, 139, 165, 208, 212, 221, 227

life expectancy, 213, 214

lymphocytes, 204, 205, 210

M

meditation, 13, 29, 33

mental strain, 57, 62, 63

metaphor, 48, 94, 102

metaphorical, 49, 65, 67, 81, 95, 100, 129, 141, 240, 241

milieu interieur, 55, 70, 71, 151, 152

multiple sclerosis, 24, 26, 213

N

natural killer cells, 206, 208

nervous tension, 11, 73, 74, 75, 76, 79, 86, 104, 251

neurasthenia, 55, 56, 59, 60, 61, 62, 63, 64, 66, 67, 69, 70, 71, 74, 78, 79, 86, 251, 256

neuroendocrine system, 191, 206

Neuroendocrinology, 271

neurology, 6, 26, 82, 199

neurosis, 51, 70, 124

neurotransmitters, 6, 17, 189, 193, 196, 207, 231, 256

noradreneline, 188, 193

norepinephrine, 188, 195

O

Osler, 67, 102, 275

P

pace of life, X, 52, 55, 57, 65, 68

Paracelsus, 46

parasympathetic nervous system, 188

passions, 46, 47, 49, 50, 51, 52

Books from Science & Humanities Press

AVOIDING Attendants from HELL: A Practical Guide to Finding, Hiring & Keeping Personal Care Attendants 2Ed June Price, (2002) ISBN 1-888725-60-5, 8¼X5½, 200 pp, $18.95

The Bridge Never Crossed — A Survivor's Search for Meaning. Captain George A. Burk (1999) Inspiring story of George Burk, lone survivor of a military plane crash, who overcame extensive burn injuries to earn a presidential award and become a highly successful motivational speaker. ISBN 1-888725-16-8, 5½X8¼, 170 pp, illustrated. $16.95

Value Centered Leadership — A Survivor's Strategy for Personal and Professional Growth — Captain George A. Burk (2002) Principles of Leadership & Total Quality Management by Captain George Burk, Principles for management and living. ISBN 1-888725-59-1, 5½X8¼, 120 pp, $16.95

Virginia Mayo — The Best Years of My Life (2002) Autobiography of film star Virginia Mayo as told to LC Van Savage. From her early days in Vaudeville and the Muny in St Louis to the dozens of hit motion pictures, with dozens of photographs. ISBN 1-888725-53-2, 5½ X 8¼, 300 pp, $16.95

To Norma Jeane With Love, Jimmie -Jim Dougherty as told to LC Van Savage (2001) ISBN 1-888725-51-6 The sensitive and touching story of Jim Dougherty's teenage bride who later became Marilyn Monroe. Dozens of photographs. "The Marilyn Monroe book of the year!" As seen on TV. 5½X8¼, 200 pp, $16.95

The Job — Eric Whitfield (2001) A story of self-discovery in the context of the death of a grandfather.. A book to read and share in times of change and Grieving. ISBN 1-888725-68-0, 5½ X 8¼, 100 pp, $14.95

Plague Legends: from the Miasmas of Hippocrates to the Microbes of Pasteur-Socrates Litsios D.Sc. (2001) Medical progress from early history through the 19th Century in understanding origins and spread of contagious disease. A thorough but readable and enlightening history of medicine. Illustrated, Bibliography, Index ISBN 1-888725-33-8, 6¼X8¼, 250pp, $24.95

The Stress Myth -Serge Doublet, PhD (2000) A thorough examination of the concept that 'stress' is the source of unexplained afflictions. Debunking mysticism, psychologist Serge Doublet reviews the history of other concepts such as 'demons', 'humors', 'hysteria' and 'neurasthenia' that had been placed in this role in the past, and provides an alternative approach for more success in coping with life's challenges. ISBN 1-888725-36-2, 5½X8¼, 280 pp, $24.95

Downloadable PDF eBook for Mac and PC (2008) ISBN 9781596300422 $12.95

Order form			
Item	Each	Quantity	Amount
Missouri (only) sales tax 6.325%			
Postage & Handling			$5.00
	Total		
Ship to Name:			
Address:			
City State Zip:			

Science & Humanities Press

PO Box 7151
Chesterfield, MO 63006-7151
(636) 394-4950
on the web at
sciencehumanitiespress.com